OECD Health Policy Studies

Cardiovascular Disease and Diabetes

POLICIES FOR BETTER HEALTH AND QUALITY OF CARE

OECD
BETTER POLICIES FOR BETTER LIVES

This work is published under the responsibility of the Secretary-General of the OECD. The opinions expressed and arguments employed herein do not necessarily reflect the official views of OECD member countries.

This document and any map included herein are without prejudice to the status of or sovereignty over any territory, to the delimitation of international frontiers and boundaries and to the name of any territory, city or area.

Please cite this publication as:
OECD (2015), *Cardiovascular Disease and Diabetes: Policies for Better Health and Quality of Care*, OECD Health Policy Studies, OECD Publishing, Paris.
DOI: *http://dx.doi.org/10.1787/9789264233010-en*

ISBN 978-92-64-23300-3 (print)
ISBN 978-92-64-23301-0 (PDF)

Series: OECD Health Policy Studies
ISSN 2074-3181 (print)
ISSN 2074-319X (online)

The statistical data for Israel are supplied by and under the responsibility of the relevant Israeli authorities. The use of such data by the OECD is without prejudice to the status of the Golan Heights, East Jerusalem and Israeli settlements in the West Bank under the terms of international law.

Photo credits: © *Zern Liew / Shutterstock.com;* © *Alexander Lukin / Shutterstock.com;* © *leremy / Shutterstock.com;* © *Oleg Babich / Thinstock.*

Corrigenda to OECD publications may be found on line at: *www.oecd.org/about/publishing/corrigenda.htm*.

Foreword

Over the last few decades, mortality from cardiovascular disease has dropped faster than mortality from other causes. Despite this great success, prospects for making further inroads are threatened by rising levels of obesity and the lack of adherence to recommended treatments.

Startling variations in the probability of being hospitalised with diabetes or surviving a heart attack or a stroke, and the cost associated to their care persist across and within OECD countries. For example, Central and Eastern European Countries, such as the Slovak Republic, Hungary, Estonia and the Czech Republic, face the greatest cardiovascular disease mortality burden, with mortality rates in excess of 400 per 100 000 population. On the other side of the spectrum, countries such as Japan and France experienced mortality rates of less than 150. The consequence of such large variation is either unacceptable waste of scarce resources or poor quality of life for the people affected. Given the large disease burden accounted for by cardiovascular disease and diabetes, better policies to improve care for patients and reduce variation in outcomes are highly needed. Cardiovascular disease accounts for around a third of all deaths in OECD countries. Rising levels of diabetes, on the other hand, lead to greater morbidity and disability from blindness, kidney failure and other serious complications. Taken together, these two conditions represent about 40% of the health burden across the OECD.

This report shows that throwing ever more resources to care services is not enough to deliver good outcomes and reduce unacceptable variation in performance for these two conditions. Both cardiovascular disease and diabetes are complex diseases to manage and treat effectively. Good primary care and early diagnosis is needed to manage risk factors such as high blood pressure and cholesterol and avoid unnecessary long-term damage being caused by the diseases. Both require timely services from the onset of the disease through to later stages when specialist and hospital treatment is necessary. And both require continuity and integration of services across the entire clinical pathway.

Sadly, many OECD countries are still a long way from making the necessary reforms in their health systems to deliver such good care. This report makes a series of recommendations that policy makers can take to reduce the gap between actual care and optimal care for both conditions. It argues that integrating evidence-based clinical recommendations into day-to-day care requires changes in governance of the system. Crucially, an improved national policy framework around these two conditions would go a long way to reducing mortality and morbidity.

Acknowledgements

This study was conducted as part of the OECD Health Care Quality Indicator (HCQI) project which monitors and evaluates quality of health care and system performance across countries. The report was developed by Kees van Gool, Nelly Biondi, Rie Fujisawa and Niek Klazinga. Chapter 6 of the report was co-authored by Professor Aldo Maggioni, Renato Urso Roberto Ferrari, Nikolaos Maniadakis, Luigi Tavazzi and members of the OECD Secretariat. The report benefited from valuable comments from Stefano Scarpetta, Mark Pearson, Francesca Colombo and Franco Sassi. The authors are grateful to Jan Alexa for his research assistance; Michael Mueller and Yuki Murakami for their assistance with expenditure data; and Gillian Sykes, Marlène Mohier and Lucy Hulett for their respective editorial contributions.

The authors are grateful to members of the OECD Health Committee and experts of the HCQI project who provided important comments and suggestions as well as inputs to this report through their responses to questionnaires, and request for data and interviews. Finally, the authors would like to acknowledge the valuable support of the European Society of Cardiology to this project.

Table of contents

Acronyms and abbreviations 10

Executive summary 13

Assessment and recommendations 15

Chapter 1. **The burden of cardiovascular disease and diabetes** 31

- Introduction 32
- Cardiovascular disease and diabetes defined 34
- Despite substantial gains, CVD remains the leading cause of mortality 36
- Fewer CVD deaths have led to greater life expectancy, but gains have not been uniform 37
- Explaining the fall in CVD mortality 39
- CVD and diabetes take a heavier toll in some countries than in others 40
- CVD and diabetes strike at different ages across countries 45
- The health care costs of CVD and diabetes 47
- Summary 49
- Notes 49
- References 49

Chapter 2. **Improving cardiovascular disease and diabetes outcomes through lifestyles: Trends and policies** 53

- Lifestyles play an important part in predicting cardiovascular disease and diabetes risk 54
- Improving lifestyles to reduce CVD and diabetes risk: Recent experiences in OECD countries 61
- Lifestyle patterns across OECD countries vary considerably 70
- Summary 73
- Note 74
- References 74
- *Annex* 2.A1. Tobacco control policies 76

Chapter 3. **Improved control of cardiovascular disease risk factors and diabetes: The central role of primary care** 77

- The ever increasing importance of primary care in managing cardiovascular disease and diabetes 78
- Opportunities to reduce cardiovascular risk in primary care 80
- Towards a better understanding of primary care quality in OECD countries 85
- Most countries provide good access to primary care but there are some important challenges 93
- Examining primary care quality initiatives 98

The growing recognition of empowering patients to take effective control of their chronic diseases 102
Summary 103
Notes 104
References 105

Chapter 4. **Improving acute cardiovascular care quality and access** 111
Advances in acute care treatments are improving CVD outcomes 112
The evidence on optimum acute treatments has widespread implications for health service delivery models 113
Out-of-hospital survival for some CVD events is low and could be improved 115
Timeliness of care: Evidence of variation across countries, but there is room for optimism 118
Access to revascularisation procedures has improved, but some countries are lagging behind 121
Care in specialised facilities improves outcomes but access remains limited in some countries 123
Hospital care resources 127
Better access and quality of care have improved survival after a heart attack and stroke 130
From onset to discharge: Full pathway monitoring and governance 131
Summary 134
Notes 135
References 135
Annex 4.A1. Data coverage for case-fatality indicators 139

Chapter 5. **Acute care cardiovascular disease: Examining hospital performance** 141
Examining the links between hospital expenditure and quality 142
New opportunities to measure hospital performance 142
Measuring hospital performance 143
Performance is linked to resources but some countries derive more quality for money 146
Payment systems, technology, quality measurement are linked to better hospital performance 155
Summary 157
Notes 157
References 158
Annex 5.A1. Empirical framework for analysing acute care CVD performance 159
Annex 5.A2. Full CVD acute care performance analysis results 160

Chapter 6. **Adherence to recommended cardiovascular care in OECD health systems** 163
Improving adherence to chronic heart failure treatment is an important health care issue 164
Combining individual patient and national health system data to study the problem of adherence 165

Results show substantial cross and within country variation found in adherence 169
Better adherence is linked to some national health system characteristics but within-country variation needs to be better understood 174
Summary 176
Notes 176
References 176

Tables

0.1. Policies to improve quality of care in primary care 21
1.1. Explaining the fall in CHD mortality: Summary of studies using the IMPACT model 39
2.1. Predicting the ten-year likelihood of a CVD event: Smoking and body mass index 55
2.2. Predicting the ten-year likelihood of developing diabetes: Exercise, body mass index and waist size 55
2.3. The relationship between tobacco policies and smoking rates 63
2.4. The relationship between tobacco policies and smoking rates 64
2.5. Smoking among males and females: Country rankings and trends 71
2.6. Overweight and obesity rates among males and females: Country rankings and trends 72
2.A1.1. Tobacco policy categories by country: Higher scores indicate stricter policy 76
3.1. Patients with CVD and diabetes often have multiple conditions 80
3.2. Predicting the ten-year likelihood of a CVD event: Diabetes, cholesterol and blood pressure 81
3.3. Policies to improve quality of care in primary care 99
4.1. Treatment times (measured in minutes) for ischemic stroke and heart attacks, 2012 (or nearest year) 119
4.2. Case-fatality rates and trends for AMI, ischemic and haemorrhagic stroke, 2011 (or nearest year) 132
4.A1.1. Observation periods for AMI, ischemic and haemorrhagic stroke case-fatality data 139
5.1. Variable definitions, descriptive statistics (selected years) and data sources 147
5.2. Regression results: Case-fatality rates by gender 148
5.3. Testing for country differences in the relationship between hospital expenditure and CVD quality 150
5.4. Country rankings for case-fatality performance 153
5.5. Summary of health system characteristic results 155
5.A2.1. CVD acute care performance analysis results 160
6.1. Descriptive national health system characteristics data by country 168
6.2. Number of patients enrolled, number of centres and non-adherence to drug treatment 169
6.3. Characteristics of the study population and odds ratio for non-adherence estimated by univariate models 172
6.4. Odds ratios by the multi-level logistic model 173

Figures

1.1. Analytical framework for the OECD project on cardiovascular disease and diabetes 33
1.2. Mortality rates for cardiovascular diseases and all other causes of death in OECD countries 36
1.3. Trends in potential years of life lost (PYLL) due to CVD and other diseases, by gender 37
1.4. Declining CVD mortality rates have improved life expectancy at birth and at age 65 38
1.5. Mortality rates for CVD per 100 000 population, 2011 (or latest year) 41
1.6. End-stage renal failure patients per 100 000 population, 2000 and 2011 (or nearest year) 43
1.7. CVD mortality rates and potential years of life lost, 2011 (or nearest year) 45
1.8. AMI admissions per 100 000 population by age group: OECD average, quartile range and selected countries, 2011 (or nearest year) 46
1.9. Diabetes prevalence in OECD countries by age, 2011 47
1.10. Proportion of hospital expenditure by major diagnostic category 48
2.1. Obesity is a strong predictor of diabetes 56
2.2. Smoking is a strong predictor of cerebrovascular disease mortality 57
2.3. Trends in OECD lifestyles: Tobacco, obesity and alcohol 59
2.4. Years of life lost in cardiovascular disease due to risky behaviours 59
2.5. Spending on prevention and public health services 60
2.6. Examples of plain cigarette packaging in Australia 65
2.7. Countries compared to the OECD average in smoking and overweight and obesity rates 73
3.1. High cholesterol and high blood pressure prevalence in OECD countries, 2008 82
3.2. Undiagnosed diabetes – percentage of diabetics unaware of their condition 84
3.3. Pharmaceutical consumption per patient with elevated CVD risk factor, defined daily doses 2008 87
3.4. The use of CVD risk-factor medication among diabetics, 2012 88
3.5. Diabetes admissions per 1 000 patients with diabetes, 2011 (or nearest year) 89
3.6. Comparing diabetes-related admissions and overall admissions across OECD countries 90
3.7. Heart failure admissions per 1 000 population, 2011 (or nearest year) 91
3.8. Comparing heart failure admissions and overall admissions across OECD countries 92
3.9. Per capita ambulatory care expenditure, 2011 (or nearest year) 94
3.10. Financing sources for ambulatory care and prescription drugs 95
3.11. Number of generalist doctors per 1 000 population, 2011 (or nearest year) 97
3.12. Unmet care needs for medical examination by income, European countries, 2012 (or nearest year) 98
4.1. Bypass surgery and percutaneous coronary interventions per 100 000 population, 2011 (or nearest year) 122
4.2. Percentage of patients treated in stroke units, 2011 (or latest year) 124
4.3. The number of PCI capable centres per million population 126
4.4. Specialist medical workforce, 2011 (or latest year) 128
4.5. Per capita hospital expenditure on cardiovascular diseases (USD PPP, 2005) 129

4.6. Per capita hospital expenditure on endocrine, nutritional and metabolic disease (USD PPP, 2005) 129
4.7. Governance and performance measurement of the full pathway of CVD acute care 133
5.1. Cross-country variation in the relationship between expenditure and quality: A hypothetical example 149
5.2. Country-specific relationships between health expenditure and AMI case fatality 151
5.3. Country-specific relationships between health expenditure and ischemic stroke case fatality 152
5.4. The role of health system characteristics in explaining performance: A hypothetical example 154
6.1. ESC-HFA Heart Failure Long-Term Registry: Patient disposition 166
6.2. Non-adherence in participating centres, within and across country variation 170

Acronyms and abbreviations

AADE	American Association of Diabetes Educators
ACC/AHA	American College of Cardiology/American Heart Association
ACE	Angiotensin-converting-enzyme
ACE-I	Angiotensin converting enzyme inhibitors
ACTION-GWTG	Acute Coronary Treatment and Intervention Outcomes Registry-Get with the Guidelines
AED	Automated external defibrillator
AHRQ	United States Agency for Healthcare Research and Quality
ALOS	Average length of stay
AMI	Acute myocardial infarction
ARBs	Angiotensin II receptor blockers
ARG	Angiotensin receptor blockers
BMI	Body mass index
CABG	Coronary artery bypass graft
CCU	Coronary care unit
CDC	United States Centres for Disease Control and Prevention
CDSMP	Chronic disease self-management programme
CHD	Coronary heart disease
CHF	Chronic heart failure
CI	Confidence intervals
CIBIS-II	Cardiac Insufficiency Bisoprolol Study II
CKD	Chronic kidney dysfunction
CONSENSUS	Cooperative North Scandinavian Enalapril Survival Study
COPD	Chronic obstructive pulmonary disease
CPR	Cardiopulmonary resuscitation
CRT	Cardiac resynchronisation therapy
CT	Computed tomography
CVD	Cardiovascular disease
D2B	Door-to-Balloon
DAK-E	Danish General Practice Quality Unit
DDD	Defined daily doses
DEA	Data Envelop Analysis

DHC	Department of Health and Children
DOH	Department of Health
DRG	Diagnosis-related group
ECG	Electrocardiogram
ECHO	European Collaboration in Healthcare Optimisation
EDLF	European Diabetes Leadership Forum
EF	Ejection fraction
ESC	European Society of Cardiology
ESC-HFA	European Society of Cardiology Heart Failure Association
ESO	European stroke organisation
ESRF	End-stage renal failure
EUBIROD	European Best Information through Regional Outcomes in Diabetes
EUROHOPE	European Health Care Outcomes, Performance and Efficiency
EU-SILC	European Statistics of Income and Living Conditions
FBG	Fasting blood glucose
FINDRISC	Finnish Diabetes Risk Score
GB	Global budget
GBD	Global Burden of Disease
GDP	Gross Domestic Product
GP	General Practitioner
HCQI	Health Care Quality Indicators
HDL-C	High-density lipoprotein cholesterol
HE	Health expenditure
HIQR	Hospital Inpatient Quality Reporting
HMO	Health Maintenance Organisations
HSC	Health System Characteristics
ICBP GWAS	International Consortium for Blood Pressure Genome-Wide Association Studies
ICCU	Intensive Cardiac Care Unit
ICD	Implantable cardioverter defibrillator
IDF	International Diabetes Federation
LDL-C	Low-density lipoprotein cholesterol
MERIT-HF	Metoprolol CR/XL Randomised intervention Trial in Congestive Heart Failure
MRI	Magnetic resonance imaging
NHS	National Health Service
NICE	National Institute of Clinical Excellence
NINDS	National Institute of Neurological Disorders and Stroke
NRT	Nicotine replacement therapy

NSTEMI	Non-ST segment elevation myocardial infarction
NTCP	National tobacco control programmes
NYHA	New York Heart Association
OGTT	Oral Glucose tolerance test
OOP	Out-of-pocket
OR	Odds ratios
PAD	Peripheral arterial diseases
PCI	Percutaneous coronary intervention
PPP	Purchasing power parities
PTCA	Percutaneous transluminal coronary angioplasty
PYLL	Potential years of life lost
QICH	Quality Indicators in Community Healthcare
QOF	Quality Outcomes Framework
Rt-PA	Recombinant tissue plasminogen activator
SBP	Systolic blood pressure
SCI-DC	Scottish Care Information – Diabetes Collaboration
SDMSG	Scottish Diabetes Monitoring Study Group
SE	Standard errors
SFA	Stochastic Frontier Analysis
SHA	System of Health Accounts
SOLVD	Studies of Left Ventricular Dysfunction
STEMI	ST segment elevation myocardial infarction
TIA	Transient Ischemic Attack
VIP	Value Incentive Program
WHO	World Health Organization
YLD	Years lost due to Disability
YLL	Years of life lost

Cardiovascular Disease and Diabetes
Policies for Better Health and Quality of Care
© OECD 2015

Executive summary

The last 50 years have witnessed remarkable improvements in cardiovascular disease (CVD) outcomes. Since 1960, CVD mortality rates have fallen by over 60% whereas mortality rates for all other causes fell by 38% in OECD countries. Advances in the prevention and treatment of CVD have outpaced those of many other diseases, and these improvements have contributed to longer and healthier lives.

There are a number of explanations behind the success. Smoking rates have fallen in virtually all OECD countries resulting in a demonstrable impact on CVD outcomes. Technological innovations are also a key reason for improvements by expanding the health system's capacity to control CVD risk factors such as high cholesterol and blood pressure, improve management of diabetes and provide more effective care in the event of an acute episode such as a stroke or heart attack. The foundation upon which these successes have been built has been the ability of health systems to deliver better and more timely access to high quality health programmes, services and technologies.

Despite these gains, CVD remains the leading cause of death in most OECD countries and prospects for further reductions are slowing. Countries face a number of significant challenges to reduce the health burden of CVD in the years to come. These include: 1) rising levels of key risk factors of CVD, obesity and diabetes; 2) delays in diagnoses of CVD risk factors and diabetes; 3) lack of adherence to recommended treatments; 4) ageing populations leading to greater complexity of health care needs; and 5) gaps in the timely access of specialised care. In addition to these overarching issues, many countries also face individual challenges. There is substantial variation across OECD countries in the prevalence of risk factors, the availability of health care resources and access to high quality of care.

This report assesses OECD health systems along the pathway by which CVD and diabetes is prevented, managed and treated. It examines prevention programmes to improve lifestyles, the strength of the primary care system to diagnose risk factors and manage disease as well as the effectiveness of the acute care sector in delivering high quality care. The report develops a better understanding of how countries can improve health system performance to reduce the burden of these two diseases.

The report highlights many policy initiatives in the area of CVD and diabetes management and care as well as draw out the key policy implications from the analysis on health system performance in relation to these two diseases. Some of these lessons point to areas where specific countries could improve performance but there are also some overarching policy implications for OECD countries. Key messages from the report are:

- There is no doubt that the health system has been instrumental in delivering better outcomes for patients but there remains substantial scope for further improvements in both CVD and diabetes care.

- Despite the success in reducing CVD mortality over recent decades, rising levels of obesity and diabetes are threatening prospects for further gains.
- The ageing population will lead not only to greater demand for health care but also change the complexity and type of care that CVD and diabetes patients require.
- Greater access to health care resources improves CVD and diabetes outcomes, but some countries are able to extract greater benefits from health resources than others. Analysis shows that better access to services and technologies, payment systems and quality of care initiatives are strongly linked to better performance.
- Though some countries have faced considerable resistance to their strong stance on prevention of unhealthy behaviour, these policies focusing on tobacco and obesity are shown to have widespread impact on promoting healthy lifestyles. More could be done to deliver an integrated approach that incorporates regulations and public health programmes to save thousands of lives.
- Primary care is central to optimising the prevention, diagnosis and management of CVD and diabetes and stops people from escalating down a path of adverse health outcomes, higher health care needs and costs. Countries can further strengthen the sector by ensuring patients have good financial and physical access to primary care and that services are of high quality through better integration and co-ordination with other parts of the health systems as well as continuity of care that is focused on the patient's needs.
- There is a need to establish better integrated systems to improve the chances of surviving out-of-hospital CVD events. Such efforts could be supported through a national policy framework to lift the community's capacity to respond and lift standards in emergency care.
- In hospitals, the quality of care has improved over the last ten years in almost all OECD countries. Performance in the acute care sector can be enhanced by developing better governance systems that are aimed at minimising the gap between recommended care guidelines and actual care delivered. This encompasses:
  - Better and more integrated information systems to monitor patient care and assess performance along the entire pathway of CVD and diabetes prevention, management and care. Such efforts should be matched by stronger governance systems that create clear lines of accountability and improve transparency. Such systems can not only create greater incentives on the part of health care funders and providers to improve quality of care but can also inform national policy formulations by highlighting aspects of the health system that are doing well and where performance could be improved.
  - Greater policy focus on reducing the variation in performance within countries, lifting not only overall standards of care but minimising the widespread differences in access and quality of care that are evident within health systems, including pre-hospital systems. Information systems are the bedrock of performance management which enable comparative health system assessment as well as evaluate the impact of policies at both the national and international levels.

Cardiovascular Disease and Diabetes
Policies for Better Health and Quality of Care
© OECD 2015

Assessment and recommendations

CVD mortality has been falling but it remains the number one killer in OECD countries

The mortality rate attributable to CVD has declined substantially in recent decades. Over the 50-year period since 1960, average mortality rates for CVD fell by 61%. CVD mortality rates started to decrease in the 1970s and in the 1980s the rate of decrease accelerated even further. Prior to 1985, CVD accounted for one in every two deaths in OECD countries, but by 2011 this had dropped to around one in every three. The reduction in CVD mortality accounts for 60% of the decline in all-cause mortality. Despite these gains, CVD remains the most common cause of death in most OECD countries.

Changes in the health care system's capacity to prevent, treat and manage CVD have been instrumental in reducing mortality rates. A number of studies have estimated the relative contribution of health care treatments and risk-factor control in explaining the reduction in coronary heart disease (CHD) mortality. Studies published in the last ten years show that treatments account for around 40% of the overall improvements in CHD mortality and improved risk factors contributed around 50% (with 10% unaccounted for in the modelling studies). More recent studies though indicate that treatments are becoming a more important contributing factor.

The prospects for reducing the CVD disease burden are diminishing and the pattern of declining mortality is coming to an end or even reversing amongst some population groups, particularly younger age groups. Rising levels of obesity and diabetes are reducing our ability to make further inroads into reducing the CVD burden. Approximately 85 million people are living with diabetes in OECD countries, representing around 7% of people aged 20-79 years. Based on current trends, the number of people with diabetes in OECD countries is projected to reach almost 108 million by 2030, a 27% increase, and a further 23 million patients with higher health care needs and higher risk of complications.

CVD and diabetes outcomes vary across countries and strike at different ages

When measured in terms of the number of deaths, CVD imposes a heavy burden in all countries, but this burden is not equally distributed. The number of deaths caused by CVD varies considerably across OECD countries. Central and Eastern European Countries, such as the Slovak Republic, Hungary, Estonia and the Czech Republic, face the greatest CVD health burden with mortality rates in excess of 400 per 100 000 population. On the other side of the spectrum, countries such as Japan and France experienced mortality rates of less than 150. While many factors such as genetics, demographics and socio-economics are outside of the control of health system policy, the degree to which countries have been able to reduce the mortality burden over the years gives some room for optimism that some of the differences between countries can be influenced by good access to high quality health care.

While diabetes and CVD risks rise with age, there is strong evidence that in some countries they affect people of younger ages. Just under 2% of 20-39 year-olds have diabetes with prevalence climbing to around 20% for those aged between 60 and 79 years. Early onset of diabetes is substantially bigger in Mexico, Chile, Portugal, the United States and Poland where prevalence exceeds 12% of the 40 to 59 year-old population, compared to an OECD average of 8.9% in this age group. The age at which diabetes or CVD strikes has important implications for a patient's health status, and also for their social and economic status. Young survivors of CVD events such as AMI (acute myocardial infarction) and stroke may face serious deterioration in their quality of life, leading to greater social and health care needs over longer periods of time, and a reduced ability to work. People living with diabetes for longer periods of time are at higher risk of suffering complications that cause high levels of morbidity.

There are also significant challenges associated with delivering care for more elderly CVD and diabetes patients. As a result of the ageing population profile of many OECD countries, health systems are increasingly caring for elderly patients who not only have greater health care needs, but also more complex needs. Elderly patients are more likely to be suffering from multiple morbidities, may be more fragile and require multiple health and social services to deliver best-practice care.

Healthy lifestyles are key to success but countries have had mixed results in reducing risky behaviours

Cardiovascular disease (CVD) and diabetes are highly preventable diseases. The majority of CVD is caused by risk factors that can be controlled, treated or modified. These risk factors include high blood pressure, cholesterol, obesity, lack of physical activity, and tobacco use. CVD and diabetes share many common risk factors, including obesity and physical activity; therefore, the prevention of these two modifiable risk factors can lead to a lower prevalence of both diseases.

An underlying role for governments and markets is to make healthy lifestyle choices easier. In the field of prevention, government actions may take at least four types of actions aimed at: 1) improving the breadth or the attractiveness of healthy choices, relative to a free market situation; 2) modifying preferences to encourage healthy choices; 3) increasing the price of selected unhealthy choices; and 4) regulating selected unhealthy choices.

There has been mixed success in improving risky behaviours. On the one hand, smoking rates have declined substantially, but the percentage of the population who are obese continues to climb. The percentage of the population who smoked daily fell from 28% in 1997 to 20% in 2009, although men are more likely to smoke than females in most countries. Obesity levels have been rising in all OECD countries. Over the 2000 to 2009 period, the percentage of the population who were measured obese rose from 17% to 22%. For countries with self-reported indicators, obesity rose from 12% to 16% over the corresponding period. The more recent data indicate that for a number of OECD countries obesity rates have not increased to the extent that was projected. This provides some positive signs that the rates of increase are falling or have stabilised. Nevertheless, rates continue to increase in other countries and remain high in many OECD countries.

Strong anti-tobacco legislation and programmes are having an impact

All OECD countries have implemented anti-tobacco programmes and policies, including mass media campaigns to warn about the dangers of smoking, services and products to help smokers quit, advertising bans and taxes. However, the types of policies and intensity of those policies varies considerably by country. Analysis of the relationship between anti-tobacco policies and smoking rates show that more stringent policy and higher tobacco taxes have led to bigger falls in smoking rates among various population groups between 1996 and 2011. Higher taxes were particularly effective among younger age groups indicating that price signals play an important part of an effective deterrent strategy to take up smoking. Comprehensive anti-tobacco policies are also effective in cutting the number of adult male and female smokers.

A number of countries have continued to strengthen their anti-tobacco policies through a variety of means. Australia, for example, has introduced a number of innovative programmes and regulations, including its plain-packaging laws which took effect in December 2012. The aim of these laws was to remove a key method by which industry promotes its products to current and potential consumers. While evidence about their effectiveness is still being gathered, these initiatives may provide the next set of policy instruments for governments to help further reduce the harmful impact of smoking in society.

Governments are becoming more innovative in encouraging healthy lifestyles

Previous OECD analysis has called for strong government action to help citizens improve diets and increase physical activity. A number of interventions are shown to provide affordable and cost-effective solutions to the ever-increasing burden of obesity, with the potential to reduce mortality and reduce costs. According to the analysis, primary care can play an important role in tackling obesity. An intervention which targets high-risk individuals and is delivered by primary care physicians and dieticians has been shown to be highly effective and cost-effective in OECD countries.

Up to the mid-2000s, governments focused more of their actions on diets rather than on active lifestyles. Most actions were focused on increasing choice and delivering information and education programmes to influence preference. In recent years, however, a considerable number of countries have implemented a range of initiatives to combat obesity including new fiscal measures to raise the prices of foods that are high in fat, sugar or salt. While fiscal measures can have an important role in the policy armoury against obesity, they can also affect consumer choice and the wider economy. This may help explain why these taxes have been controversial in some countries. In fact, the "fat tax" was rescinded in Denmark at the start of 2013 following widespread criticism. In Mexico, the tax was met with an extensive public campaign both in favour of and opposed to the tax. These controversies highlight the need for careful consideration of the design of such fiscal measures in order to minimise any potential negative impacts.

Aside from the recent policy action against obesity, more countries are turning their attention to improving physical activity and levels of salt consumption to reduce the prevalence of high-blood pressure. Countries such as Canada, Finland, and the United Kingdom have used a variety of policy instruments to reduce salt intake amongst their citizens. These include public information, food labelling, taxation, regulation and marketing controls and food reformulation. These countries have successfully worked with food industries to set new salt targets for processed foods. Initiatives that have used multifaceted and reinforcing approaches have had real impact on consumption levels and health outcomes. Similar approaches are also being used to encourage more active lifestyles, particularly among the young. For example, the nationally co-ordinated programme "Let's Move" was launched in the United States in 2010. Programmes such as these have included multi-stakeholder frameworks, involving business and civil society to develop and implement public health policies. Evaluations of the effectiveness of such initiatives are only beginning to emerge and should be monitored closely for their potential effect on physical activity levels and obesity.

Strengthening primary care for better management of risk factors, diabetes and chronic CVD

Primary care is the centre of the health care system, and is particularly so for CVD and diabetes. Not only are primary care providers the first point-of-contact with the health system for many patients, they also deliver a range of health care services that are vital to the early diagnosis and control of cardiovascular risk factors and diabetes. Early diagnosis is an essential first step towards patients taking effective control, and limits the potential long-term damage that these risk factors can cause to the body.

The role of primary health care systems is likely to expand in the future. The ageing population is driving changes in health care needs, with more patients likely to: 1) suffer from multiple morbidities; 2) be more fragile; and 3) require multiple health and social services to deliver best-practice care. From age 75, the majority of people with any chronic condition have three or more conditions. Many patients with diabetes, for example, are also likely to have CVD, or chronic obstructive pulmonary disease (COPD) or mental illnesses. More than one in five patients with dementia also had coronary heart disease.

Such changing health needs have required reconfiguration of health care delivery models, including more effective co-ordination of care and greater continuity of care. Patients with multiple morbidities require more frequent access to a range of multi-disciplinary care providers that are well co-ordinated to tightly monitor treatments, avoid potential duplication and reduce the risks of ineffective or unsafe care. Multiple morbidities also raise some important issues around the need to broaden the clinical evidence upon which clinical guidelines' recommendations are often made.

Delivering the health care needs for older populations with CVD, diabetes and other comorbidities will place greater pressure on existing primary health care resources. A key challenge for OECD health care systems is therefore to realign health delivery systems with these evolving needs.

At the same time, to alleviate the burden in health systems through better health outcomes, efforts can be made to change health care needs of people with CVD and diabetes by involving them in managing their own care. Structured patient education programmes are known to reduce the risk of diabetes-related complications and a number of evidence-based programmes are already widely used in different countries including Australia, Canada, Denmark, Ireland, Spain, the United Kingdom and the United States. Educational programmes mixed with behavioural or psychological approaches contribute to increasing knowledge of diabetic care and achieving metabolic control. Interventions that mix patient collaboration and didactic presentations alongside regular follow-up have been shown to be effective in improving health outcomes. Programmes adapted to specific cultural background and age groups can also improve outcomes more effectively.

Good access is the foundation of a strong primary care system

Many OECD countries have achieved good access to primary care even among those in lower socio-economic groups. A highly accessible primary care system has the capacity to reduce inequalities in health outcomes and deliver care to those who stand to benefit most. This is particularly important for diseases such as diabetes which is far more prevalent among lower socio-economic groups. Aside from good financial access, patients also require easy physical access to primary care providers including short waiting times, low transaction costs such as travel expenses and time and out-of-hours care.

The two main financing sources for primary care are government contributions and patient out-of-pocket (OOP) costs. A relatively small contribution is made through private sources such as private health insurance. All countries use a mix of financing sources to fund primary care, although there is substantial variation between countries in the importance placed on these sources. On average, patients directly contribute around 19% of primary care expenditure but in countries such as Estonia, Luxembourg and France the percentage is less than 10% whereas in Turkey, Greece and Hungary it exceeds 40%. A number of countries have put in place additional measures to protect people with chronic diseases from high OOP costs. In Chile, for example, both diabetes and CVD risk factors are part of eighty health conditions that are guaranteed by law. This means that patients diagnosed with these conditions receive 100% reimbursement for a range of health care services and products used to treat these conditions. Similarly, countries such as Portugal, France and Mexico, provide additional coverage for specific treatments for identified diseases including diabetes and CVD.

The method by which care is financed has enormous implications on the access that patients have to health care. Higher OOP costs will lead to a lower use of primary care services, particularly among the poor. Reducing access to primary care also has wider ramifications. By foregoing routine visits to primary care physicians, patients are exposed to greater risk leading to a worsening of health status which, in turn, may require more intensive (and costly) acute care. It is therefore essential that primary care remains highly accessible to all. Good access is a necessary requirement to enable primary care practitioners to have regular contacts with patients, assess patient risk, monitor progress, deliver care, and adjust treatments when required.

Quality in primary care: Evidence of variation across countries

Although governments and professional organisations have invested substantial resources in the development and dissemination of clinical practice guidelines, there remains a substantial gap between recommended care and actual care. Some of the most common barriers to the implementation of CVD and diabetes guidelines in primary care relate to the lack of physician time, prescribing costs, poor patient compliance and a lack of dedicated health care resources for preventive medicine. Such systematic barriers can lead to suboptimal quality of care, poor compliance with recommended guidelines and, as a result, adverse health outcomes and higher resource use as patients suffer more complications.

Hospitalisation rates for conditions such as diabetes are commonly used as an indicator of primary care quality. With high-quality primary care, hospitalisations can often be avoided. However, these indicators are also a measure of the access that patients have to hospitals, as well as the role that hospitals play in the overall health care system. In some countries, access to hospitals is restricted due to financial or physical barriers, whereas in others countries they remain the predominant institution within which health care is provided. These two factors can explain some but not all the variation observed across countries for diabetes-related hospital admissions. However, there are a number of countries where diabetes-related hospitalisations go beyond that which can be explained by the general use of hospitals. Countries such as Hungary, Sweden, Belgium, France and Korea have a particularly high rate of diabetes-related hospitalisations, even after controlling for general hospital use. On the other hand, diabetic patients in countries such as Israel, Slovenia and Switzerland have fewer diabetes-related hospitalisations.

Quality of care for patients with chronic heart failure: Evidence of within country variation

Survival of patients with chronic heart failure (CHF) has improved over the last two decades, with trials concluding that outpatient medical treatment combined with fluid management and controlled exercise can improve survival rates. This evidence has now been widely incorporated in clinical practice guidelines that provide practitioners and patients with recommendations on optimum care. However, despite the potential for practice guidelines to improve health care outcomes, they are adopted too slowly or are applied inconsistently. This often leads to suboptimal care and fails to deliver further improvements in the quality of heart failure care and patient outcomes.

From the analysis presented in this report, adherence to recommended medication treatments among a sample of CHF treating centres show substantial variations not only across countries but also within OECD countries. Among the sample countries, within country variation is lowest in Portugal but relatively high in the Czech Republic, France, Israel and Italy. Analysis also shows that a number of country health system characteristics are associated with non-adherence. Higher levels of unmet needs and fewer doctors per head of population are associated with greater non-adherence. A number of quality initiatives such as the availability of information systems to exchange information across providers, primary care accreditation and provider incentives to comply with guidelines were all significantly associated with better adherence. These results suggest that greater access to health care and the implementation of quality initiatives are linked to greater guideline adherence among patients. However, these findings should be interpreted as mere associations and no causal relationship has been established.

The degree of variation in adherence within and across countries present important policy challenges. It suggests a need to identify the reasons why systematic variation exists and develop a better understanding of the factors that could help lift performance among providers and institutions that deliver poor quality care. Such factors may not only involve variation in local health care characteristics such as the number of available doctors within a region, but also the ability of national health system characteristics to reduce unwanted practice variation. These results also highlight the fact that international comparison of overall performance as well as the distribution of performance within health systems is a promising avenue for future benchmarking exercises.

Recent efforts to improve primary care quality show promise but no magic potion

Rising levels of chronic diseases such as diabetes and CVD have led many countries to introduce reforms to improve the quality and accessibility of primary care. As part of this renewed focus, there have also been concerted efforts to improve the measurement of primary care quality at both the national and international levels. Good primary care systems have the following strengths:

- *Structure*: Appropriate policies include primary care policies and regulations (e.g. population coverage for primary care services, resourcing and funding, policies to reduce mal-distribution of primary care providers and facilities; workforce development and training for primary care.
- *Accessibility*: Ease of access to primary care services requires a national and geographic supply of primary care services, appointment systems and access to after-hours care as well as the affordability and acceptability of services as perceived by patients.
- *Continuity*: The set of conditions are put in place to develop enduring doctor-patient relationships (e.g. patient registration systems, electronic health records, indicators of the doctor-patient relationship).
- *Co-ordination*: Primary care providers are able to co-ordinate patients' use of other parts of the health care system (e.g. the existence of a gatekeeping system, the skill mix of primary care providers, collaboration with other providers, and the integration of public health functions).
- *Comprehensiveness*: Breadth of services is available in primary care (e.g. procedures and certain preventive services).

Governments have introduced substantive reforms and invested significant resources to improve the quality of care provided to patients. The instruments by which governments can try to influence quality of care are summarised in Table 0.1. Many OECD countries are recognising the need to transform their health care systems and place greater focus on primary care and its role in managing complex patients. As part of this transformation, policy makers face the challenging task of making their health system more responsive to their population's health needs. This entails, in part, shaping the health care work force, its institutions as well as the co-ordination of care around the health care needs of patients with multiple chronic diseases.

Table 0.1. **Policies to improve quality of care in primary care**

Policy type	Examples
Health system inputs (professionals, organisations, technologies)	Accreditation and certification of health care institutes. Professional licensing including GPs and specialised nurses (e.g. diabetes or heart failure) and credentialing. Assessment and control of pharmaceutical products.
Health system design (allocation of responsibilities)	Accountability requirements at the primary care level. Quality governance structures in recognition of shifting focus of CVD and diabetes care towards primary care and social care. Quality as part of contracting and patient choice.
Monitoring (standards and information systems)	National standards and guidelines. Regulation on public reporting (including policies and support for registries, use of administrative databases, electronic health records, data sharing across health sectors, and patient surveys). Audit studies. Integrated guidelines on chronic diseases
Improvement (incentive structures and programmes)	Financial incentives such as pay for performance, care bundling, patient self-management. Programmes on patient safety and quality improvement.

Source: Adapted from OECD (2010), *Improving Value in Health Care: Measuring Quality*, OECD Publishing, Paris, *http://dx.doi.org/10.1787/9789264094819-en*.

Integrated and co-ordinated care

The proper management of patients with long-term diseases such as diabetes and CVD poses challenges to the organisation of health care delivery. In particular, fragmented health care systems between primary and specialist care have led to a number of structural barriers that prevent strong continuity of care and care co-ordination between providers. Without a well-coordinated care, patients with complex needs such as CVD or diabetes may find it difficult to navigate the health care system and receive the right type of care at the right time. Good information flows about a patient's health care needs may also be lacking in fragmented systems, leading to potential duplication of services, unnecessary or ineffective care or, worse, adverse events through prescribing errors.

Countries such as the Netherlands, Germany and the United States have responded to this challenge by developing new models of integrated care, designed to deliver patient-centred care to people with complex health care needs such as is required by many people with CVD. Most integrated care programmes have had a positive impact on patient functional status and outcomes as well as guideline adherence. Whilst almost all studies concluded that integrated care reduced the number of hospitalisations, these did not result in overall cost savings. Most reviews found mixed or insignificant evidence on the effects of integrated care on health care cost.

Better information systems to monitor performance

The use of information technology is becoming an important tool for performance management in primary care. A number of countries are making better use of electronic patient records to automatically derive information that can be used to improve patient care as well as measure performance within and outside the practice. Systems such as the Danish General Practice Quality Unit (DAK-E), and Israel's National Programme for Quality Indicators in Community Healthcare (QICH) are showing notable improvements in primary care quality, particularly on process indicators relating to cardiovascular risk factors and diabetes. Yet other measures such as glycaemic control are proving more difficult, with the percentage of patients with good blood glucose control staying relative stable over recent years. While some countries have made substantial progress in this field, measuring primary care quality remains a complex task. The sector is characterised by thousands of independent practices which makes system-wide changes more difficult. This, in part, explains why countries have also invested time and effort into developing better governance structures for primary care.

Pay-for-performance

Over the last 20 years, pay-for-performance schemes have become an increasingly common method for paying primary care providers in OECD countries. Pay-for-performance schemes operate in around half of all OECD countries, focusing mainly on preventive care and care for chronic disease. While the design of these schemes varies considerably across countries, the central element is to make some part of provider reimbursement conditional on the quality of care delivered. All schemes include a common set of four basic elements: 1) performance domains and measures; 2) basis for reward; 3) reward; and 4) data reporting and verification.

A recent systematic review found that pay-for-performance schemes have led to an improvement in performance of incentivised aspects of care. The effects were generally stronger in primary care than in secondary care. The results suggest that pay-for-performance schemes appear to have had a small positive impact on the quality of care for diabetes in countries such as the United Kingdom and the United States. Evaluations of the UK Quality Outcomes Framework also show improvements in quality measures relating to diabetes, hypertension, heart disease, and stroke. Despite these successes, the evidence is frequently limited to measuring impact on short-term clinical processes (e.g., periodically performing eye exams for diabetes patients) and, to a lesser extent, intermediate outcomes (e.g., HbA1c levels of diabetes patients).

Nevertheless, pay-for-performance schemes can potentially form a useful part of a blended payment system to drive longer term changes, particularly if it promotes development and measurement of quality indicators in primary care. It can be part of an important move towards better purchasing arrangements where the quality of care delivered plays a more prominent role. However, it is becoming increasingly recognised that such schemes are highly context specific, suggesting that there are other conditions that need to be met in order for pay-for-performance to have a positive impact on outcomes.

Better access to high quality acute care

Recent decades have witnessed substantial innovations in the acute treatment of patients. In 1970 the first vein bypass surgery was performed and in 1978 the first angioplasty was carried out. Since their introduction, the acute care sector has become increasingly sophisticated in dealing with acute CVD events safely and effectively. For instance, for ischemic stroke care, clinical trials have demonstrated the benefits of thrombolytic treatment and, in the case of haemorrhagic stroke, more surgical options have become available. However, patient access to evidence-based technologies is only part of the optimum treatment pathway. In order to derive maximum benefit from these innovations, access to care must be swift, available at all times, and delivered in high-quality facilities. In this way, the clinical evidence has enormous implications for the way that health care services are delivered. This includes the way that services are organised and co-ordinated, the resources available, the timeliness of care and the processes by which quality of care is monitored.

This complex pathway is sometimes referred to as the *chain of survival* in recognition of the importance of each link in the pathway from the moment a person suffers a CVD event. A well-functioning chain is one where: patients or bystanders recognise symptoms and take action; first medical responders are on the scene in the fastest possible time and provide appropriate diagnosis, care and transport; and, once in hospital, the patient receives the right care at the right time provided by the right clinical staff.

More can be done to improve pre-hospital systems for CVD

The speed at which a person receives emergency care after suffering a CVD event can often mean the difference between life and death. In the case of cardiac arrest, for example, there is a 10% decrease in the likelihood of survival for every minute that defibrillation (administration of a controlled electric shock to the heart to allow restoration of a normal rhythm) is delayed. Survival after an out-of-hospital cardiac arrest is low, ranging from 1.2% for studies conducted in Asian regions to 12.8% for studies conducted in Australian cities. European and North American studies recorded survival rates of 10% and 6.8%, respectively.

To improve out-of-hospital survival many jurisdictions have sought to: 1) raise public awareness and education about recognising the symptoms of heart attack and stroke; 2) improve the ability of bystanders to respond appropriately; 3) develop a high-functioning ambulance system, delivering fast response times and a highly professional workforce able to deliver an appropriate first response; and 4) a high level of integration between emergency services and acute care facilities. There are many examples that show how some jurisdictions such as London and Seattle have successfully responded to the challenge of pre-hospital care, including the enhanced diagnostic capabilities of their ambulances and reduced time to hospital treatment. Nevertheless, the decentralised nature of emergency medical services in many OECD countries limits the ability to report comparative national data. Most studies in this field are on a regional basis and show considerable heterogeneity in not only patient outcomes, but also processes of care, emergency services resources and organisation. This suggests that there may be a role for a national policy framework for the measurement, benchmarking and continuous quality improvement of emergency services to lift overall standards and reduce heterogeneity within countries.

From the hospital door to treatment: Moving towards faster access to quality care

The uptake and diffusion patterns of acute care procedures such as bypass surgery and percutaneous coronary intervention (PCI) have varied considerably across OECD countries. Countries with greater resources and technical skills are known to be early adopters of these technologies. However, as the evidence gathers, costs fall, and skills are developed, countries that may have been late starters have the ability to catch up to the early adopters. Nevertheless, there remain wide-ranging variations in the use of these coronary care interventions across countries; even after several decades following the publication of evidence that demonstrate the clinical benefit of these procedures. The widespread disparity has led to programmes such as the European "Stent 4 Life" initiative which have increased PCI use substantially.

Not only is access to treatment important but so is the timing. Clinical practice guidelines have set out clear recommendations on the maximum times for the commencement of treatment following acute CVD events such as stroke or heart attack. More countries such as the Czech Republic, France, Israel, Japan, Korea, Poland and Singapore are starting to use the timeliness of intervention as an important process indicator of hospital performance, with a number of those showing substantial improvements in the timeliness of care over recent years. Nevertheless, this is an area where further improvements can have a real impact on clinical outcomes and also where better measurement could help lift standards.

Although the benefits of stroke units have been known for a considerable amount of time, adoption of stroke units has been slow in many countries and still too many patients do not receive optimal care due to several obstacles. National efforts that involve not only additional resources but also better networking of facilities and performance monitoring are having demonstrable effects on patient access to specialised care. In delivering greater geographic access, there are important resource and staffing constraints that may restrict the expansion of specialised coronary centres. Countries face a delicate trade-off between providing greater access to specialised care but at the same time ensuring that the quality of care is not compromised by lack of workforce skills or low volumes of care.

Better access and quality of care have improved survival after a heart attack and stroke

Acute care quality for CVD has improved over the last ten years. Thirty day case-fatality rates for both AMI and stroke have fallen across the OECD as a whole, as well as in almost every single OECD country. Case-fatality rates reflect the percentage of patients who die within the 30 days following an admission to hospital for AMI, ischemic stroke and haemorrhagic stroke.

For AMI, the OECD average case-fatality rate for the admission-based indicators is 8.8% and most countries now report a case-fatality rate of less than 10%. The average rate of decline in AMI case-fatality rates was between 4.2% and 4.9%, depending on the type of case-fatality rate indicator used. For ischemic stroke, the average admission-based case-fatality rate is 8.7%. Again, almost all countries were able to reduce their case-fatality rates over the last ten years. Case-fatality rates for haemorrhagic stroke are not only substantial higher than either AMI or ischemic stroke, there is also greater variation between countries. The case-fatality rate for admission-based haemorrhagic stroke averaged 22% and 30% for the patient-based indicator. The average rate of decline in case-fatality rate was around 2.4% over the ten year period, but there are some signs that the rate of decline has accelerated since 2005.

There are encouraging signs across most countries that case-fatality rates are falling, and that these are reflecting better access to high-quality acute care for patients. Countries such as Austria, the Czech Republic, Korea, the Netherlands, the Slovak Republic and the United Kingdom have done well in reducing case-fatality rates for both AMI and strokes over recent years. Nevertheless, the figures also provide some warning signs for countries with very high case-fatality rates or where the decline has not been as extensive as other OECD countries. Case-fatality rates in countries such as Hungary and Mexico are not only very high compared to their OECD peers, the rate of improvement has been slower than many of their peers. Countries such as Finland, Japan, Latvia and New Zealand face more specific challenges where their performance could be improved for some case-fatality rates.

Improved resourcing is associated with better quality care

Recent developments in monitoring acute care quality at an international level have made it possible to undertake cross-country analysis of hospital performance. In particular, it can develop a better understanding of how health system characteristics and policies can influence the relationship between hospital expenditure and the quality of acute CVD care, using 30-day case-fatality rates for 1) AMI; 2) ischemic stroke; and 3) haemorrhagic stroke as indicators.

Analysis of OECD Health Statistics covering the period from 2001 to 2011 reveals that, across OECD countries, higher hospital care expenditure is related to better quality of CVD acute care. This relationship is highly significant when measuring acute care quality through case-fatality rates for AMI and ischemic stroke but not for haemorrhagic stroke. Results show that a 1% *increase* in health expenditure is associated with an approximate 0.37% and 0.53% *decrease* in the female and male AMI 30-day case fatality rate, respectively. Hospital expenditure is even more strongly related to ischemic stroke, where a 1% increase in expenditure is associated with a 0.61% drop in female case-fatalities and a 0.69% drop among males. It should be noted that these results are an OECD average and is based on a small sample covering a relatively short time-frame.

But some countries are getting more quality from extra spending than others

Analysis shows that the relationship between hospital expenditure and CVD acute care quality varies across countries, particularly with respect to the ischemic stroke and AMI. This implies that some countries have derived greater improvements in acute care quality from additional expenditure than others. For the majority of countries though, the relationship between expenditure and case fatality is not statistically different from the OECD average. However, in terms of female AMI case-fatality rates and hospital expenditure, performance in Finland and Poland is lower than the OECD average, whereas Denmark has a significantly better than average performance. For males, Finland and Poland are joined by Spain and Chile in the lower than average performance, whereas Luxembourg joins Denmark in the better than average performance ledger. For ischemic stroke, the best performance was found in the Netherlands for both males and females. Less than average performances were estimated for Chile, Hungary, Mexico and Israel. The results show a substantial degree of consistency in country rankings across both AMI and ischemic stroke case-fatality rates and genders. Countries such as Denmark, Luxembourg and Norway, for example, consistently rank in the top five of high performing countries. It should be noted that these results are not predictive of future success. The relationship between health care resources and quality may change over time. In particular, it is feasible that the way in which resources are deployed and organised will become a bigger determinant of future success than the volume of resources.

Better access and quality initiatives can help explain hospital performance

The analysis in this report indicates that some health system characteristics help explain why the relationship between expenditure and quality differs between countries. The results show that greater access to acute care (as proxied by the percentage of hospital expenditure that is public funded) is associated with improved hospital performance. There is also some evidence that countries that pay hospitals on the basis of global budgets and those that systematically measure hospital performance have been able to extract greater quality improvements from additional expenditure.

While these results offer some insights into understanding hospital performance, there are several limitations that should be taken into account when interpreting the findings. First and foremost is the small sample size. Second, is that the performance analysis has only focused on the relationship between expenditure and quality when other objectives are also important. Third, is that the key explanatory variable in this analysis has been hospital expenditure. This variable can only serve as a proxy for the hospital resources devoted to CVD care.

Some of the limitations in the current analysis may be resolved in future years, as current OECD work is developing more detailed expenditure data that can be used to examine the relationship between disease-specific resources and outcomes. Similarly, work is also being undertaken to develop health-specific purchasing power parity (PPP) estimates that will permit a more appropriate method of converting expenditure data into common resource units. It may therefore be of value to repeat this type of analysis in future years, as the OECD Health Statistics develops into a stronger longitudinal dataset.

From onset to discharge: Full pathway monitoring and governance

While acute CVD care quality has improved over recent decades, further gains are feasible. Experiences have shown that further improvements along the entire *chain of survival* are feasible and can have a real impact on the quality of care and health outcomes. The *chain of survival* involves the effective operation and interaction of many parts of the acute care system: public awareness and first response capabilities, high functioning emergency response teams, adequate resources and access to specialised care and treatments. What is evident is that each of these links needs to perform well as individual units and they also need to be integrated in order to optimise health care outcomes. There is increasing recognition that stronger governance over the full pathway of acute CVD care can strengthen the acute care pathway.

In France, for example, numerous professional organisations and other stakeholders have worked together with the National Authority for Health (Haute Autorité de Santé – HAS) to develop a common and shared base of Clinical Practice Indicators (CPI) for AMI. These indicators measure the optimal clinical pathway over the full patient care cycle, capturing health system performance in three distinct phases of care: 1) from pain to reperfusion; 2) reperfusion to discharge; and 3) post-infarction one-year follow-up.[1]

Some examples of full pathway monitoring could include:

- the time interval between onset of symptoms and treatment,
- delivery of the right treatment within recommended timeframe,
- rate of patients receiving appropriate medications upon discharge,
- rate of patients receiving specialist diabetes advice on severe hyperglycaemia,
- proportion of patients seen by allied health professionals to assess longer term needs and plan services upon discharge,
- rates of patients receiving appropriate medication at short and medium term follow-up,
- rate of correspondence between the GP and the cardiologist at short and medium term follow-up.

This wider frame of reference encapsulates the many initiatives that countries have used to deliver better CVD acute care for their patients, incorporating first responders, emergency care, diagnosis, acute care treatment and rehabilitative services, and the return back home. Such a wider perspective of optimum care can help policy makers and clinical managers to identify potential weaknesses as well as develop more comprehensive plans to improve performance along the pathway.

Policy conclusions and implications

The successes

The health system's capacity to prevent, manage and treat CVD and diabetes has improved markedly over recent decades, leading to substantial gains in health outcomes for patients. Healthier lifestyles have had a major role in improving outcomes, and more patients are benefiting from high quality primary and acute care services and greater access to effective technologies. Health care programmes and policies have underpinned many of these successes. For example,

Lifestyles

- Smoking policies have been shown to be highly effective. Tobacco control policies involving public health, education, regulation and health services have saved lives. The multifaceted policy approach used to cut smoking provides lessons for other lifestyle policies. A key factor behind the anti-smoking campaigns' success has been that, collectively, the tobacco control policies have changed the cultural status attached to smoking.

- Policies that involve a co-operative approach between government, industry and other stakeholders are having a measurable impact on salt consumption and hypertension.
- Countries are enlarging their policy armouries to combat unhealthy lifestyles. Fiscal measures to combat obesity and plain package tobacco products to restrict branding are examples that are worth monitoring for their impact.

Primary care

- Most countries deliver equitable access to primary care for patients with CVD and diabetes through high levels of public funding and insurance coverage.
- Countries have put in place specially designed chronic disease initiatives to enhance access to primary care for patients with CVD and diabetes.
- New and innovative primary care initiatives are showing some promise in improving quality of care through pay-for-performance, integrated care, monitoring and governance.

Acute care

- Many countries are investing in highly specialised care and more patients have greater access to such care after a heart-attack or stroke.
- Hospitals are delivering better quality care with 30-day case-fatality rates for heart attacks, ischemic stroke and haemorrhagic stroke all falling in virtually all OECD countries.
- Better hospital performance is linked to better quality systems for monitoring, and benchmarking, as well as greater access to care and payment mechanisms.

The challenges

The report has also identified a number of policy challenges that need to be addressed so that health system performance can be improved and that further inroads into the CVD and diabetes health burden can be made. Some of these challenges are common to many OECD health systems, whereas others are more specific to particular countries. The report has found the following key challenges for OECD countries:

- Rising levels of obesity stand in the way of reducing the burden of CVD and diabetes even further, particularly among younger age groups.
- Some lifestyle policies have faced strong criticism on the basis that these may interfere with personal choice or impose costs on the wider economy. At the same time, many of these policies are shown to be highly effective tools in changing unhealthy behaviours that, in turn, save lives and costs.
- Management of CVD risk factors and diabetes can be improved. Less than half of all patients attain their clinical goals for blood pressure and cholesterol and for the majority of diabetes patients, blood glucose levels remain well above recommended clinical targets.
- Quality of care varies not only across countries but also within countries. This suggests that part of the policy challenge is to not only lift overall standards but also minimise unwanted variation in quality.
- The ageing population will lead to more patients with multiple comorbidities which will generate not only greater demand for health care but also change the complexity and type of care that patients require.

- The decentralised nature of emergency care has contributed to widespread variation in resources, organisation and performance across and within countries.
- Health care systems have faced difficulties in providing patients with access to specialised acute care facilities and technologies as set out in clinical practice guidelines.

The recommendations

The main recommendations identified here seek to help countries by building on the policy successes experienced in many OECD countries and also take into account many of the challenges that policy makers currently face.

Improving lifestyles

- Tobacco control policies have been effective and further strengthening of policies, particularly in countries where smoking rates remain high, can have a real impact on health outcomes.
- Strong advocacy and stakeholder engagement is needed to develop support for making healthy lifestyle choices easier and less costly.
- Single policy measures are likely to have less impact than multifaceted approaches. Policy makers should use all available tools, including regulations, education, incentives, as well as health care programmes and services to work in unison and strengthen their effectiveness.

Strengthening primary care

- Access to primary care should be maintained or strengthened further for patients with diabetes and CVD. Good access involves not only financial access through adequate provision of insurance coverage, but also good physical access that minimises waiting times and other barriers to care.
- Develop better information systems to monitor patient care and primary care performance to improve adherence to evidence-based recommended care. Information systems should also be able to monitor and develop a better understanding of variation in the quality of care within countries.
- Strengthen governance systems to improve accountability and transparency of primary care performance and use available performance management tools to incentivise (financial or otherwise) the delivery of quality care.
- Continue development and research into models of primary care delivery that are aligned to increasingly complex patient needs and can facilitate improved continuity of care as well as highly integrated and co-ordinated care across providers.

Towards high quality acute care

- Consider the development of a national policy framework to improve pre-hospital performance following an acute CVD event. Such a framework should seek to develop policies for:
  - Raising awareness and improving the capacity of the community to respond to acute CVD events.
  - Planning emergency system resource requirement, professional skills needs and training capacity.

- ❖ Setting national standards for the measurement, bench-marking and continuous quality improvement of emergency services to lift overall standards and reduce heterogeneity within countries.
- Develop policy instruments that support the widespread adoption of effective CVD and diabetes health care services, including a stronger role for national government, professional bodies and other stakeholders to monitor and set standards around best-practice care.
- Strengthen governance and monitoring systems along full *chain of survival* that incorporates pre-hospital, hospital and post-hospital phases.

Summary

The mortality burden of CVD has fallen over recent decades. Health care systems and innovative policies have made a substantial contribution to this success by reducing smoking rates, improving access to primary care, and improving the quality of acute care. Nevertheless, substantial challenges remain. CVD remains the number one killer in most OECD countries, diabetes and obesity is on the rise and despite improvements, gaps between actual care and recommended care persist.

The analysis shows that resources are an important driver of health system performance in the area of CVD and diabetes, but they do not automatically deliver the best outcomes. Health care resources need to be well managed and effectively used to deliver care that is in line with the best available evidence. This is where many OECD health systems continue to struggle. The evidence on what constitutes good quality care has been in public domain for decades but many OECD countries are still coming to terms with the changes that need to be made in their health systems to deliver such care.

One of the most significant challenges facing policy makers is to improve health system's capacity to effectively integrate evidence-based care recommendations into usual care. This capacity should not only lift overall standards of care but also reduce the variability in the quality of care provided within OECD health systems. Such reforms can be addressed through improved national policy frameworks that involve all government, professional organisations, insurers, patients as well as other stakeholders. Such a framework would establish stronger systems of governance that focuses on the whole pathway of CVD and diabetes as well as develop better monitoring systems as a necessary requirement for further improvements.

Note

1. For more details see: *www.has-sante.fr/portail/jcms/c_1561455/en/myocardial-infarction-mi-full-care-cycle-and-patient-outcomes.*

Cardiovascular Disease and Diabetes
Policies for Better Health and Quality of Care

Chapter 1

The burden of cardiovascular disease and diabetes

Cardiovascular disease (CVD) and diabetes are both major drivers of the global burden of disease. They are a complex set of diseases involving a wide array of health sectors that place considerable pressure on health systems across countries. Chapter 1 describes the burden of CVD and diabetes across OECD countries and examines trends in mortality and morbidity burdens according to gender and age across countries over time. This chapter summarises recent findings that seek to explain some of these recent trends and then describes the economic burden of CVD and diabetes in terms of direct health care cost.

The statistical data for Israel are supplied by and under the responsibility of the relevant Israeli authorities. The use of such data by the OECD is without prejudice to the status of the Golan Heights, East Jerusalem and Israeli settlements in the West Bank under the terms of international law.

Introduction

Cardiovascular disease (CVD) and diabetes are both major drivers of the global burden of disease. In 2011, CVD accounted for nearly one-third of deaths across all OECD countries and was the number one cause of death in most countries (OECD, 2013a). Over 85 million people living in OECD countries were estimated to have diabetes in 2011, representing around 7% of people aged 20-79 years (IDF, 2013). While diabetes and CVD are two distinct diseases, they are closely connected because they share common risk factors (e.g. obesity) and people with diabetes are at greater risk of CVD.

CVD and diabetes are a complex set of diseases involving a wide array of health sectors. As shown in Figure 1.1, CVD and diabetes involve all aspects of the health care system, including public health programmes and preventive services, primary care, emergency and acute care, as well as rehabilitative and long-term care.

Each aspect of the health system has an important set of functions that can help reduce the health burden of CVD and diabetes. The role of health promotion programmes and services is to promote healthy lifestyles and reduce the prevalence of obesity, tobacco smoking and excessive alcohol consumption, as well as improve physical activity in the population. Primary care services have an important role in promoting healthy lifestyles for individual patients and, in addition, are instrumental in the diagnosis and treatment of risk factors, such as high blood pressure and high cholesterol. These services also help patients to manage their diabetes. In the case of an acute episode such as stroke and heart attack, the acute care sector is responsible for providing effective and timely treatment to maximise the likelihood of survival and improve long-term prognosis. Following acute care, services including not only rehabilitative care but also primary care, play a vital role in managing CVD, diabetes and associated complications that may have arisen after an acute episode. Such health care services are integral to minimising the morbidity associated with such events.

To deliver effective services and programmes along the CVD and diabetes pathway, a health care system needs to ensure that: 1) there are adequate financial and physical resources such as doctors, nurses, hospital beds and technologies; 2) those services and technologies are highly accessible to the people in need of those services. This implies both financial access, so that cost does not impose unnecessary barriers to care, and physical access, to ensure that care is timely; and 3) the health care system delivers high quality care.

This report examines how countries perform in their ability to prevent, manage and treat CVD and diabetes. The analysis in this report examines the pathways by which OECD countries deliver the programmes and services related to CVD and diabetes, namely health promotion, public health, primary care and acute care. Chapters 2, 3 and 4 of this report describe the main health sectors involved in CVD and diabetes prevention and care. In doing so, the report will describe the resources available to prevent disease and deliver care, the accessibility and utilisation of those services, as well as the effectiveness and quality of care delivered.

Figure 1.1. **Analytical framework for the OECD project on cardiovascular disease and diabetes**

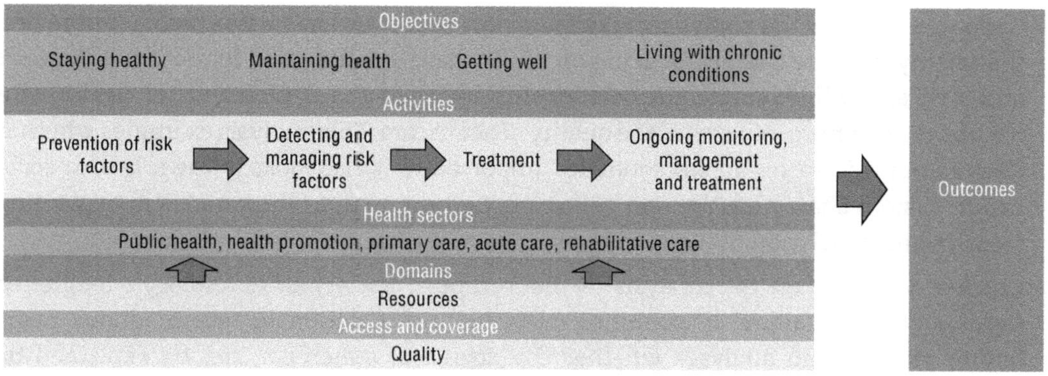

Source: Adapted from OECD (2013), *Cancer Care: Assuring Quality to Improve Survival*, OECD Publishing, Paris, *http://dx.doi.org/10.1787/9789264181052-en.*

The main aim of this analysis is to explore the reasons behind the reported differences in the overall health outcomes resulting from cardiovascular disease and diabetes. The analytical components examine how countries have used available health care resources to reduce the overall burden of CVD and diabetes. It will focus on the variation in OECD health systems' ability to convert health care inputs (such as expenditure) into health gains. This part of the analysis will also examine the role of health system characteristics and policy settings in explaining cross-country differences in performance. The findings of these analyses are reported in Chapters 5 and 6.

This report is structured as follows:

- The remainder of Chapter 1 describes the burden of CVD and diabetes across OECD countries. After a short description of CVD and diabetes, it will examine trends in mortality and morbidity. It summarises recent findings that seek to explain some of these recent trends. This chapter will also assess the mortality and morbidity burden across countries according to gender and age. Finally, this chapter will describe the economic burden in terms of direct health care cost.
- Chapter 2 looks at the health promotion and public health contribution to maintaining healthy lifestyles in OECD countries. It examines recent trends in obesity, tobacco and alcohol consumption, and physical exercise. This chapter will outline policies that health systems have introduced recently to combat unhealthy lifestyles. The chapter will benchmark OECD countries in relation to their CVD and diabetes lifestyle rankings.
- Chapter 3 focuses on the role of the primary care system and its ability to diagnose and control common CVD-related risk factors. It will examine the strengths and weaknesses of primary care by looking at the resources available, its accessibility, and quality. It will include data on prescribing patterns for diabetic patients and the rates of CVD and diabetes-related hospital admissions that are largely avoidable through proper primary care management. It will assess country performance on the basis of its relative incidence of high blood pressure and cholesterol levels, avoidable hospital admissions, and quality prescribing and diabetes-related complications.
- Chapter 4 describes the resources, accessibility and quality of the acute care sector. It will describe cross-country variation in available resources and accessibility to timely treatments for acute CVD episodes and diabetes complications. It will examine the use

of procedures such as bypass surgery and other coronary interventions. It will also show recent trends in acute care quality for stroke and heart attack.

- Chapter 5 presents the analytical results on how countries have performed in improving the quality of acute care by focusing on 30-day case-fatality rates for both heart attack and stroke. It will examine the relationship between the deployment of health care resources and improvements in the quality of acute care. This analysis examines whether this relationship varies across countries. Importantly, it also looks at the role of specific health system characteristics and policies to determine their importance in explaining cross-country variation in the quality of CVD acute care.
- Chapter 6 reports on the analysis of the European Society of Cardiology's long-term registry of heart failure. It examines cross-country variation in recommended heart failure practice and analyses whether the degree of adherence can be explained by health system characteristics and policies.

The primary data source used in this report is OECD Health Statistics 2013. These data provide a comprehensive picture of health care expenditure, health care use and resources, lifestyles and risk factors, health care quality and health outcomes. The statistics that relate directly to CVD and diabetes care and outcomes provide the basis for the statistical analysis presented in this report. In addition, the analysis uses information from the 2012 OECD Health Systems Characteristics (HSC) Survey which provides details of countries' health care institutional arrangements, funding and financing provisions and governance structure (see *www.oecd.org/els/health-systems/characteristics.htm* for more details). This data source was supplemented with information collected through the OECD's CVD and Diabetes Health System Characteristics Survey. This survey was completed in 16 OECD countries as well as Singapore.[1]

Cardiovascular disease and diabetes defined

According to the American Heart Foundation, cardiovascular disease is a collective term for a range of problems, many of which are related to a process called atherosclerosis. Atherosclerosis refers to the build-up of plaque which narrows the arteries and makes it harder for blood to flow. A heart attack, also referred to as an acute myocardial infarction (AMI), occurs when the blood flow that brings oxygen to the heart muscle is severely reduced or cut off completely. In severe cases, or if timely treatments are unavailable, a patient suffering a heart attack may die. Nevertheless, a person who has had a heart attack can often go back to normal activities, particularly if the heart attack was less severe or if the damage to the heart muscle was limited by timely and effective treatments. The long-term prognosis will depend on the damage to the heart muscle and heart valves, as well as where that damage is located.

Cardiovascular disease also refers to two common types of stroke: ischemic stroke and haemorrhagic stroke. Both types of stroke can cause brain cells to die, leading to a potential loss in functions such as walking or talking. Depending on the extent of damage to the brain cells, some effects of stroke are permanent. However, over time some injured cells can repair themselves and, through rehabilitation, other brain cells may take control of those areas that were injured. Through these processes, physical functions such as speech, memory and mobility may all improve. CVD also refers to a range of other diseases related to the circulatory system, including heart failure, vascular diseases of the brain and kidney, and peripheral arterial disease. Box 1.1 provides further details of the definitions of other common types of cardiovascular disease that will be referred to in this report.

Box 1.1. Common terms used in this report: Cardiovascular diseases and diabetes

Common types of cardiovascular diseases

Heart attack or acute myocardial infarction (AMI) occurs when the supply of blood to the heart muscle is suddenly blocked, usually by a blood clot. There are two types of heart attack:

- ST segment elevation myocardial infarction (STEMI) is the most serious type of heart attack. It is caused by a total blockage of the coronary artery, leading to a prolonged interruption to the blood supply. This can cause extensive damage to a large area of the heart.
- Non-ST segment elevation myocardial infarctions (NSTEMI) tend to be less serious than STEMI. It involves a partial blockage to the supply of blood to the heart, and damage to a smaller area of the heart.

Cardiac arrest occurs when the heart stops pumping blood around the body. It is most commonly caused by an abnormal heart rhythm called ventricular fibrillation. Many cardiac arrests happen to people who are already having a heart attack.

Cerebrovascular disease refers to conditions that develop as a result of problems with the brain's blood vessels. Stroke is a common type of cerebrovascular disease. A stroke occurs when the blood supply to part of the brain is interrupted, causing brain cells to become damaged or to die. There are two main types of stroke:

- Ischemic stroke occurs when something, like a blood clot, blocks an artery that carries blood to the brain.
- Haemorrhagic stroke occurs when a blood vessel bursts and bleeds into the brain.

Heart failure is when the heart is unable to pump blood around the body as well as it used to. It usually occurs when the heart muscle becomes too weak to work properly.

Coronary heart disease (CHD), also known as ischemic heart disease (IHD), occurs when the blood supply to the heart is blocked or interrupted by a slow build-up of fatty substances in the coronary arteries (the blood vessels that supply the heart muscle with blood).

Atherosclerosis is the process by which fatty substances, such as cholesterol, clog the arteries and reduce the flow of blood to the heart. These substances are called plaques or atheromas.

Diabetes

Diabetes is a condition that causes a person's blood sugar level to become too high. There are two main types of diabetes:

- Type 1 diabetes is where the body's immune system attacks and destroys the cells which produce insulin. It is also sometimes known as insulin-dependent diabetes, juvenile diabetes or early-onset diabetes.
- Type 2 diabetes is where either the body fails to produce enough insulin, or the body's cells fail to respond to insulin. This, the most common type of diabetes, is often linked to obesity.

Diabetes is a chronic disease, characterised by high levels of glucose in the blood. It occurs either because the pancreas stops producing the hormone insulin (type 1 diabetes), or through a reduced ability to produce insulin (type 2 diabetes). People with diabetes are at a greater risk of developing cardiovascular diseases such as heart attack and stroke. They also have elevated risks for sight loss, foot and leg amputation due to damage to nerves and blood vessels, and renal failure requiring dialysis or transplantation. It is increasingly recognised that many people who have type-2 diabetes also have multiple risk factors that commonly appear together. This has become known as metabolic syndrome, which appears to place additional cardiovascular risk on patients (IDF, 2006). The recognition of metabolic syndrome can lead to important new understanding of how risk factors interact and affect patients. In turn, this can lead to better diagnosis, risk assessment and treatments. While the science around metabolic syndrome is continuously evolving, at present little data are available on its prevalence or health care burden. This is why, for the purposes of this report, the focus is on type 2 diabetes, risk factors and CVD.

Despite substantial gains, CVD remains the leading cause of mortality

While CVD remains the most common cause of death, the mortality rate attributable to CVD has declined substantially in recent decades. Over the 50-year period since 1960, average mortality rates for CVD fell from 776 to 299 per 100 000 population. Across OECD countries, this represents a drop of 61% over the 50-year period. Figure 1.2 shows that CVD mortality rates were fairly steady over the 1960s and then started to decrease in the 1970s. The rate of decrease accelerated after 1985 and has been consistent since that time.

Mortality rates from all other causes have also fallen since the 1960s. Over a 50-year period, the annual rate of decline was just under 1%, representing a 38% drop over the entire period. Interestingly, the rate of decline for all other causes of death was similar to the rate of decline in CVD mortality up to the mid-1980s, but has since fallen behind. Up until the mid-1980s, CVD accounted for one in every two deaths in OECD countries, but by 2011 this had dropped to around one in every three. The reduction in CVD mortality accounts for 60% of the decline in all-cause mortality.

Figure 1.2. **Mortality rates for cardiovascular diseases and all other causes of death in OECD countries**

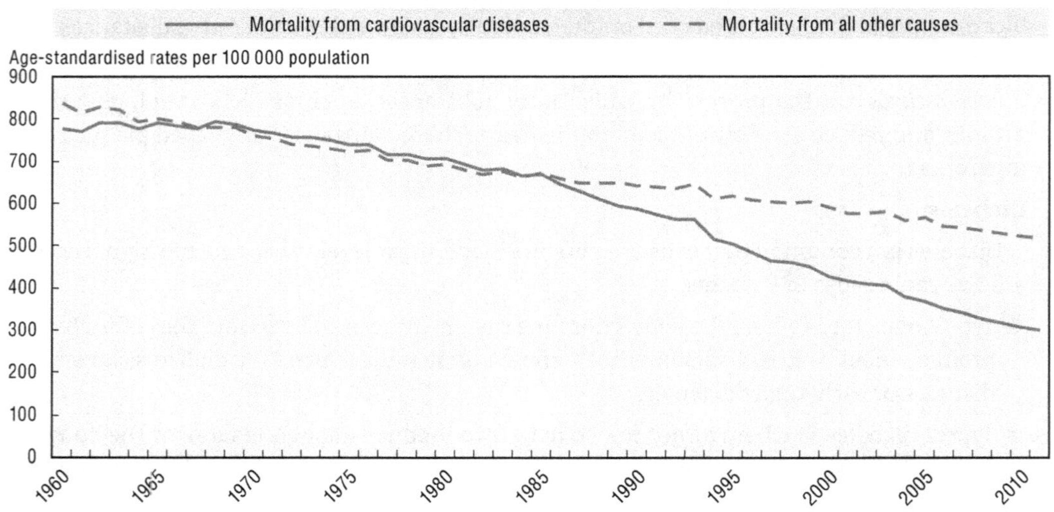

Source: OECD Health Statistics 2013, http://dx.doi.org/10.1787/health-data-en.

While the risk of CVD rises with age, its burden is not restricted to the elderly. CVD affects many people in their middle age and is a leading cause of premature death. The number of potential years of life lost (PYLL) is a commonly used measure of premature mortality which provides an explicit way of weighing deaths occurring at younger ages, which are, a priori, preventable. Figure 1.3 presents time-series data on the number of PYLL due to CVD as well as for all other causes of death by using the age limit of 70. The vertical axis represents the average number of PYLL per 100 000 population across OECD countries. Among men, CVD accounts for approximately 18% of the total number of PYLL. The corresponding figure for women is 12%.

Over time, the number of PYLL for CVD and other diseases has fallen considerably. Similar to the trend in mortality, the number of PYLL due to CVD have declined substantially between 1960 and 2011. For women, the average PYLL across OECD countries fell from 1 300 life years lost per 100 000 population in 1960 to less than 300 in 2011; this represents a drop of 75%. For men, the PYLL due to CVD fell from 2 352 in 1960 to less than 900 in 2011, reflecting a 62% drop. The decline for men has been particularly strong since 1985.

Figure 1.3. **Trends in potential years of life lost (PYLL) due to CVD and other diseases, by gender**

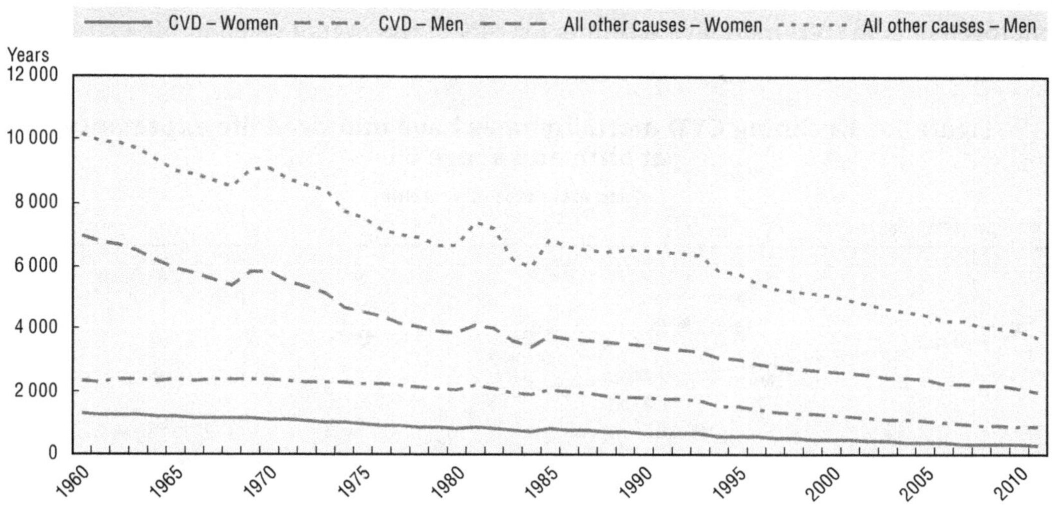

Source: OECD Health Statistics 2013, http://dx.doi.org/10.1787/health-data-en.

Fewer CVD deaths have led to greater life expectancy, but gains have not been uniform

The decline in CVD mortality has had a real impact on improving life expectancy in all countries, particularly since the mid-1980s. Figure 1.4 shows the relationship between declining rates of CVD morality and gains in life expectancy. The horizontal axis represents the reduction in CVD mortality (in percentage terms) achieved by OECD countries between 1985 and 2011. For example, in the Netherlands the CVD mortality rate fell from 501 per 100 000 population in 1985 to 217 in 2011, representing a 57% fall. Countries such as Israel and Australia have been able to reduce CVD-related mortality by more than 65% over this period, whereas other countries such as Greece, the Slovak Republic and Mexico have reduced their rates by 40% or less. Importantly, countries that have had a historically low burden of CVD disease, such as Switzerland and Japan, have still managed to make substantial gains. This suggests not only that other countries can also make further gains, but also raises important questions about why success has varied so much across countries.

The vertical axis of Figure 1.4 shows the gains made in reducing CVD mortality and increasing life expectancy at birth (panel A) and at age 65 (panel B) between 1985 and 2011. All countries have been successful in improving life expectancy at birth and at age 65.

Countries such as Norway and Poland improved life expectancy by more than 10% between 1985 and 2011, although the degree of success was large in countries such as Sweden and Canada. In percentage terms, life expectancy has improved even more once a person reaches 65 years of age.

Not surprisingly, there is a strong association between the fall in CVD mortality and improvements in life expectancy over time, particularly for those aged 65. Panel A of Figure 1.4 indicates that for every 10% reduction in CVD mortality, countries have, on average, increased life expectancy at birth by around 0.7%. The fall in CVD mortality between 1985 and 2011 accounts for around 15% of the total variation in life expectancy across countries. The relationship between CVD mortality and life expectancy is even stronger for those aged 65 (panel B). Across OECD countries, for every 10% reduction in CVD mortality, life expectancy at age 65 increased by around 4.3%. The decline in CVD mortality accounts for around 30% of the cross-country variation in life expectancy gains. Change in CVD mortality is a stronger predictor of life expectancy at 65 among males than females. Improvements in CVD mortality accounts for 44% of the overall gains in life expectancy among men and 21% among women aged 65.

Figure 1.4. **Declining CVD mortality rates have improved life expectancy at birth and at age 65**

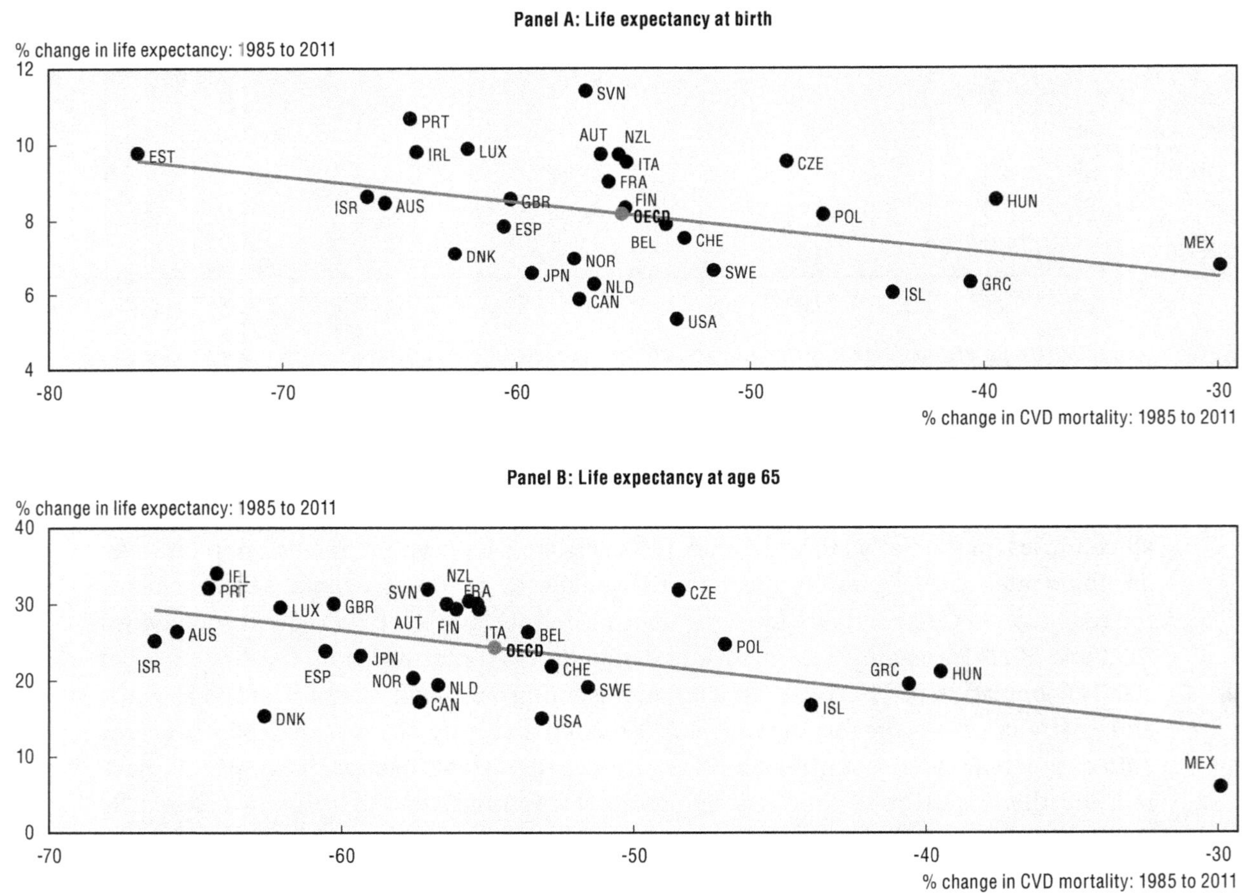

Source: OECD Health Statistics 2013, *http://dx.doi.org/10.1787/health-data-en.*

Explaining the fall in CVD mortality

Changes in the health care system's capacity to prevent, treat and manage CVD have been instrumental in reducing mortality rates. At the time that the decline in CVD mortality was first observed, three major hypotheses emerged as possible explanations: 1) improved primary prevention through risk factor reduction, including public health and clinical measures; 2) improved acute care through emergency services and better access to more effective treatments; and 3) secondary prevention in those with known CVD (Luepker, 2008). The introduction and diffusion of new technologies such as cholesterol and blood pressure lowering medications, coronary angioplasty and thrombolysis over recent decades have had a marked effect on the quality of care. In addition, primary prevention activities such as tobacco control programmes have also had a real impact on CVD mortality.

A number of studies have estimated the relative contributions of treatments and risk factor management in improving coronary heart disease mortality, which is a major contributor of overall CVD mortality. A number of countries have used the so-called IMPACT model to explain the changes in coronary heart disease (CHD) mortality rates observed in a population. This model, developed by academics at the University of Liverpool, uses longitudinal data on major population risk factors (smoking, high systolic blood pressure, elevated total blood cholesterol, obesity, diabetes and physical inactivity), and from medical and surgical treatments to quantify the contribution that treatments and risk factor reductions has made to the decline in CHD mortality (Capewell et al., 2010).

The IMPACT model has been applied to an extensive number of OECD countries, producing country-specific estimates. Table 1.1 summarises the main results from the studies published in the last ten years that have applied a similar methodology. For example, in Poland CHD mortality rates began to decline in the 1990s, coinciding with substantial social and economic change. The IMPACT model estimates that of the 50% decline in CHD mortality achieved in Poland between 1991 and 2005, around 37% was attributable to treatments, including treatments for heart failure (12%) and initial treatments for acute

Table 1.1. **Explaining the fall in CHD mortality: Summary of studies using the IMPACT model**

	Observation period	% annual change in CHD mortality	% explained by improved		Reference
			treatment	risk factors	
Canada (Ontario)	1994-2005	-4.3	42.6	48.3	Wijeysundera (2010)
Czech Republic	1985-2007	-5.0	43	52	Bruthans (2012)
Finland	1982-1997	-6.8	27	53	Laatikainen (2005)
Iceland	1981-2006	-6.4	27	72	O'Flaherty (2009)
Ireland	1985-2006	-5.5	40	48	Kabir (2013)
Italy	1980-2000	-4.4 (males) -3.7 (females)	40	55	Palmieri (2010)
Poland	1991-2005	-5.1	37	54	Bandosz (2012)
Portugal	1995-2008	-2.8 (males) -1.9 (females)	50	42	Pereira (2013)
Spain	1985-2005	-2.6	49	51	Mateo (2010)
Sweden	1986-2002	-4.9 (males) -4.7 (females)	36	55	Björck (2009)
Turkey	1995-2008	-5.1	47	42	Unal (2013)
United Kingdom (England/Wales)	1981-2000	-4.2	42	58	Unal (2004)
United Kingdom (England)	2000-2007	-7.1	52	34	Bajekal (2012)
United Kingdom (Scotland)	2000-2010	-6.0	43	39	Hotchkiss (2014)
United States	1980-2000	-3.6 (males) -3.4 (females)	47	44	Ford (2007)

coronary syndrome (9%). It also estimated that around 54% of the fall was attributed to changes in risk factors, including reductions in total cholesterol concentration (39%) and an increase in physical activity (10%) (Bandosz et al., 2012).

The IMPACT model, as applied in numerous OECD countries, has consistently shown that changes in treatments and risk factors have both made major contributions to the decline in CVD-related deaths, although the importance of these two contributing factors varies between countries (Ford et al., 2011; Bots et al., 1996; Capewell et al., 2000; Unal et al., 2004; Laatikainen et al., 2005; Wijeysundera et al., 2010; and Bandosdz et al., 2012). Across all studies reported in Table 1.1, treatments account for 41% of the overall improvements in CHD mortality, whereas improved risk factors have contributed 49%. However, more recent studies indicate that treatments have become a more important contributing factor of late. For example, a study conducted in England using data from 1981 to 2000 estimated that treatments accounted for approximately 42% of the total CHD mortality reduction, whereas a more recent study covering the 2000 to 2010 period assigned 52% to improved treatments. This suggests that the pathway to success has not only varied across countries but also over time. It also implies that some countries may be able to achieve higher relative returns through risk-factor reduction programmes, whereas others may make greater gains through better access to high quality treatments.

Importantly, all of the impact studies show that the reduction in CHD mortality could have been bigger had it not been for the rising prevalence of obesity and diabetes. For example, a study using US data showed that increases in mean body mass index and the prevalence of diabetes decreased the estimated numbers of the deaths prevented or postponed by 8% and 10%, respectively (Ford et al., 2007). The most recent studies, such those conducted in England and Scotland (Bajekal et al., 2012; Hotchkiss et al., 2014), reveal that the rising prevalence of these two risk factors is having a negative impact on CHD mortality, and a differential impact depending on socio-economic status. To a great extent, both the English and Scottish studies show that better treatments and improvements in risk factors are equally distributed among various socio-economic groups. However, the rising prevalence of diabetes and obesity, particularly in lower socio-economic areas, has partly negated the improvements in mortality increases. In England, the rise in diabetes was estimated to have offset mortality improvements by 7.4% overall, but by 14% in the more deprived areas of England and by only 2% in wealthier areas (Bajekal et al., 2012). Such results indicate that the advancements in equal access to high quality treatments are being threatened by the unequal distribution in risk factors such as diabetes.

CVD and diabetes take a heavier toll in some countries than in others

When measured in terms of the number of deaths, CVD imposes a heavy burden in all countries, but this burden is not equally distributed. The number of deaths caused by CVD varies considerably across OECD countries. Figure 1.5 shows that Central and Eastern European Countries, such as the Slovak Republic, Hungary, Estonia and the Czech Republic, face the greatest CVD mortality burden with mortality rates in excess of 500 per 100 000 population. On the other side of the spectrum, countries such as Japan, France, Korea and Israel experienced mortality rates of less than 200. The mortality burden is almost four-times bigger in the Slovak Republic compared to Japan. This degree of variation has an enormous bearing on the differences between countries in the number of deaths each year. For example, if Germany was able to achieve the same mortality rates as France, each year there would be around 108 000 fewer deaths caused by CVD among German citizens. If

Figure 1.5. **Mortality rates for CVD per 100 000 population, 2011 (or latest year)**

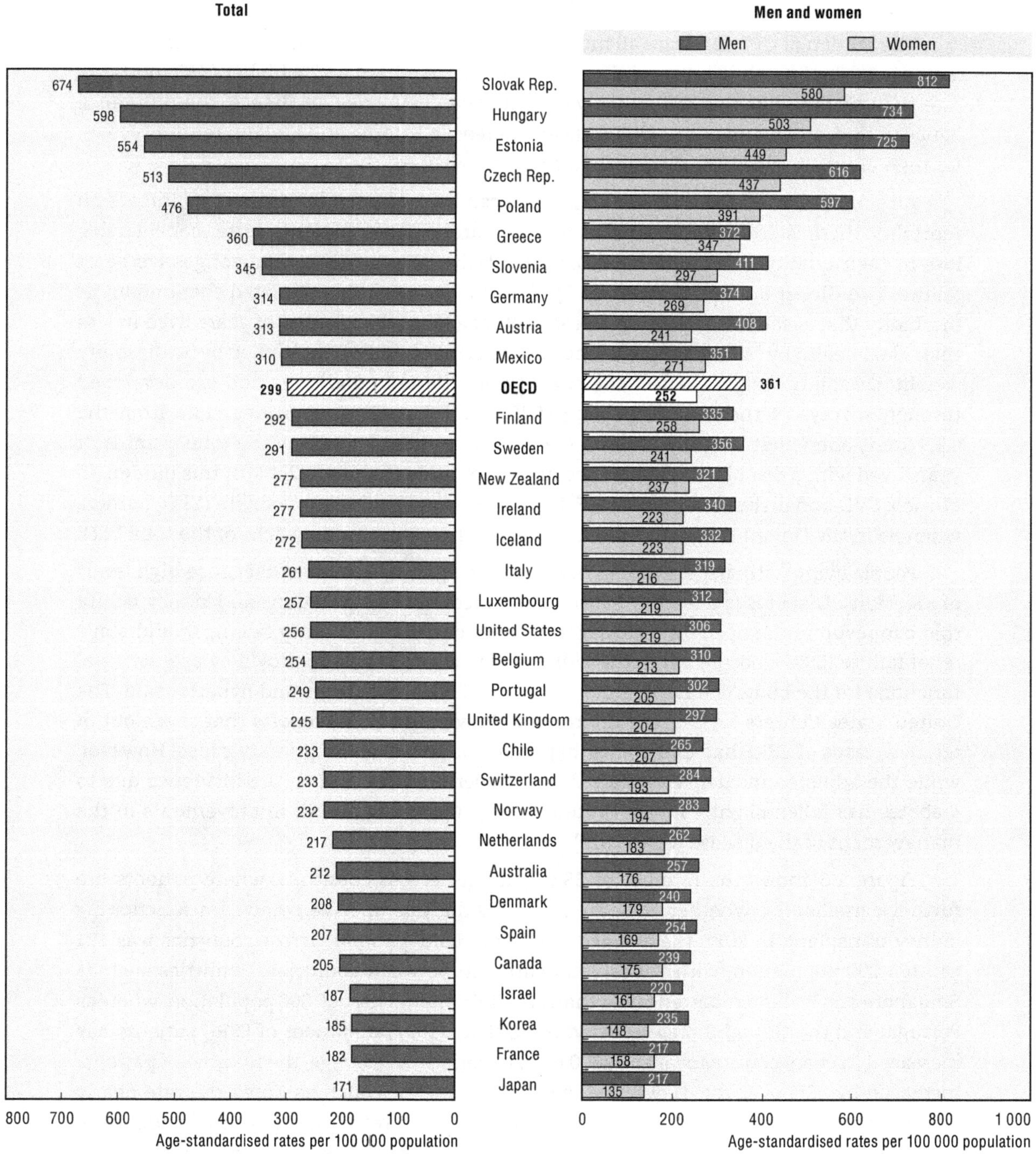

Source: *OECD Health Statistics 2013, http://dx.doi.org/10.1787/health-data-en.*

the United States could replicate Canada's mortality rates, around 160 000 fewer Americans would die from CVD each year. These numbers only serve to illustrate the scale of CVD as a leading cause of death. It should not be inferred that health systems have capacity or know-how to reduce all the variation observed in the data. Many factors such as genetics, demographics and the environment are outside of the control of health systems and policy, and therefore some variation between countries may always persist. Nevertheless, the degree to which countries have been able to reduce the mortality burden over the years gives some room for optimism; it suggests that some of the differences between countries can be influenced by good access to high quality health care.

The burden of CVD tends to fall more heavily on males than females, but it remains the leading cause of death in both genders. On average, men have a 22% higher CVD mortality rate than women but this difference varies between countries. In Greece, the difference between men and women is negligible (3%) whereas in Estonia and Finland mortality rates for men are more than 30% greater than those for women.

Although most of the CVD health burden can be measured in terms of its impact on mortality, there is also a substantial morbidity burden. Many patients suffer considerable loss in their quality of life due to CVD, particularly through stroke and congestive heart failure. The Global Burden of Disease (GBD) study has recently estimated the amount of morbidity that is caused by leading diseases. It measured the number of years lived in less than ideal health by taking the prevalence of a specific condition multiplied by its disability weight. Disability weights reflect the severity of different conditions and are developed through surveys of the general public (IMHE, 2013). For OECD countries, data from the GBD Study show that in 2010, CVD and diabetes accounted for 5.2% of the total number of years lived with a disability. Diabetes accounted for more than half (2.8%) of this burden. In Mexico, CVD and diabetes account for 8.1% of the years lost due to disability (YLD) burden, whereas in the United Kingdom these two diseases account for only 3.2% of the total YLD.

People living with diabetes are at risk of suffering complications that cause high levels of morbidity. Diabetes is a leading cause of blindness, foot amputations and kidney failure that can result in the need for a kidney transplant or dialysis.[2] Kidney failure, or end-stage renal failure (ESRF), occurs when the kidneys are no longer able to provide waste removal functions for the body. The two leading causes of ESRF are diabetes and hypertension. The United States Centers for Disease Control and Prevention (CDC) reports that seven out of ten new cases of ESRF had diabetes or hypertension listed as the primary cause. However, while the adjusted incidence of ESRF due to hypertension is rising, the incidence due to diabetes has fallen slightly in the United States, suggesting overall improvements in the management of the disease (CDC, 2010).

Figure 1.6 shows the number of ESRF patients across countries, where patients are further classified by whether they are receiving dialysis or have received a functioning kidney transplant. In 2011, the average number of ESRF patients across countries was 101 per 100 000 population, with widespread variation between countries. Countries such as Singapore and Iceland reported fewer than 70 ESRF patients per 100 000 population, whereas Portugal and the United States reported more than 150. The number of ESRF patients has increased in every country over the 2000 to 2011 period. On average, the number of patients increased by 36% over the 11-year period, but in countries such as Korea the rate nearly doubled over this timeframe. In part, this rise is likely to reflect the growing incidence of diabetes as well as improved access to dialysis care. Nevertheless, the increasing number of patients on dialysis also indicates the potential for reducing the burden of disease through effective preventive actions aimed at reducing disease incidence as well as better management of disease to minimise the risk of serious complications such as ESRF.

Across countries, around 59% of ESRF patient are treated via dialysis and the remaining 41% receive a functioning kidney transplant. There is a much greater reliance on dialysis in countries such as Greece, Italy, Japan and Korea, where over 75% of patients are treated this way. In countries such as Iceland and the Netherlands, on the other hand, over 60% of ESRF patients receive a functioning kidney transplant. The reliance on dialysis to treat ESRF patients has reduced somewhat over time. Over the 11-year period to 2011, the percentage of ESRF patients receiving dialysis fell from 64% to 59%, with a corresponding increase in the percentage of patients with functioning kidney transplants. However, some countries have increased the number of kidney transplants substantially over this period, particularly in countries where the number of transplants had been historically low. For example, Italy, the Slovak Republic and Singapore have witnessed rapid rises in the number of kidney transplants.

The quality of life is severely impaired for people with ESRF and who are on dialysis. A systematic review of symptoms found that patients experienced multiple symptoms, and that pain, fatigue and constipation were reported in more than one in two patients (Murtagh et al., 2007). Other studies suggest that the loss in quality of life for ESRF patients is comparable to patients with advanced cancer (Saini et al., 2006). End-stage renal disease not only has severe human costs but also very high financial costs. An Israeli study found that the health care costs for diabetes patients on dialysis were almost six times greater than diabetic patients not on dialysis (Chodick et al., 2005). As dialysis and kidney transplant are highly substitutable treatments for many ESRF patients, a number of studies have looked at their cost-effectiveness. Many studies found that kidney transplant is more cost-effective than dialysis across countries including Australia (Howard et al., 2009), Chile (Domínguez et al., 2010), Denmark (Jensen et al., 2014), England (NHS Blood and Transplant, 2009), and the Netherlands (de Wit et al., 2002). According to a cross-national review (Winkelmayer et al., 2002), the cost-effectiveness ratio is approaching to USD 10 000 per life year gained for kidney transplant while the ratio is between USD 33 000 and 50 000 for home dialysis and USD 55 000 and 80 000 for dialysis at a medical centre. It should be noted that these treatment options are not alternatives for all patients but depend on medical and other eligibility criteria.

Figure 1.6. **End-stage renal failure patients per 100 000 population, 2000 and 2011 (or nearest year)**

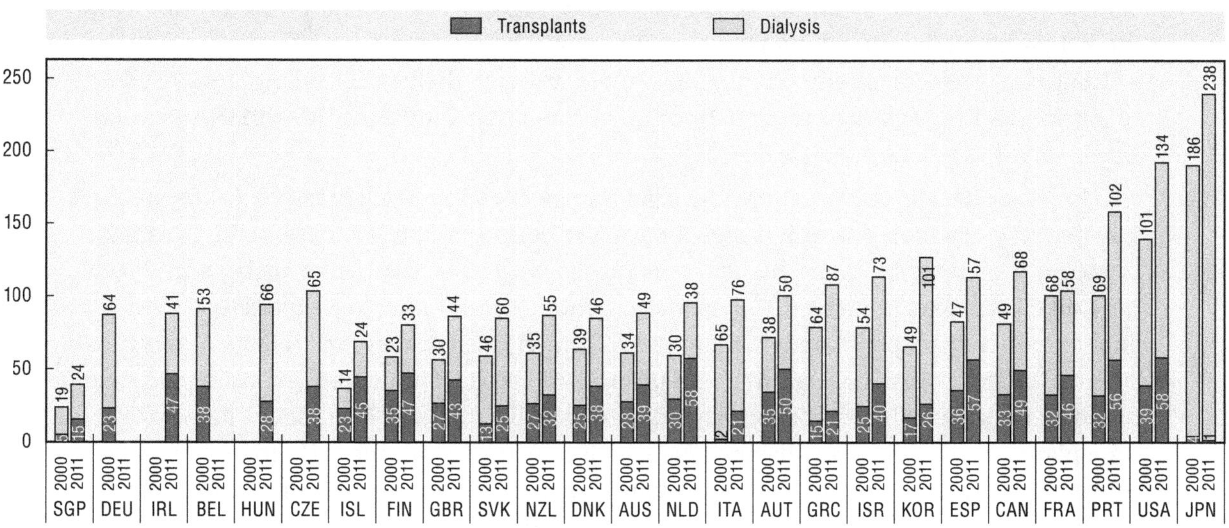

Source: *OECD Health Statistics 2013, http://dx.doi.org/10.1787/health-data-en.*

The cost-effectiveness studies indicate that for many ESRF patients, a kidney transplant is an effective and efficient alternative to dialysis. Despite their benefit, the supply of kidney donors falls short of the demand in many countries. Barriers for kidney transplants include the legal framework requiring explicit consent for organ donation, eligibility criteria for organ donation, rules around the use of kidney from incompatible donor/recipient pairs, the cost associated with organ donation and the lack of standard procedures for organ donation in the critical care unit of hospitals. In Japan, the number of transplants is extremely low (4.1 and 1.3 per 100 000 population in 2000 and 2011, respectively) while the number of dialysis per population is the highest due to additional barriers; low out-of-pocket payment and highly effective and established clinical standards for dialysis, compared with transplants which have some risks of side effects related to immunosuppressant medication (Ishikawa, 2004). Given the speed of super-ageing population, this dichotomous trend is not sustainable for the country's health system and also health financing. In recent years, some efforts are being made to increase the number of kidney transplants in the country and some hospitals have adopted Donor Action.

A number of jurisdictions have recently introduced programmes to increase the number of kidneys available for transplant. One of these initiatives is the kidney exchange programmes designed to overcome problems of incompatibility between a donor and recipient when there is a mismatch in blood group or tissue type. This is a particular problem when a donor's willingness is conditional on the recipient being an identified person such as a family member. Incompatibility therefore affects the supply of donors when willing donors cannot be matched to suitable recipients. Several countries, including Australia, Canada, Korea, the Netherlands, the United Kingdom and the United States, have introduced paired kidney exchanges which allow the donation of kidney from an incompatible donor/recipient pair to a compatible recipient. A paired kidney exchange will help find compatible donors amongst registered pairs of donors/recipients. Such initiatives expand the pool of kidney donors by extending donor eligibility to a wider group of potential recipients within the chain (for more information, see, for example Roth et al., 2005).

The introduction of kidney exchanges has formed part of increased efforts in some countries to improve the number of transplantations. For instance, countries such as the United States provide a compensation to donors through a tax credit of up to USD 5 000 for kidney donation to compensate for the unreimbursed costs and lost wage (Library of Congress, 2009). Australia has a pilot project to cover the cost of taking a leave of up to six weeks from work to recover from organ donation until June 30th 2015 (Australian Government Department of Health, 2014).

In relation to deceased donors, the legal framework supporting presumed consent and a systematic hospital donation protocol have also contributed to an increase in transplant rates. Kidney transplants are higher in countries with presumed consent laws in which no explicit consent is needed to become potential donors and the change of law from explicit consent to presumed consent actually increased transplant rates in countries such as Belgium (Roel and Rahmel, 2011). Standardised hospital organ donation protocols based on multidisciplinary consensus and team-building can also be effective in increasing transplants, and one of the widespread and well-known programme is Donor Action which sets out quality management standards to maximise a hospital's organ donation potential through training for medical and nursing critical care professionals to improve clinical practices. It has been used in hospitals in an increasing number of European countries and beyond with positive impact on transplant rates (Roel and Rahmel, 2011). In several European countries and the United States, age criteria for eligible donors have also been relaxed to optimise available organs from older donors and to shorten the waiting time particularly for the elderly patients (Roel and Rahmel, 2011).

CVD and diabetes strike at different ages across countries

One further difference between countries is the age at which CVD and diabetes strike. While CVD risks rise with age in all countries, there is strong evidence that, in some countries, CVD affects people of younger ages. Figure 1.7 provides an indication of these differences. It shows the relationship between a country's mortality rate and the potential years of life lost (PYLL) due to CVD. The diagonal line in Figure 1.7 shows the average relationship between the two measures across countries. It indicates that, on average, for every death due to CVD, countries lose around 2.32 years of life. As would be expected, there is a high correlation between the two measures; however, some observations are worth noting. In the United States, for example, CVD mortality rates are similar to the OECD average, but its measure of PYLL is considerably higher than the OECD average. This suggests that CVD is striking people who are relatively young in the United States. By contrast, the mortality rate in the Slovak Republic is considerably higher than in Estonia, but the number of PYLL is similar for the two countries. This indicates that CVD is affecting people who are relatively older in the Slovak Republic compared to Estonia.

Figure 1.7. **CVD mortality rates and potential years of life lost, 2011 (or nearest year)**

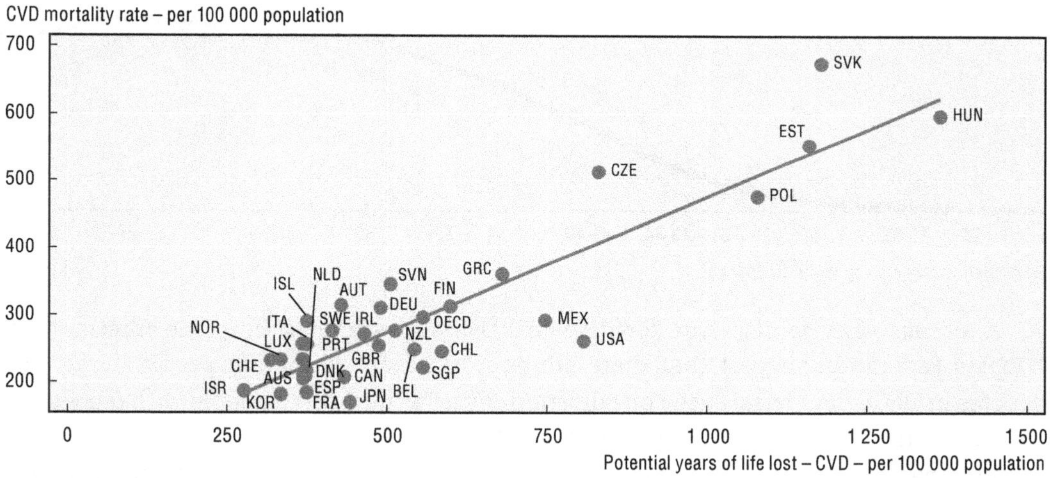

Source: *OECD Health Statistics 2013, http://dx.doi.org/10.1787/health-data-en.*

Aside from mortality, it is also possible to look at the age at which CVD strikes by using hospital admissions data. Figure 1.8 reveals the age-specific AMI admission rates per 100 000 population across the OECD, using the OECD HCQI (Health Care Quality Indicators) database. These data give an insight into the different age profiles of AMI incidence across countries for those patients who make it to hospital. In line with expectations the age specific admission rates rise with age. For those aged 45 to 49 years, the OECD mean is around 120 admissions for every 100 000 population, rising to over 1 000 admissions per 100 000 population for those aged 85 and over. The rising trend with age, underscore the additional demand on health care systems as population age.

The 25th and 75th per cent quartile lines in Figure 1.8 provide an indication of the range in age-specific admission rates across OECD countries. Admission rate vary considerably across countries for all age groups but the gap widens at older ages. Furthermore, there are some important differences between countries at different ages. Admissions rates in the Netherlands and the United Kingdom follow a similar trend up to age 79, but with rates slightly higher in the former compared to the latter. From age 80 onwards, the age specific admission rate rises sharply in the United Kingdom when compared to the Netherlands.

The age profile at which CVD strikes has important implications for a patient's longevity and health status, and also for their social and economic status. Young survivors of CVD events such as AMI and stroke may be incapacitated and have a lower quality of life at the prime of their lives. This can lead to greater social and health care needs over longer periods of time, and a reduced ability to work and earn an income. In turn, it can affect labour force participation and productivity not only for the patient, but also for their families, who often provide informal care and support.

Figure 1.8. **AMI admissions per 100 000 population by age group: OECD average, quartile range and selected countries, 2011 (or nearest year)**

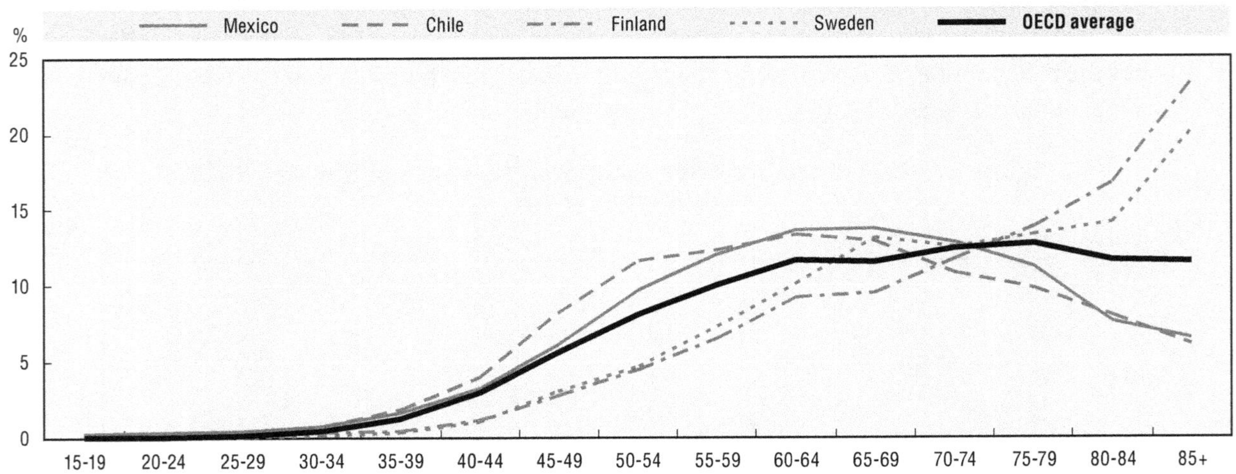

Source: OECD Health Care Quality Indicators 2013.

A similar story is also true for diabetes. Overall, estimates from the International Diabetes Federation suggest that there are approximately 85 million people living with diabetes in OECD countries. Based on current trends, the number of people with diabetes in OECD countries is projected to reach almost 108 million by 2030 (IDF, 2013). This represents a 27% increase over the 2011 estimates, and a further 23 million patients with higher health care needs and higher risk of complications. Prevalence varies widely across countries. In many Nordic countries, diabetes is estimated to affect less than 5% of the population, whereas in Mexico, Portugal, Chile and the United States estimates exceed 9.5%.

Figure 1.9 shows the estimated prevalence of diabetes across OECD countries by different age groups. The graph shows that prevalence rises sharply with age: it is estimated to be 1.7% among 20-39 year-olds, 8.9% among those aged 40 to 59 years, and 19.6% for those aged between 60 and 79 years. The data suggest that early onset of diabetes is substantially bigger in Mexico, Chile, Portugal and Poland than in Israel, Canada and Austria. This has enormous implications for diabetes-related outcomes and health care; in countries with higher early onset, diabetes has to be managed more effectively for longer periods of time in order to minimise the likelihood of complications such as CVD, blindness and renal disease.

As a result of the ageing population profile of many OECD countries, health systems are increasingly caring for elderly patients who not only have greater health care needs, but also more complex needs. Elderly patients are more likely to be suffering from multiple morbidities, may be more fragile and require multiple health and social services to deliver best-practice care. A recent Scottish study used electronic clinical record systems to examine the prevalence of multiple morbidities for patients presenting to a general practice (Barnett et al., 2012). As expected, the study found that the number of conditions rises with age. From age 65, over half the population have two or more chronic conditions. Evidence suggests that people with multiple morbidities are at greater risk of: care co-ordination problems, ineffective or unsafe combinations of prescriptions, and of receiving unsafe care (Guthrie et al., 2011). They are more frequent and intensive users of the health care system and pose a substantial challenge in the delivery of health care.

Figure 1.9. **Diabetes prevalence in OECD countries by age, 2011**

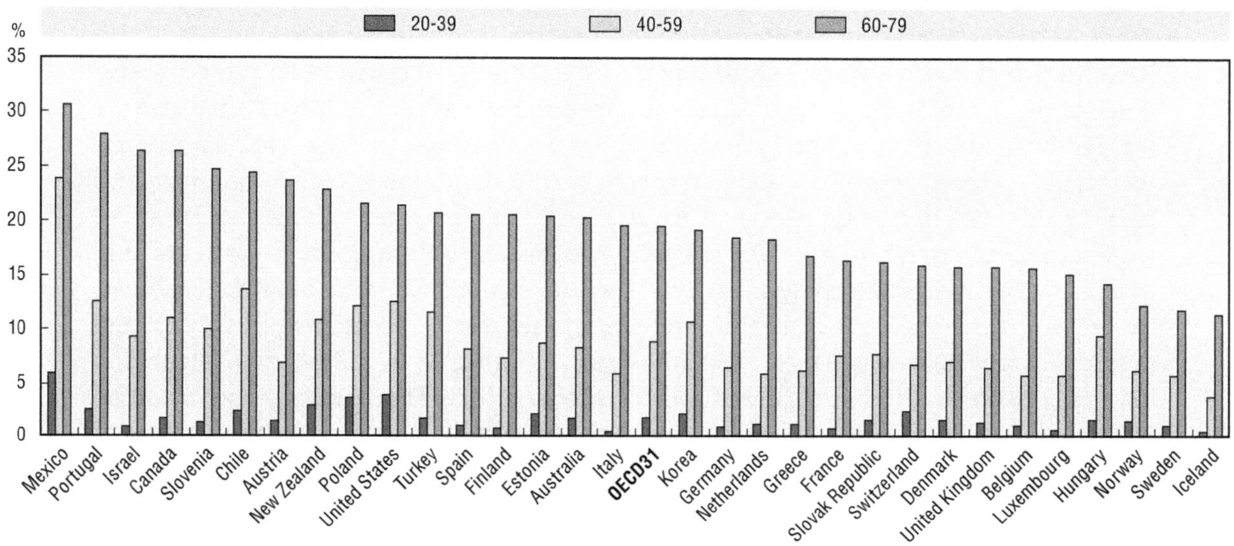

Source: IDF (2013), *IDF Diabetes Atlas, 6th Edition*, International Diabetes Federation, Brussels, *www.idf.org/diabetesatlas/previouseditions*. Only includes countries with direct diabetes prevalence estimates.

The health care costs of CVD and diabetes

In addition to the enormous health and social burden of CVD and diabetes, the direct health care costs are substantial. The OECD has developed a methodology to estimate the direct health care costs of various types of disease. Generally this refers to expenditure items for which some form of payment has been made, including costs directly related to the detection, treatment, prevention and rehabilitation of the disease (i.e. medical care expenses such as hospitalisation, outpatient clinical care, care in rehabilitation and long-term care facilities, physician care, pharmaceuticals, medical care equipment).

A variety of studies have been carried out to estimate the costs of CVD and diabetes at the country level. However, given the various methodologies and data sources used in these studies it is difficult to validly compare results across countries. In order to increase the comparability of the estimates of spending on diseases across countries, the OECD has used the System of Health Accounts (SHA) framework to derive expenditures by disease. It is currently only feasible to derive these estimates for a limited number of countries and observation years. However, it is hoped that in future years it will be possible to expand the scope of the project by increasing the number of countries for which similar data can be derived and expand the scope of countries and expenditure items.

Figure 1.10 presents data from 11 OECD countries on hospital expenditures assigned to various diseases. In the majority of countries, cardiovascular disease accounts for the largest percentage share of hospital expenditure. Only in Korea and the Netherlands is a greater proportion of expenditure allocated to cancer and mental health, respectively. On average, CVD accounts for 17% of total hospital expenditure, ranging from 12% in Australia to 22% in Japan. The large percentage observed for Japan is somewhat surprising given the low CVD mortality and incidence rates observed in this country. However, this may be explained by long average lengths of stay in Japan, particularly for some of the specific CVD such as stroke (OECD, 2013b).

The IDF estimates that, for OECD countries, average health care costs equate to around USD 5 000 per diabetic patient. When this figure is compared to overall health expenditure from OECD Health Statistics, it shows that costs per diabetic patient are around 18% higher than health care costs for the general population. This is consistent with more detailed studies which reveal that most medical costs incurred by patients with type 2 diabetes are caused by their complications and comorbidities. For example, the direct annual medical cost in the United States for a male diagnosed with diabetes (but with no complications) was found to be USD 2 465. However, these costs escalated when the disease advanced and complications set in. Annual costs rose by between 70% and 150% for patients with coronary heart disease, congestive heart failure, hemiplegia, and amputation. Costs were approximately 300% higher for end-stage renal disease treated with dialysis, and approximately 500% higher for end-stage renal disease with kidney transplantation (Li et al., 2013). Furthermore, patients with diabetes complication find themselves on an escalating health care cost trajectory. An Israeli study found that over a short three-year period, the annual costs for diabetic dialysis patients more than tripled, whereas health care cost for non-dialysis diabetic patients grew by 30% (Chodick et al., 2005). These studies underline the importance of effectively preventing and managing diabetes to reduce both the health burden and health care costs.

Figure 1.10. **Proportion of hospital expenditure by major diagnostic category**

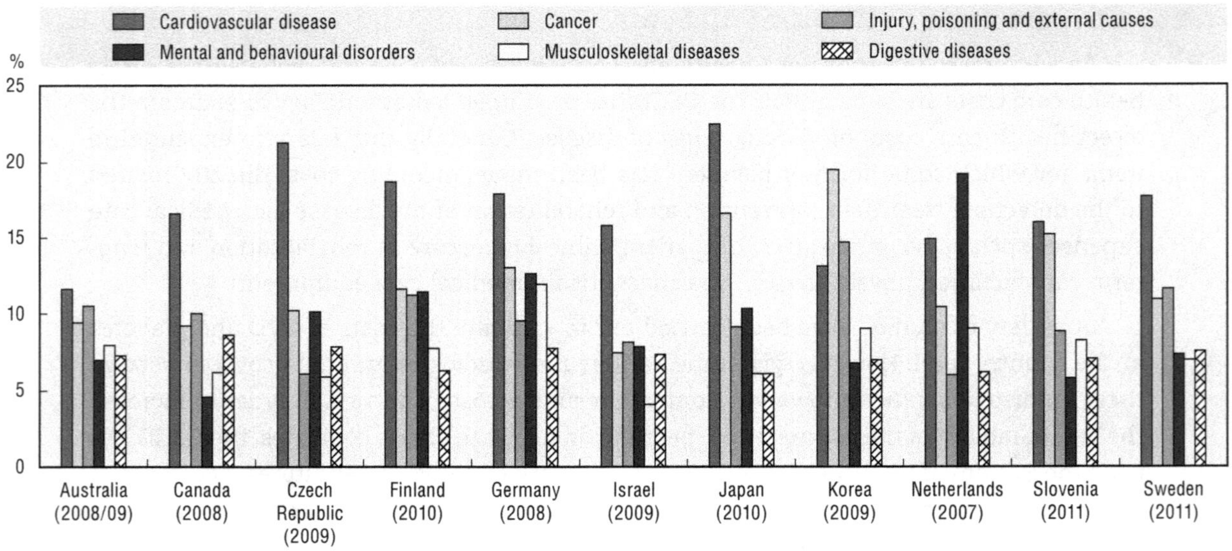

Source: OECD (2013), *Health at a Glance 2013: OECD Indicators*. OECD Publishing, Paris, *http://dx.doi.org/10.1787/health_glance-2013-en*.

Summary

While CVD remains the number one cause of mortality, its burden varies considerably across countries, with some countries reporting nearly four times as many CVD deaths than others. Nevertheless, the decline in CVD mortality is an unambiguous success story. On average, OECD countries have reduced their CVD mortality rate by over 50% since 1985. However, the improvements are not uniform across countries, with some countries able to reduce CVD-related mortality by more than 60% and others reducing their rates by less than 30%. These figures raise important questions about why success has varied so much across countries, and to what extent health care systems and policies help to explain this variation.

Despite these positive developments, there is evidence that prospects for reducing the CVD disease burden are diminishing. Numerous studies have shown that rising levels of obesity and diabetes are reducing our ability to make further inroads into reducing the CVD burden. Some studies are showing that the pattern of declining mortality is coming to an end or even reversing amongst some population groups, particularly younger age groups (Wilson and Siskind., 1995; Ford et al., 2007; Allender et al., 2008). In fact, by 2030 over 40% of the US population is projected to have some form of CVD, with the total direct medical costs of CVD set to triple (Heindenreich et al., 2011). These figures present some considerable challenges for policy makers. The remaining chapters of this report examine the performance of each aspect of health system across countries relating to CVD and diabetes. The emphasis is on examining the role of policy in improving CVD and diabetes outcomes and health system performance.

Notes

1. Singapore is a participant to OECD's Health Care Quality Indicator Expert Group. For the purposes of this project, Singapore provided additional information which has been incorporated in this report.
2. Chapter 3 of this report will further discuss diabetes-related complications.

References

Allender, S. et al. (2008), "Patterns of Coronary Heart Disease Mortality Over the 20th Century in England and Wales: Possible Plateaus in the Rate of Decline", *BMC Public Health*, Vol. 8, No. 1, p.148.

Ardine de Wita, G., P.G. Ramsteijnb and F.Th. de Charroa (1998), "Economic Evaluation of End Stage Renal Disease Treatment", *Health Policy*, Vol. 44, No. 3, pp. 215-232, June.

Australian Government Department of Health (2014), *www.health.gov.au/internet/main/publishing.nsf/Content/Leave-for-living-organ-donors.*

Bajekal, M. et al. (2012), "Analysing Recent Socioeconomic Trends in Coronary Heart Disease Mortality in England, 2000-2007: A Population Modelling Study", *PLOS Medicine*, Vol. 9, No. 6, Cambridge.

Bandosz, P. et al. (2012), "Decline in Mortality from Coronary Heart Disease in Poland after Socioeconomic Transformation: Modelling Study", *British Medical Journal*, Vol. 344, BMJ Publishing, London.

Barnett, K. et al. (2012), "Epidemiology of Multimorbidity and Implications for Health Care, Research, and Medical Education: A Cross-sectional Study", *The Lancet*, Vol. 380, No. 9836, London, pp. 37-43.

Björck, L. et al. (2009), "Modelling the Decreasing Coronary Heart Disease Mortality in Sweden Between 1986 and 2002", *European Heart Journal*, Vol. 30, No. 9, pp. 1046-1056.

Bots, M.L. and D.E. Grobbee (1996), "Decline of Coronary Heart Disease Mortality in the Netherlands from 1978 to 1985: Contribution of Medical Care and Changes Over Time in Presence of Major Cardiovascular Risk Factors", *Journal of Cardiovascular Risk*, Vol. 3, pp. 271-276.

Bruthans, J. et al. (2012), "Explaining the Decline in Coronary Heart Disease Mortality in the Czech Republic Between 1985 and 2007", *European Journal of Preventive Cardiology*, Vol. 21, No. 7, pp. 829-839.

Capewell, S. et al. (2010), "Cardiovascular Risk Factor Trends and Potential for Reducing Coronary Heart Disease Mortality in the United States of America", *Bulletin of the World Health Organization*, Vol. 88, No. 2, World Health Organization, Geneva, pp. 120-130.

Capewell, S. et al. (2000), "Explanation for the Decline in Coronary Heart Disease Mortality Rates in Auckland, New Zealand, Between 1982 and 1993", *Circulation*, Vol. 102, pp. 1511-1516.

CDC – Centers for Disease Control and Prevention (2010), *National Chronic Kidney Disease Fact Sheet: General Information and National Estimates on Chronic Kidney Disease in the United States, 2010*, Department of Health and Human Services, Atlanta.

Chodick, G. et al. (2005), "The Direct Medical Cost of Diabetes in Israel", *European Journal of Health Economics*, Vol. 6, No. 2, pp. 166-171.

Domínguez, J., R. Harrison and R. Atal (2010), "Cost-Benefit Estimation of Cadaveric Kidney Transplantation, the Case of a Developing Country", *Documento de Trabajo No. 382*, Instituto de Economia, Santiago, *www.economia.puc.cl/docs/dt_382.pdf*.

Ford, E.S. and S. Capewell (2011), "Proportion of the Decline in Cardiovascular Mortality Disease Due to Prevention Versus Treatment: Public Health Versus Clinical Care", *Annual Review of Public Health*, Vol. 32, Annual Reviews, Palo Alto, pp. 5-22.

Ford, E.S. et al. (2007), "Explaining the Decrease in U.S. Deaths from Coronary Disease, 1980-2000", *New England Journal of Medicine*, Vol. 356, pp. 2388-2398.

Guthrie, B. et al. (2011), "Multicomorbidity: The Impact on Health Systems and their Development", Chapter 6 in *Health Reform: Meeting the Challenge of Ageing and Multiple Morbidities*, OECD Publishing, Paris, *http://dx.doi.org/10.1787/9789264122314-en*.

Heidenreich, P.A. et al. (2011), "Forecasting the Future of Cardiovascular Disease in the United States: A Policy Statement from the American Heart Association", *Circulation*, Vol. 123, No. 8, pp. 933-944.

Hotchkiss, J.W. et al. (2014), "Explaining Trends in Scottish Coronary Heart Disease Mortality Between 2000 and 2010 Using IMPACTSEC Model: Retrospective Analysis Using Routine Data", *British Medical Journal*, Vol. 348, BMJ Publishing, London.

Howard, K. et al. (2009), "The Cost-effectiveness of Increasing Kidney Transplantation and Home-based Dialysis", *Nephrology*, Vol. 14, No. 1, pp. 123-132.

IDF – International Diabetes Federation (2013), *IDF Diabetes Atlas, 6th Edition*, International Diabetes Federation, Brussels, *www.idf.org/diabetesatlas/previouseditions*.

IDF (2006), *The IDF Consensus Worldwide Definition of the Metabolic Syndrome*, International Diabetes Federation, Brussels, *www.idf.org/webdata/docs/IDF_Meta_def_final.pdf*.

IHME – Institute for Health Metrics and Evaluation (2013), *The Global Burden of Disease: Generating Evidence, Guiding Policy*, Institute for Health Metrics and Evaluation, Seattle.

Ishikawa, I. (2004), "Saishin no jinishoku toukei: oubei to nihon no makki jinfuzen chiryou no taihi" [The latest statistics on kidney transplant: comparisons of treating end-stage kidney failures across Japan, the United States and Europe], *Journal of the Japan Society of Nephrology*, Vol. 46, No. 1, Japan Society of Nephrology, Tokyo, pp. 12-19.

Jensen, C.E, P. Sørensen and K.D. Petersen (2014), "In Denmark Kidney Transplantation Is More Cost-effective than Dialysis", *Danish Medical Journal*, Vol. 61, No. 3, A4796, The Danish Medical Association, København, March.

Kabir, Z. et al. (2013), "Modelling Coronary Heart Disease Mortality Declines in the Republic of Ireland, 1985–2006", *International Journal of Cardiology*, Vol. 168, No. 3, pp. 2462-2467.

Laatikainen, T. et al. (2005), "Explaining the Decline in Coronary Heart Disease Mortality in Finland Between 1982 and 1997", *American Journal of Epidemiology*, Vol. 162, No. 8, pp. 764-773.

Laupacis, A. et al. (1996), "A Study of the Quality of Life and Cost-utility of Renal Transplantation", *Kidney International*, Vol. 50, International Society of Nephrology, pp. 235-242.

Li, R. et al. (2013), "Medical Costs Associated with Type 2 Diabetes Complications and Comorbidities", *American Journal of Managed Care*, Vol. 19, No. 5, pp. 421-430.

Library of Congress (2009), *www.congress.gov/bill/111th-congress/house-bill/218*.

Mateo, G.F. et al. (2010), "P02 Risk Factor and Treatment Contributions to the Coronary Heart Disease Mortality Decline in a Low Risk Mediterranean Population: Spain 1988-2005", *Journal of Epidemiology and Community Health*, Vol. 64, Suppl. 1, pp. A34-A34.

Murtagh, F.E., J. Addington-Hall and I.J. Higginson (2007), "The Prevalence of Symptoms in End-stage Renal Disease: A Systematic Review", *Advances in Chronic Kidney Disease*, Vol. 14, No. 1, pp. 82-99.

NHS Blood and Transplant (2009), *www.organdonation.nhs.uk/newsroom/fact_sheets/cost_effectiveness_of_transplantation.asp*.

OECD (2013a), *OECD Health Statistics*. OECD publishing, Paris, *http://dx.doi.org/10.1787/health-data-en*.

OECD (2013b), *Health at a Glance 2013: OECD Indicators*. OECD Publishing, Paris, *http://dx.doi.org/10.1787/health_glance-2013-en*.

O'Flahert, M. et al. (2009), "Explaining the Massive Decline in Coronary Heart Disease Mortality in Iceland Between 1981 and 2006", *Journal of Epidemiology and Community Health*, Vol. 63, Suppl. 2, p. 31.

Palmieri, L. et al. (2010), "Explaining the Decrease in Coronary Heart Disease Mortality in Italy Between 1980 and 2000", *American Journal of Public Health*, Vol. 100, No. 4, pp. 684-692.

Pereira, M. et al. (2013), "Explaining the Decline in Coronary Heart Disease Mortality in Portugal Between 1995 and 2008", *Circulation: Cardiovascular Quality and Outcomes*, Vol. 6, No. 6, pp. 634-642.

Roels, L. and A. Rahmel (2011), "The European Experience", *Transplant International*, Vol. 24, pp. 350-367.

Roth, A.E., T. Sönmez and M.U. Ünver (2005), "A Kidney Exchange Clearinghouse in New England", *American Economic Review*, pp. 376-380.

Saini, T. et al. (2006), "Comparative Pilot Study of Symptoms and Quality of Life in Cancer Patients and Patients with End Stage Renal Disease", *Palliative Medicine*, Vol. 20, pp. 631-636.

Unal, B., J. Critchley and S. Capewell (2004), "Explaining the Decline in Coronary Heart Disease Mortality in England and Wales, 1981-2000", *Circulation*, Vol. 109, pp. 1101-1107.

Unal, B. et al. (2013), "Explaining the Decline in Coronary Heart Disease Mortality in Turkey Between 1995 and 2008", *BMC Public Health*, Vol. 13, No. 1, p. 1135.

Valderrábano, F., R. Jofre, and J.M. López-Gómez, (2001), "Quality of Life in End-stage Renal Disease Patients", *American Journal of Kidney Diseases*, Vol. 38, No. 3, pp. 443-464.

Wijeysundera, H.C. et al. (2010), "Association of Temporal Trends in Risk Factors and Treatment Uptake with Coronary Heart Disease Mortality, 1994-2005", *Journal of the American Medical Association*, Vol. 303, No. 18, pp. 1841-1847.

Wilson, A. and V. Siskind (1995), "Coronary Heart Disease Mortality in Australia: Is Mortality Starting to Increase Among Young Men?", *International Journal of Epidemiology*, Vol. 24, No. 4, pp. 678-684.

Winkelmayer, W.C. et al. (2002), "Health Economic Evaluations: The Special Case of End-Stage Renal Disease Treatment", *Medical Decision Making*, Vol. 22, p. 417.

Cardiovascular Disease and Diabetes
Policies for Better Health and Quality of Care

Chapter 2

Improving cardiovascular disease and diabetes outcomes through lifestyles: Trends and policies

Lifestyles play an important part in predicting cardiovascular disease (CVD) and diabetes risk, although prevention services have to cope with fewer resources in some countries. Lifestyles help explain variations in CVD and diabetes across OECD countries. Chapter 2 looks at the health promotion and public health contribution to maintaining healthy lifestyles in OECD countries. It examines recent trends in obesity, tobacco and alcohol consumption, and physical exercise. This chapter outlines policies that health systems have introduced recently to combat unhealthy lifestyles such as tobacco consumption and high salt intake and to promote physical activities in adults and children in order to reduce overweight and obesity. It also benchmarks OECD countries in relation to their CVD and diabetes lifestyle rankings.

The statistical data for Israel are supplied by and under the responsibility of the relevant Israeli authorities. The use of such data by the OECD is without prejudice to the status of the Golan Heights, East Jerusalem and Israeli settlements in the West Bank under the terms of international law.

Lifestyles play an important part in predicting cardiovascular disease and diabetes risk

Cardiovascular disease (CVD) and diabetes are highly preventable diseases. The majority of CVD is caused by risk factors that can be controlled, treated or modified. These risk factors include high blood pressure, cholesterol, obesity, lack of physical activity, tobacco use and excessive alcohol consumption. CVD and diabetes share many common risk factors, including obesity and physical activity; therefore, the prevention of these two modifiable risk factors can lead to a lower prevalence of both diseases.

As noted in Chapter 1, improvements in lifestyles have made a substantial contribution towards the falling CVD mortality burden. For example, estimates suggest that around 54% of the fall in coronary heart disease (CHD) mortality can be explained by risk-factor improvements. This chapter focuses on the four risk factors that are most strongly associated with lifestyles and amenable to primary prevention activities. Chapter 3 looks at some other risk factors, such as blood pressure and cholesterol, which involve both primary and secondary prevention activities.

Unhealthy lifestyles increase the odds of suffering from CVD and diabetes. An extensive literature has shown that obesity, smoking and lack of exercise independently increase the chances of an individual suffering from these diseases. The Framingham Study, for example, followed over 8 000 participants over a 12-year period to calculate the importance of risk factors in predicting the likelihood of suffering a CVD event (D'Agostino et al., 2008). Here, a CVD event includes coronary death, heart attack, coronary insufficiency, angina, stroke and heart failure. Table 2.1 reports the chances of a person experiencing a CVD event over a ten-year period, based on estimates from the Framingham Study. The risks have been calculated on the basis of a 60-year-old person who does not suffer from hypertension and is not a diabetic.

The likelihood of a non-smoking female with a healthy body mass index (BMI) of 20 suffering a CVD event is 6.5%. These chances virtually double if that person is a smoker. In addition, BMI increases the risk profile. Holding all other risk factors constant, a person who is obese (BMI > 30) is around 20% to 30% more likely to suffer a CVD event than a person who is in a healthy weight category. Importantly, some non-modifiable risk factors also have an important bearing on CVD. As shown in Table 2.1, being a male doubles the chances of a CVD event when keeping other risk factors constant. For obese and smoking 60-year-old males, the ten-year likelihood of a CVD event is in excess of 30%. Age is another important risk factor. For example, the likelihood of a CVD event would increase from 6.5% to 9.7% for a healthy 70-year-old female, compared to her 60-year-old counterpart.

The relationship between risk factors and developing type 2 diabetes has also been studied extensively. The FINDRISC study, for example, has developed a widely used clinical tool to predict the risk of developing diabetes for patients (Lindström and Tuomilehto, 2003). This Finnish study was based on over 4 400 participants, aged 35 to 64, who were followed

Table 2.1. **Predicting the ten-year likelihood of a CVD event: Smoking and body mass index**

BMI	Females		Males	
	Non-smoker	Smoker	Non-smoker	Smoker
	%	%	%	%
20	6.5	11.8	13.2	25.0
25	7.3	13.1	15.5	29.0
30	8.0	14.3	17.7	32.7
35	8.6	15.3	19.8	36.1

Note: Predicted risk scores have been calculated on the basis of a 60-year-old person who does not suffer from hypertension and is not a diabetic.

Source: Based on estimates from D'Agostino, R.B. et al. (2008), "General Cardiovascular Risk Profile for Use in Primary Care: The Framingham Heart Study", *Circulation*, Vol. 117, No. 6, pp. 743-753.

over a ten-year period to determine whether they had developed diabetes. Table 2.2 shows the likelihood of developing diabetes for a range of risk factor values. These estimates are based on the FINDRISC results and are reported for a person who is aged 50-64, has no history of high blood glucose, does not take hypertension medication and consumes vegetables or fruits daily.

The figures in Table 2.2 indicate that a healthy 55 to 64 year-old person who is not overweight and exercises more than four hours per week has a 1% chance of developing diabetes. Without exercise this risk rises by around 40% to 1.4%. Obesity more than doubles the risk of diabetes. The distribution of body weight is also an important determinant of diabetes risk. People with a greater waist circumference have a much higher risk. Diabetes also has a number of non-modifiable risk factors, with the chance of developing diabetes rising with age. Males are more susceptible as are those who have close family members with diabetes.

Table 2.2. **Predicting the ten-year likelihood of developing diabetes: Exercise, body mass index and waist size**

BMI	> 4 hours physical exercise per week			< 4 hours physical exercise per week		
	Waist circumference			Waist circumference		
	Cat. 1	Cat. 2	Cat. 3	Cat. 1	Cat. 2	Cat. 3
	%	%	%	%	%	%
≤ 25	1.0	2.8	4.2	1.4	3.7	5.4
> 25 to 30	1.1	2.9	4.3	1.4	3.7	5.5
> 30	2.6	7.0	10.1	3.4	8.9	12.8

Waist circumference: Cat. 1= Female (male) < 80 (94) cm; Cat. 2 = 80(94) cm ≤ Female (male) < 88(102) cm; Cat. 3 = Female(male) ≥ 88(102) cm

Note: Predicted risk scores calculated on the basis of a person who is aged 50-64, has no history of high blood glucose, does not take hypertension medication and consumes vegetables or fruits daily.

Source: Based on estimates from Lindström, J. and J. Tuomilehto (2003), "The Diabetes Risk Score: A Practical Tool to Predict Type 2 Diabetes Risk", *Diabetes Care*, Vol. 26, No. 3, pp. 725-731.

Tables 2.1 and 2.2 provide a clear overview of the additional risks that individuals face of experiencing a CVD event or developing diabetes. The increased likelihood of worsening health status, associated with many of these modifiable risk factors, provides a clear motivation for individuals to alter their behaviour.

For many people, however, the additional risk of illness and death is insufficient for them to choose healthy options. Numerous other factors may influence their choice, such as the relative price of healthy and unhealthy options, the transaction costs of consumption (e.g. time and skills required to make a healthy dinner versus buying fast food on the way home from work), as well as the perceived benefits of consumption. At the same time, people trade off the benefits and costs of immediate consumption versus the long-term (possibly negative) consequences of their consumption. All these factors can lead to sub-optimal decisions from the perspective of health outcomes. They provide reasons for governments and markets to play an active role in encouraging citizens to change their behaviour and adopt healthier lifestyle choices.

An underlying role for governments and markets is to make healthy lifestyle choices easier. In the field of prevention, government actions may take at least four types of actions aimed at (Sassi, 2010):

- improving the breadth or the attractiveness of healthy choices, relative to a free market situation,
- modifying preferences to encourage healthy choices,
- increasing the price of selected unhealthy choices,
- regulating and banning of selected unhealthy choices.

This chapter will examine the overall trends that OECD countries have experienced in lifestyle choices. In particular, it will focus on smoking rates, alcohol consumption, and obesity levels that are reported in OECD Health Statistics. For each of the main lifestyle indicators, it will show how countries are positioned in relation to their OECD peers, as well as indicate whether the trend over time for a country is substantially different from the OECD average. This chapter will also describe some of the main policy initiatives in this field and analyse the role that these have had in altering lifestyle behaviours.

Lifestyles help explain variation in diabetes and CVD across OECD countries

Figure 2.1 shows the percentage of the population who are obese as well as the percentage with diabetes. The percentage of the population who are obese ranges from less than 5% in Korea to over 35% in the United States. The diabetes prevalence ranges from less than 4% in Iceland to around 16% in Mexico. There is a strong positive association between the two measures. Obesity can account for around 25% of the variation in diabetes prevalence across countries. These figures indicate that the variation in unhealthy lifestyles is strongly associated with differences in the prevalence of diseases such as diabetes across countries.

Figure 2.1. **Obesity is a strong predictor of diabetes**

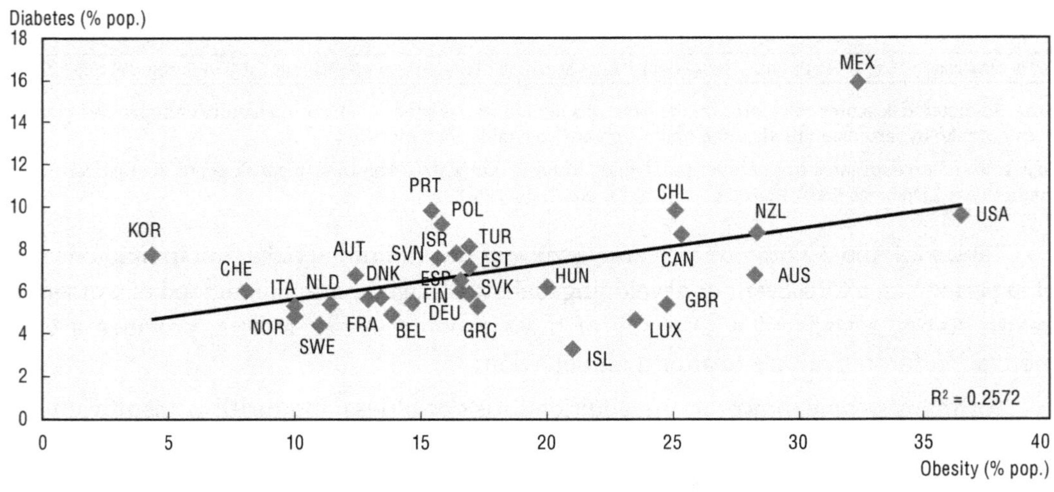

Source: IDF (2013), *IDF Diabetes Atlas, 6th Edition*, International Diabetes Federation, Brussels, *www.idf.org/diabetesatlas/previouseditions* for diabetes prevalence data and OECD Health Statistics 2013 for obesity prevalence data.

Similarly, smoking prevalence can account for a substantial amount of CVD mortality across countries. Figure 2.2 shows the relationship between smoking prevalence among those aged 15 and up and the cerebrovascular disease mortality rate per 100 000 population. The lowest smoking rates for men and women combined are found in Sweden, where only 13.1% of the population aged 15 and over smoke. On the opposite end of the smoking scale is Greece, where over 30% smoke. In terms of cerebrovascular mortality, the lowest rates can be found in France and the highest rates in the Slovak Republic. The relationship between these two variables indicates that around 17% of the cross-country variation in cerebrovascular mortality can be explained by smoking prevalence. Higher smoking rates are also associated with increased CVD mortality, although this relationship is not quite as strong as with cerebrovascular disease.

Figure 2.2. **Smoking is a strong predictor of cerebrovascular disease mortality**

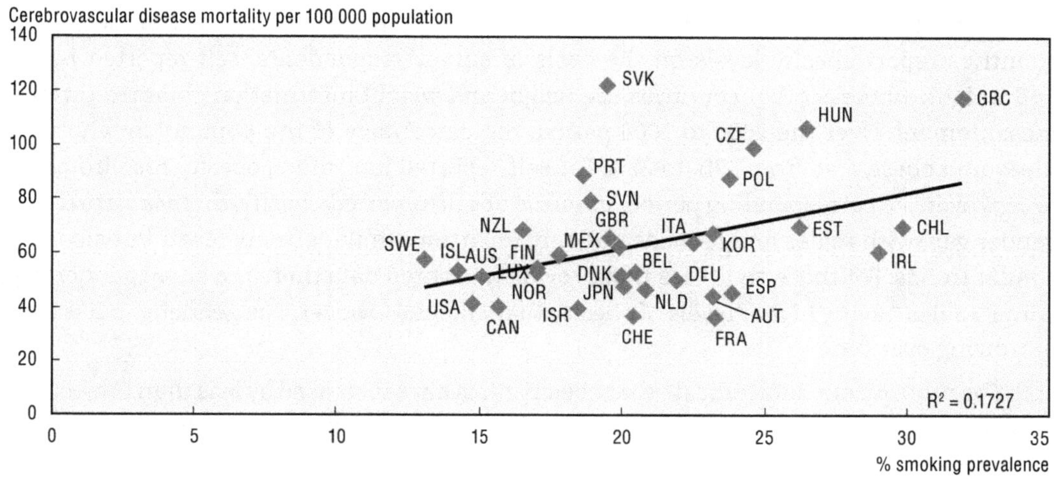

Source: *OECD Health Statistics 2013, http://dx.doi.org/10.1787/health-data-en.*

OECD countries have had mixed success in improving lifestyles and reducing risky behaviours

The lifestyle factors discussed in this chapter are to a considerable degree associated with risky behaviours on the part of individuals. The decision to pursue such behaviours is determined by a complex set of factors, including the perceived costs and benefits, prices, income and information (Lundberg and Shapira, 2014). Risky behaviours are based on a subjective decision that trades off the value of current consumption against the long-term consequences of that consumption. For example, a person who chooses to smoke is trading off the short-term impulse to consume tobacco against the longer-term risk of adverse health. The value that an individual places on their future health and well-being can depend on their education, wealth, and competing health risks. Furthermore, social norms can influence the perceived benefit of such behaviours.

OECD countries have had mixed success in improving risky behaviours. On the one hand, smoking rates have declined substantially, but the percentage of the population who are obese continues to climb. Figure 2.3 shows the trends reported in OECD Health Statistics. The period over which trends were observed was chosen on the basis of the largest and most consistent number of countries able to report these data.

The figure shows declining trends in the percentage of the population who smoke for males and females, and younger smokers aged between 15 and 24. Overall, the percentage of the population who smoked daily fell from 28% in 1997 to 20% in 2009. Men are more likely to smoke than females, but the rate of decline was similar in both sexes. While there has also been a decline in the percentage of younger smokers, this trend is only evident in the latter years. Between 1997 and 2004, the percentage of younger smokers was fairly stable, but then started to decline among males and, more recently, among females as well. The gender gap in smoking varies enormously between countries. In 2010, smoking rates were, on average, over 90% higher among males than females. In the United Kingdom, though, the gap between males and females was only 5%. In Korea, only 5% of females smoke, but smoking rates among males is over 40%. These gender gaps have an important bearing on the differential CVD risks faced by men and women in some countries.

Obesity levels have been rising in all OECD countries. Figure 2.3 shows the trends for males and females as well as for two different obesity measurement techniques. Some countries report obesity levels on the basis of survey respondents' self-reported height and weight, whereas other countries use height and weight information obtained through measurement. Over the 2000 to 2009 period, the percentage of the population who were measured obese rose from 17% to 22%. For self-reported indicators, obesity rose from 12% to 16% over the corresponding period. In terms of self-reported obesity, there is virtually no gender gap, with males and females not only reporting similar obesity levels but also very similar trends. For those countries that provide measured data there is a small gender gap, with females having higher levels of obesity than males. However, this gender gap has been narrowing over time.

The more recent data indicate that obesity rates have increased by less than projections in a large number of OECD countries, providing some positive signs that the rates of increase are falling (OECD, 2012). The most recent observations provide some tentative signs that the prevalence of obesity has stabilised or the rate of increase has slowed in some countries. Nevertheless, rates continue to increase in other countries and remain high in many OECD countries.

The percentage of children who are reportedly either overweight or obese has also been rising. Figure 2.3 indicates that the percentage of overweight or obese 15-year-olds rose from 13% to 15% between 2001 and 2009. Alcohol consumption, on the other hand, has been stable across OECD countries, with evidence of a small reduction after 2008.

The Global Burden of Disease (GBD) study has estimated the years of life lost (YLL) that can be attributed to 67 risk factors, including risky behaviours. The GBD study approach is to calculate the proportion of deaths caused by specific risk factors, holding other independent factors unchanged. Calculations were made for 187 countries and for 1990, 2005 and 2010 (Lim et al., 2013).

Figure 2.4 presents the YLL due to cardiovascular disease in 1990 and 2010 that can be attributed to a number of lifestyle choices. The figures shown are for all OECD countries as well as Singapore and Latvia. As shown in Chapter 1, cardiovascular disease mortality fell considerably over the 1990 to 2010 period, and this is reflected in the overall drop in YLL (note: physical inactivity was not part of the 1990 study). The number of cardiovascular-related YLL due to smoking more than halved over the 20-year period, whereas those due to high body mass index (obese or overweight) fell by around 25%. It should be noted that the addition of the physical inactivity risk factor in 2010 may have influenced the

Figure 2.3. **Trends in OECD lifestyles: Tobacco, obesity and alcohol**

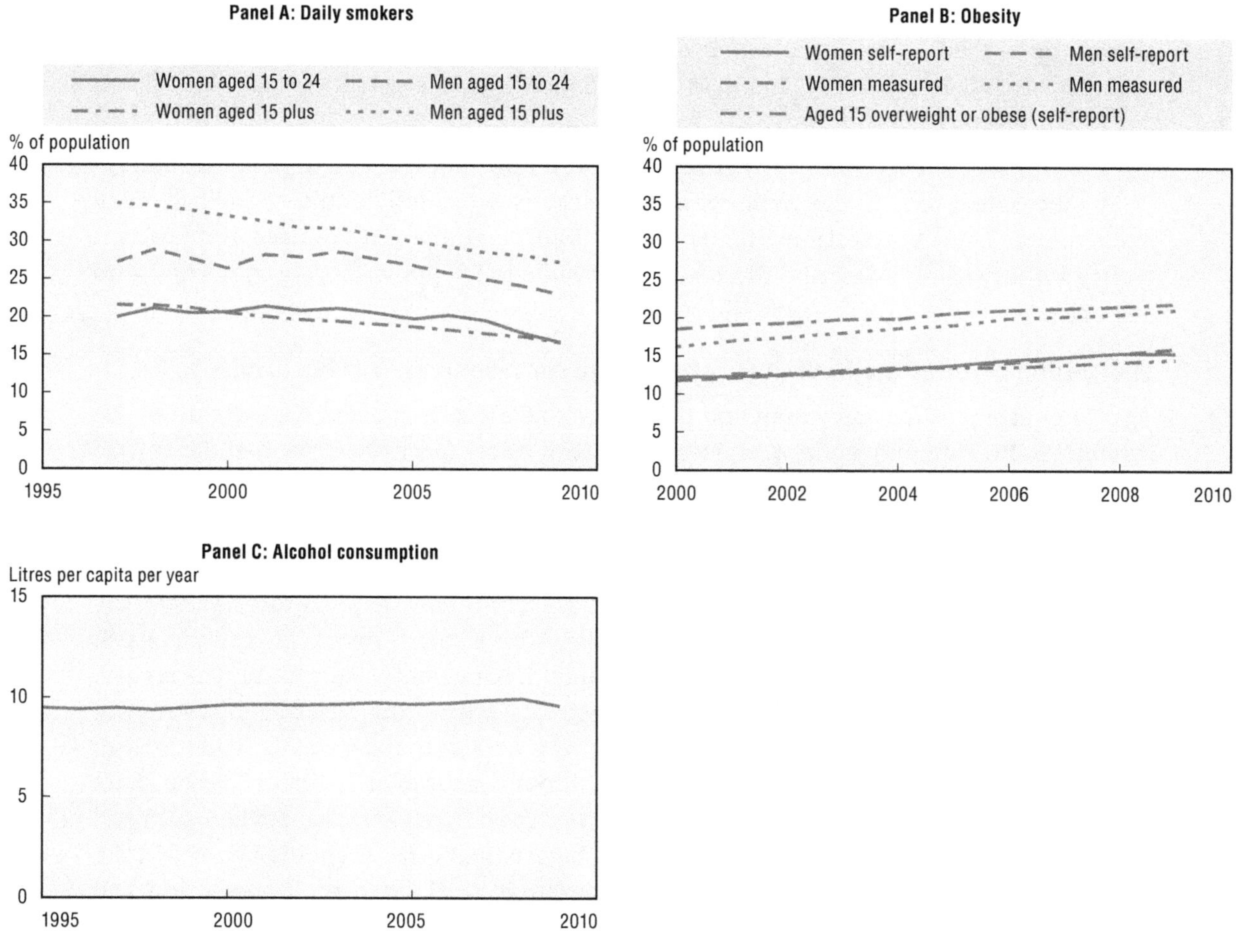

Source: *OECD Health Statistics 2013, http://dx.doi.org/10.1787/health-data-en.*

Figure 2.4. **Years of life lost in cardiovascular disease due to risky behaviours**

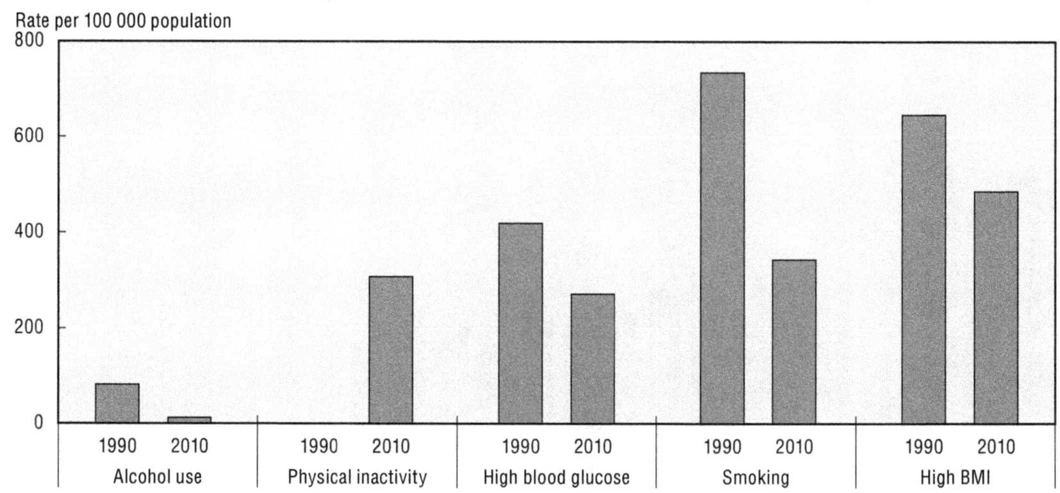

Source: IHME (2013), "The Global Burden of Disease: Generating Evidence, Guiding Policy", Institute for Health Metrics and Evaluation, Seattle.

risk attributed to high body mass. Nevertheless, the fact of being obese or overweight has overtaken smoking as the number one lifestyle risk factor in cardiovascular disease. According to the GBD results, alcohol consumption is a relatively small contributor to the number of CVD-related YLL. This is in concordance with the evidence that alcohol can provide protective CVD effects.

To improve lifestyle choices, governments require multi-faceted policy responses that take into account the heterogeneous reasons why individuals engage in risky behaviours. The next section of this chapter will examine experiences from recent policy initiatives and describe the resources available for prevention programmes and services.

Prevention services are having to cope with fewer resources in some countries

The resources for prevention and public health services represent a small part of the overall health care budget. In 2011, less than 3% of total current health expenditure was devoted to the prevention and public health sector in OECD countries overall. However, this percentage ranged from less than 1% in Italy and Israel to over 6% in Canada and New Zealand (Figure 2.5).

Following the start of the financial crisis in 2008, total health expenditure has been the target of many governments' austerity measures. After a steady period of growth, health care expenditure was constrained to zero real growth between 2009 and 2011. The biggest target for health savings has been pharmaceutical expenditures. However, preventive care services and public health programmes have also witnessed small reductions in their share of health expenditure. In 15 of the 27 countries shown in Figure 2.5, the share devoted to prevention and public health programmes went backwards between 2008 and 2011. In eight of those countries, the drop was bigger than 0.2%. It should be noted that, due to data limitations, these figures are representative of the overall prevention and public health sector, not just those devoted to the prevention of cardiovascular disease and diabetes.

Figure 2.5. **Spending on prevention and public health services**

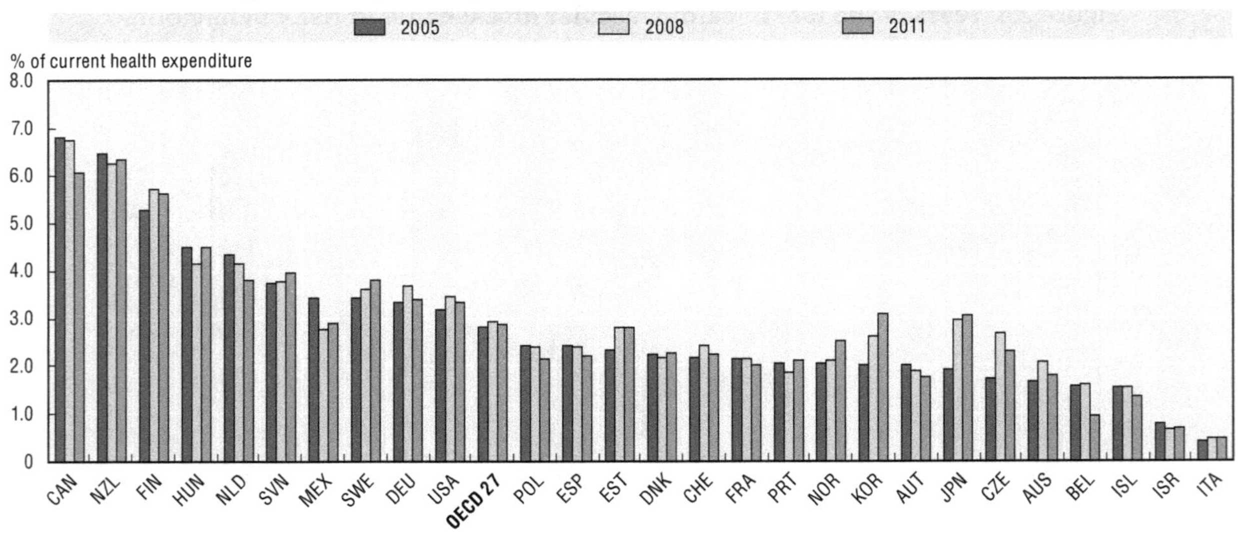

Source: OECD Health Statistics 2013, *http://dx.doi.org/10.1787/health-data-en.*

Improving lifestyles to reduce CVD and diabetes risk: Recent experiences in OECD countries

OECD countries have introduced strong anti-tobacco legislation and programmes

The World Health Organization (WHO) has recently undertaken national surveys to help characterise the type of policies that have been implemented to reduce smoking rates and cut tobacco consumption. All OECD countries have implemented anti-tobacco programmes and policies, including mass media campaigns to warn about the dangers of smoking, services and products to help smokers quit, advertising bans and taxes. However, the types of policies and intensity of those policies varies considerably by country. Box 2.1 describes these eight different types of policies in more detail, as well as the categories that describe the intensity by which countries have implemented the policy.

Stronger tobacco control policies are having an effect

To estimate the relationship between tobacco control policies and smoking rates, a fixed effects econometric model is employed. The first analysis examines whether countries that have adopted more comprehensive tobacco control programmes have been able to reduce their smoking rates at a faster rate compared to countries with less comprehensive strategies. This analysis takes into account the different smoking rates across countries at the start of the observation period, which is 1996. Separate models were estimated for the population aged 15 and above and for the population aged between 15 and 24, as well as for females and males.

For the purpose of this analysis, countries were classified into two groups: comprehensive or less comprehensive tobacco policy regimes. This classification was based on actual scores given to countries by the WHO Global Health Observatory based on the survey of policies described in Box 2.1 above. The actual scores are presented in Annex 2.A1.[1] In 2010, almost all countries indicated that they routinely monitored smoking rates for their populations. However, only eight countries indicated that they had implemented mass media campaigns that were in accordance with all the WHO desirable characteristics. The survey results show that countries such as Australia, New Zealand, Ireland, the United Kingdom and Turkey were amongst the set of countries with the most stringent and comprehensive set of anti-tobacco policies (WHO, 2010). Countries that belonged to the most stringent policy category (as outlined in Annex 2.A1) on more than three occasions were grouped in the comprehensive category, and countries with scores of three or below were grouped in the less comprehensive category. The dependent variable was transformed into log units.

The results of the regression results are shown in Table 2.3. For the population aged 15 and over, countries with less comprehensive tobacco policies were able to reduce their smoking rates by an average of 2.4% per year. Countries with more stringent policy were able to reduce their smoking rate by an additional 0.3% per year. This represents a 15% additional reduction in the percentage of smokers in the more stringent countries. The result was the same for males and females aged 15 and over and for males aged 15 to 24. For younger females, the estimate is similar to other population groups but not statistically significant at conventional levels.

Box 2.1. **Anti-tobacco policies**

WHO description of seven anti-tobacco policies:

Protection from tobacco smoke: Describes the extent to which smoke-free environments have been created. Countries are grouped into one of five groups: 1) data not reported/not categorised; 2) up to two public places completely smoke-free; 3) 3-5 public places completely smoke-free; 4) 6-7 public places completely smoke-free; and 5) all public places completely smoke-free.

Offering help to quit: Classifies countries on the extent to which they provide and cover the cost of products and services to help smokers quit. Countries were categorised into one of five groups: The groupings for this indicator are: 1) data not reported; 2) none; 3) nicotine replacement therapy (NRT) and/or some cessation services (but neither cost-covered); 4) NRT and/or some cessation services (at least one of which is cost-covered); and 5) national quit line, and both NRT and some cessation services are cost-covered.

Health warnings: Measures the extent to which tobacco products carry health warnings about the dangers of smoking. Countries were classified into five groups: 1) data not reported; 2) warnings cover < 30% of pack surface; 3) warnings cover ≥ 30% but no pictures or pictograms; 4) warnings cover 31%-49% including pictures or pictograms; and 5) warnings cover = ≥ 50% including pictures or pictograms.

Bans on advertising: Measures the implementation status and describes the extent to which countries have regulated advertising of tobacco products. Countries were categorised into one of five groups: 1) data not reported; 2) complete or almost complete absence of ban; 3) ban on national TV, radio and print media only; 4) ban on national TV, radio and print media as well as on some but not all other forms of direct and/or indirect advertising; and 5) ban on all forms of direct and indirect advertising.

Tax: describes the amount of tax levied on the most commonly sold tobacco product as a percentage of the final retail price. Taxes assessed include excise tax, value added tax, import duty and any other taxes levied. Countries were categorised into one of five groups: 1) data not reported; 2) ≤ 25% of retail price is tax; 3) between 26–50% of retail price is tax; 4) between 51-75% of retail price is tax; and 5) > 75% of retail price is tax.

Mass media campaign: Assesses the intensiveness, effectiveness and recent nature of mass media campaigns. Countries were classified into five groups: 1) data not reported; 2) no campaign conducted recently with a duration of at least three weeks; 3) campaign conducted with 1-4 appropriate characteristics; 4) campaign conducted with 5-6 appropriate characteristics; and 5) campaign conducted with all appropriate characteristics. Characteristics of a high-quality campaign are 1) part of a tobacco control programme; 2) research was undertaken to understand the target audience; 3) materials were pre-tested and refined in line with campaign objectives; 4) advertising was purchased using either the organisation's own internal resources or an external media planner or agency; 5) journalists were informed to gain publicity or news coverage; 6) process evaluation was undertaken; and 7) outcome evaluation was implemented to assess the campaign impact.

National tobacco control programmes (NTCP): Determines whether a country has established a national agency for tobacco control as well as its functions and resources. Countries were categorised into one of four groups: 1) data not reported; 2) no national agency on tobacco control; 3) national agency with responsibility for tobacco control objectives with less than five staff; and 4) national agency with responsibility for tobacco control objectives and at least five staff.

Monitoring: Determines whether countries actively monitor smoking patterns amongst its population. Countries were grouped into one of four categories: 1) no known, recent or representative data; 2) recent representative data for either adults or youth; 3) recent representative data for both adults and youth; and 4) recent, representative and periodic data for both adults and youth.

Source: Global Health Observatory of the World Health Organization.

Table 2.3. **The relationship between tobacco policies and smoking rates**

	Age greater than 15			Age between 15 and 24		
	Population	Females	Males	Population	Males	Females
Change in smoking rates per year in less comprehensive countries	-0.024***	-0.02***	-0.025***	-0.03***	-0.024***	-0.032***
(SE)	(.001)	(.002)	(.001)	(.003)	(.004)	(.004)
Additional change in smoking rates in more comprehensive tobacco control countries	-0.003**	-0.005**	-0.002**	-0.005**	-0.006***	-0.002
(SE)	(.001)	(.002)	(.001)	(.002)	(.002)	(.002)
Observations	468	468	468	288	283	283

Note: Regression controls for country fixed and country-specific time trend effects. *** = $p < 0.01$; ** = $p < 0.05$; * = $p < 0.1$.
Source: OECD Health Statistics 2013 and Global Health Observatory of the World Health Organization, 2010.

The figures presented in Table 2.3 should only be interpreted as associations because it is not possible to determine exactly when these policies were introduced prior to 2008. Unfortunately, there is no further information on when countries introduced these various anti-tobacco policies. If such information existed, it would be feasible to produce estimates of the impact of individual policies (rather than the impact of overall policy), and be more definitive about the direct impact of policy on smoking rates.

In addition to the tobacco control policy information, WHO also collected information on the prices of the most commonly sold tobacco products. These data are used to examine the empirical relationship between tobacco pricing and smoking in OECD countries. In particular, the analysis focuses on the effect of price changes and smoking rates observed in 2008 and 2010 within countries.

Similar to the tobacco control policy models shown above, a fixed effects model was employed to estimate the effect of price-level changes on smoking rates for males and females, for those aged 15 and above, and for those aged 15 to 24. To present the results in percentage terms, the models were estimated in a log-log form. Prices were only observed in 2008 and 2010, which implies that there are a maximum of two observations per country. The model accounts for general changes in smoking trends by including a time effect.

Despite the short time span between the two price observation, tobacco price increased substantially between 2008 and 2010. When measured in USD PPP, the average price in OECD countries of the most commonly sold tobacco product was USD 5.46 in 2010 compared to USD 4.70 in 2008, representing a 16% increase. However, price level changes varied considerably across countries. In countries such as Finland, Mexico, Estonia and Italy, prices increased by less than 1.5% over the two-year period, whereas in countries such as Spain, Turkey, the United States and Australia, prices increased by more than 20%.

Table 2.4 presents the regression results for the price models. Across all population groups there is a negative relationship between price changes and tobacco smoking, indicating that higher prices can lead to a reduction in smoking rates. The coefficients for the price (log) variable can be interpreted as price elasticities, reflecting the percentage change relationship between prices and smoking rates. For example, for females aged 15 to 24, a 1% increase in the price of cigarettes is associated with a (approximately) 1.3% reduction in smoking rates. The results are significant for the younger smoking group, particularly for younger females, suggesting that they are more sensitive to price changes. These results may also indicate that price rises have a more immediate impact on people taking up smoking.

Table 2.4. **The relationship between tobacco policies and smoking rates**

	Age greater than 15			Age between 15 and 24		
Dependent variable: % smoke daily	Population	Females	Males	Population	Females	Males
Price (log)	-0.178	-0.098	-0.194	-0.866**	-1.287**	-0.544
	(0.1336)	(0.2087)	(0.1489)	(.3647)	(0.473)	(0.3378)
Observations	48	48	48	34	34	34

Note: Regression controls for country fixed effects and time effects. *** = p<0.01; ** = p< 0.05; * = p<0.1.

Source: OECD Health Statistics 2013 and Global Health Observatory of the World Health Organization.2010.

The analysis above examines the impact of the strong anti-tobacco policy on the percentage of the population who smoke, however this is likely to underestimate the full effect of such initiatives. Policies will also have an impact on passive smoking. For example, the ban to smoke in public places is likely to reduce the exposure of non-smokers to harmful tobacco smoke. In fact, numerous evaluations have linked the ban to smoke in public places with a reduction in heart-attack admissions among non-smokers and smokers alike (Pell et al., 2008).

It should be noted that the period over which this analysis took place coincided with the arrival of the 2008 global financial crisis, which may impact on the generalisability of the results. It is not straight forward to predict how individuals respond in terms of their risky behaviours when faced with loss of income or greater financial stress. Increased stress may arise due to greater employment uncertainty which, in turn, induces depression or anxiety which, in turn, may invoke some people to engage in more risky behaviours. For others, the loss of income may induce them to look for ways to reduce household expenditures, including reducing the consumption of risky goods such as tobacco. Empirically, a systematic review has found that the effect of unemployment on smoking is still not clear (Henkel, 2011). However, unemployment is linked to decreasing levels of tobacco consumption among smokers (Ruhm, 2005). In Iceland, smoking prevalence fell significantly after the financial crisis, with evidence that income falls and price changes were among the most important reasons for the fall (McClure et al., 2012; Ásgeirsdóttir et al., 2013).

Since the 2010 WHO survey, a number of countries have further strengthened their anti-tobacco policies through a variety of means. Australia, for example, has set a target to cut smoking rates from around 15% of the population to 10% by 2018. As part of its comprehensive anti-tobacco plan, Australia has introduced a number of innovative programmes and regulations, including its plain-packaging laws. Under this law, logos and branding on cigarette packages have been banned. All cigarettes and tobacco products must be sold in plain olive green packets without branding. The packets carry graphic health warnings and the laws took effect as of December 2012 (see Figure 2.6 for examples). Plain packaging aims to remove a key remaining means for industry to promote its products to current and potential consumers (Freeman et al., 2008). The legislation withstood serious industry opposition and was upheld in the High Court of Australia. While it is still early days for measuring the impact of the legislation, studies are showing some positive signs. The implementation of the legislation coincided with a 78% rise in the number of calls to the national "quit line", which was equivalent to the increase in calls when graphic health warnings were introduced in 2006 (Young et al., 2014). Public support for the Australia's anti-tobacco policies is also high, with 75% of survey respondents supporting or feeling neutral about plain packaging and only one in three smokers opposing the measure (Rosenberg et al., 2012). Furthermore, the decline in the proportion of daily smokers appears to have accelerated in period during which plain packaging was introduced in Australia (AIHW, 2014). While further evidence about the effectiveness of plain packaging is still being gathered, these initiatives may provide the next set of policy instruments for governments to help further reduce the harmful impact of smoking in society.

Figure 2.6. **Examples of plain cigarette packaging in Australia**

Source: © Commonwealth of Australia.

Comprehensive programmes to reduce obesity represent good investments

As part of its Economics of Prevention programme of work, the OECD undertook a major study on obesity. The results of this study were reported in the 2010 OECD publication *Obesity and the Economics of Prevention: Fit not Fat.* This section draws on this work, the OECD's Obesity Update published 2012, as well as the most recent data.

On the basis of its analysis, the OECD has consistently called for strong government action in obesity prevention. Its research shows that programmes and supportive regulations to improve diets and increase physical activity provide affordable and cost-effective solutions to the ever-increasing burden of obesity. The results from a micro-simulation model suggest that investments in a range of population-based programmes have the potential to save hundreds of thousands of deaths from chronic diseases every year in OECD countries. The cost and effect of a comprehensive obesity prevention strategy was modelled as part of the micro-simulation exercise. This strategy includes fiscal measures, food advertising restrictions to children, and food labelling, as well as a mass media campaign, worksite and school-based interventions and intensive counselling of high-risk individuals in the primary care setting.

According to the analysis, primary care can play an important role in tackling obesity. An intervention which targets high-risk individuals and is delivered by primary care physicians and dieticians has been shown to be effective. Through intensive counselling and provision of information to patients, a primary care intervention has been shown to modify a number of risk factors; for example, it has led to a reduction in total energy intake from fats, a fall in BMI, and lower blood cholesterol and systolic blood pressure. While the primary care intervention was the mostly costly intervention, it was also the most effective (when compared to the other interventions) in the countries for which the analysis was undertaken. The analysis for the primary care intervention is sensitive to assumptions made about programme participation (by both doctors and patients) and it is likely that the best results will be obtained in countries with strong primary care systems, or where participation could be encouraged through incentives.

The results of the OECD micro-simulation exercise show that, on average, over 1 000 life years per million population could be saved in countries such as Japan, Italy, England and Canada, and around 500 life years in Mexico. The cost of delivering the comprehensive strategy ranges from USD 12 (Japan) to USD 24 (Canada) per capita per year. However, over the longer term, the strategy actually becomes cost saving as the impact takes effect and reduces downstream costs through fewer hospitalisations and other expensive medical care needs.

While such comprehensive strategies have the potential to improve health outcomes and reduce costs, they are not easily implemented. There is a complex array of agents that have a stake in these policies. Industry may perceive some regulations as threatening the bottom line, if the regulations lead to increased cost or falls in market shares. As noted previously, there are a number of examples of policies that have caused considerable conflict between stakeholders; and as a result strategies have become lost in claims and counter claims as well as judgements on individual rights and freedoms. The OECD has therefore called for co-operation among multiple stakeholders, including government and industry. The most promising policies are those that align the aims of government with the objectives of industry.

Obesity and physical activity in adults and kids: Recent policies and evidence

Government policy can play an active role in encouraging healthy behaviours. Policy actions vary in the degree of interference, ranging from fairly light-touch actions that provide individuals with more choice, to more heavy handed approaches which involve banning products or enforcing certain types of behaviours. The type of role that governments chose to take will, to some degree, depend on the level of interference in individual choices that will be tolerated by the public and can be justified. In the context of obesity prevention, governments can direct their actions through at least four different types of interventions (Sassi, 2010):

- *Increasing choices for healthy lifestyles.* Policy can play a role in expanding the range of choices considered beneficial for healthy lifestyles. This could include actions to expand the range of choices available, or to reduce the prices of products and services that encourage healthy choices. Direct investments in active transportation services such as bicycle rental schemes, or subsidies to make public transportation more convenient and less expensive, are examples of these types of interventions.
- *Inform and educate population about the benefits of healthy lifestyles.* This type of intervention aims to influence personal preferences and thereby influence un/healthy choices through education (especially among children) and provision of information to persuade adults to adopt virtuous behaviours.

- *Raising prices on unhealthy choices*. Governments can also influence choice through fiscal measures that aim to create financial disincentives for unhealthy behaviours. It can involve the use of indirect taxes and other levies charged on the consumption of unhealthy foods or drinks.
- *Banning unhealthy behaviours*. These actions result in the complete ban of one or more choices. A ban can selectively hinder certain choices, with the aim of limiting the overall consumption of a commodity or incidence of a given behaviour.

A 2007/08 OECD/EU survey sought information from national governments on the type of policies and initiatives being used across countries to tackle unhealthy diets and sedentary lifestyles. The results of the survey revealed that governments have focused more of their actions on diets rather than on active lifestyles; although action relating to the latter is the responsibility of regional or municipal levels of government in many countries. The survey also revealed that most actions were focused on increasing choice and delivering information and education programmes to influence preference. At the time the survey was conducted in 2007 and 2008, no country stated that they used fiscal measures to raise the prices of unhealthy products. Since that time, a considerable number of countries have implemented a range of taxation measures designed to raise the prices of foods that are high in fat, sugar or salt (OECD, 2012).

Since 2010, several OECD countries introduced taxes on foods and non-alcoholic beverages deemed potentially unhealthy (Sassi et al., 2013). These taxes have been part of national public health efforts to reduce obesity; but in a time of budgetary pressures, these taxes can also generate important revenues. Examples of countries that have introduced fiscal measures include:

- *Denmark* introduced a "fat tax" in 2011. Foods containing more than 2.3% saturated fats were taxed, adding around 16 kroner (EUR 2.15) per kilogram of saturated fat. Tax revenues were expected to be over EUR 200 million per year.
- *Hungary* introduced a tax on selected manufactured foods in 2011 with high sugar, salt or caffeine content. This only affects products that have healthier alternatives. The Hungarian Government is reportedly expecting to raise in excess of EUR 70 million per year from the tax.
- *Finland* introduced a tax on confectionery products in 2011 which is set at EUR 0.75 per kilogram of product. Existing excise taxes on soft drinks were raised from 4.5 cents to 7.5 cents per litre.
- *France* introduced a tax on soft drinks in 2012, including drinks with added sugars and drinks with artificial sweeteners. The tax is set at EUR 0.072 per litre. The tax is payable by manufacturers established in France and importers and is expected to generate revenues in the region of EUR 280 million per year.
- *Mexico*, in 2014, implemented a new tax set at 10% on sugar-sweetened beverages (SSB) and 8% on processed food that contains more than 275 calories per 100 g. The effect of the tax will put one peso (EUR 0.05) on a litre of sugary drinks. The tax is expected to raise 15 billion peso (EUR 0.82 billion) and is earmarked for health programmes and increased access to drinking water in schools.

The introduction of these taxes has not been without controversy. In fact, the "fat tax" was rescinded in Denmark at the start 2013 following widespread critique. In particular, there was public concern over 1) the increase in prices, which in some instances was higher than the amount of the new tax; 2) the impact on lower socio-economic groups who incur a higher burden of the tax; and 3) the much publicised cross-border shopping in order to evade the tax.

Other attempts at fiscal measures and regulating food and beverages have been contested. The introduction of the Mexican tax was met with an extensive public campaign both in favour of and opposed to the tax, and was eventually set at 10% rather than the 20% rate advocated by public health groups. In New York, the Health Board's attempt to limit the size of beverages that could be sold by restaurants and many other types of food outlets have been caught up in legal challenges and appeals. Nevertheless, fiscal measures can have an important role in the policy armoury against obesity. But they can also have clear effects on consumer choice as well as impact some aspects of the wider economy. This is why countries that are considering such fiscal measures need to consider these wider impacts and carefully design tax measures that can minimise any potential negative impacts (Sassi, 2013).

Aside from developments on fiscal measures, a number of countries have implemented programmes aimed at improving lifestyles, including increasing physical activity. A number of governments have taken further actions to fight obesity through health promotion efforts. Nationally co-ordinated programmes have been launched in countries such as the United States (Let's Move), United Kingdom (Change4Life), Switzerland (Actionsanté), and others (OECD, 2012). There is a trend in these programmes to include multi-stakeholder frameworks, involving business and civil society actors in the development of public health policies. These comprehensive programmes target obesity through an extensive variety of measures that include mass education campaigns as well as more targeted interventions aimed at high-risk individuals. Improving the level of physical activity, especially among children, has also been a key feature of these programmes. For example, since 2010 when the Let's Move campaign was launched by First Lady Michelle Obama the programme has worked Sports associations to build or refurbish sporting facilities across the country and provide beginner athletic programmes for free or low costs to actively participate in a range of sports. Institutions such as museums and gardens have pledged to offer active exhibits and healthy food choices. New resources have been devoted by local and national associations to assist local elected officials advance the goals of "Let's Move!" in their communities and street-closings are taking place to increase safe places kids and families to run, walk, bike, or play outside freely without traffic (see: *www.letsmove.gov*). Evaluations of the effectiveness of such multi-stakeholder initiatives are only beginning to emerge and should be monitored closely for their potential effect on physical activity levels and obesity.

Lowering salt consumption is achievable

There is a clear link between increased levels of sodium (salt) consumption and high blood pressure. Studies have also shown an association between salt and cardiovascular disease, although the evidence is somewhat more ambiguous (WHO, 2012). The World Health Organization recommends that adults consume less than five grams of salt a day. In most countries, average salt consumption is considerably higher than the recommended level (Brown et al., 2009), and well above the minimum physiological levels required. In the United States, for example, average salt intake has been estimated to be in excess of 10 grams a day in males and 7 grams for females (Bibbins-Domingo et al., 2010).

Reducing salt consumption can have clear benefits on cardiovascular outcomes. Modelling studies have shown that, in the United States alone, a modest reduction of three grams in daily salt can reduce the annual number strokes by 32 000 to 66 000, and myocardial infarction by 54 000 to 99 000 (Bibbins-Domingo et al., 2010). A controlled trial in Japan showed that a moderate-intensity dietary counselling intervention achieved significant dietary changes, including salt consumption, amongst subjects, which resulted in a significant decrease in systolic blood pressure (Takahashi et al., 2006).

Many countries have used a variety of policy instruments to reduce salt intake amongst their citizens. These include public information, food labelling, taxation, regulation and marketing controls and food reformulation. Many countries have successfully worked with food industries to set new salt targets for reformulating existing processed food (Cappuccio et al., 2011). In Canada, a multi-pronged approach is used which includes a multi-media campaign to enable consumers to make informed food choices; setting guidance for industry to reduce salt in processed foods; mandatory labelling; and restrictions on nutritional claims. In addition, Canada's Heart and Stroke Foundation certifies foods with a tick of approval if they can meet strict nutrient (including salt) criteria. It has been estimated that between 2004 and 2008, 150 products saw a reduction in salt content, resulting in a total drop in salt consumption of 800 000 kg.

As part its programme to reduce obesity and improve diets, the UK Government has implemented the "The Responsibility Deal" to encourage businesses and organisations to make it easier for consumers and staff members to make healthier choices. Organisations can sign up and pledge to take actions to 1) reduce ingredients that can be harmful, such as salt and fat; 2) encourage people to eat more fruit and vegetables; 3) put calorie information on menus; 4) help people to eat fewer calories by, for example, reducing portion size or changing the recipe of a product (UK DOH, 2014). The "Responsibility Deal" is part of the government's programme "Healthy Lives, Healthy People" which was developed following the release of the Foresight Report. This report recognises the wider role and responsibilities of civil society in reducing obesity. By 2012, a number of organisations had signed a pledge to achieve a number of programme goals. For example, over 80 organisations have committed to the salt targets, which aim to collectively reduce salt consumption by an additional 15% compared to 2010 targets. Such voluntary initiatives provide a more co-operative framework for achieving objectives, but it is not yet clear if they are effective in terms of improving diets in populations (DOH, 2014).

There have been clear wins in the battle to reduce salt. In Finland, salt intake has fallen from over 14 to less than 9 grams per day over a 30-year period (Karppanen et al., 2006)). In the United Kingdom, daily average salt intake fell by around 14% between 2003 and 2007 (Millett, 2012). A cost-effectiveness analysis of the UK salt reduction campaigns revealed that, by 2008, the campaigns had cost GBP 15 million and achieved a 0.9 g/day reduction in salt intake, which led to about 6 000 fewer deaths from cardiovascular disease a year. This resulted in savings to the UK economy of around GBP 1.5 billion a year (NICE, 2010). These measures provide confidence that multifaceted and reinforcing approaches can have a real impact on consumption levels and health outcomes, as well as have positive economic impact (He et al., 2013).

Lifestyle patterns across OECD countries vary considerably

Smoking in OECD countries: Most are doing well but some could do better

Despite the substantial improvements in the percentage of people who smoke, there are significant differences in overall smoking rates across countries and in trends over time. Table 2.5 presents information on smoking rates and trends by country and gender. Countries with smoking rates in the highest third of OECD countries are marked dark grey, those in the middle are marked grey, and those countries in the bottom third are marked light grey. On average, 16% of females and 26% of males smoked in OECD countries in 2011 (or latest year). To be in the top third of countries (dark grey), the percentage of females and males who smoked had to be higher than 18% and 29%, respectively. To be among the lowest third (light grey), the percentage of female and male smokers had to be less than 14% and 21%, respectively.

In terms of trends, the average annual decrease in the percentage of male smokers was 2.7%. Over the last ten years, male smoking rates have fallen in almost all countries, with the exception of Korea, where the percentage of smokers has been increasing by 1% per year. Countries where the decline in smoking rates among males was more than -2.2% belonged to the top third (dark grey) of OECD country trends, whereas countries that exhibited falls of less than -3% were in the bottom third (light grey) of trends.

Females exhibited more varied results across countries. Here, the average annual decrease in the percentage of smokers was 1.7%. Over the last ten years, female smoking rates fell in 24 countries but increased in the Czech Republic, Greece, Korea and Portugal, although no recent Portuguese data are available in OECD Health Statistics. Countries that showed a fall of less than -0.75% per year belonged to the worst third (dark grey) of OECD country trends, whereas countries with reductions in excess of -2.9% per year were in the best performing third (light grey) of country trends.

The various experiences suggest that further declines in smoking rates are feasible. Countries such as Australia, Canada, Sweden, the United Kingdom, and the United States provide evidence that those with more comprehensive and stricter tobacco control policies tend to not only have lower smoking rates overall, but to also build on that success over time. These experiences should encourage other countries that such successes can be replicated by introducing further tobacco control policies, as well as tightening and enforcing existing policies.

Overweight and obesity patterns: Worrying overall trends but some positive signs in more recent years

Despite the overall rising trends in the percentage of people who are either overweight or obese, there are considerable differences between countries and genders. To be ranked in the worst third of countries (dark grey), the percentage who were overweight or obese had to be higher than 48% for females and for 61.5% for males. To belong to the best third, the percentage had to be less than 41% and 55% for females and males, respectively.

In terms of trends, countries with annual rates of growth higher than 0.9% for females and 1.3% for males were in the worst third (dark grey) of OECD peers. To belong to the best third, countries had to exhibit growth rates of less than 0.5% and 0.7% for females and males, respectively. Over the ten-year observation period, only Ireland and Japan have managed to make a small reduction in the percentage of women who are overweight or

Table 2.5. **Smoking among males and females: Country rankings and trends**

	Female smoking daily		Male smoking daily	
	Rank	Trend	Rank	Trend
Australia	2010	2001-2010	2010	2001-2010
Austria	2006	-	2006	-
Belgium	2008	2001-2008	2008	2001-2008
Canada	2011	2001-2012	2011	2001-2012
Chile	2009	-	2009	-
Czech Republic	2011	2003-2012	2011	2003-2012
Denmark	2010	2000-2010	2010	2000-2010
Estonia	2011	2000-2010	2011	2000-2010
Finland	2011	2000-2012	2011	2000-2012
France	2010	2002-2010	2010	2002-2010
Germany	2009	1999-2009	2009	1999-2009
Greece	2010	2006-2010	2010	2006-2010
Hungary	2009	2000-2009	2009	2000-2009
Iceland	2011	2000-2013	2011	2000-2013
Ireland	2007	-	2007	-
Israel	2010	2002-2013	2010	2002-2013
Italy	2011	2000-2013	2011	2000-2013
Japan	2011	2000-2012	2011	2000-2012
Korea	2011	2001-2012	2011	2001-2012
Luxembourg	2011	2001-2013	2011	2001-2013
Mexico	2012	2000-2012	2012	2000-2012
Netherlands	2011	2000-2012	2011	2000-2012
New Zealand	2012	2007-2012	2012	2007-2012
Norway	2011	2000-2012	2011	2000-2012
Poland	2009	2004-2009	2009	2004-2009
Portugal	2006	1999-2006	2006	1999-2006
Slovak Republic	2009	-	2009	-
Slovenia	2007	-	2007	-
Spain	2011	2001-2011	2011	2001-2011
Sweden	2011	2002-2011	2011	2002-2011
Switzerland	2012	2002-2012	2012	2002-2012
Turkey	2012	2008-2012	2012	2008-2012
United Kingdom	2011	2000-2011	2011	2000-2011
United States	2011	2000-2012	2011	2000-2012

Best third	Middle third	Worst third

Rank females: Dark grey = smoking rates > 18%; Grey = between 18% and 14%; Light grey = less than 14%. **Trend females**: Dark grey = average annual percentage decline > -0.75%; Grey = average annual percentage between -0.75% and -2.9%; Light grey = average annual percentage < -2.9%; **Rank males**: Dark grey = smoking rates > 29%; Grey = between 29% and 21%; Light grey = less than 21%. **Trend males**: Dark grey = average annual percentage decline > -2.2%; Grey = average annual percentage between -2.2% and -3.0%; Light grey = average annual percentage < -3.0%.

Source: OECD Health Statistics 2013, http://dx.doi.org/10.1787/health-data-en.

obese (Table 2.6). It should be noted that the Irish data for this calculation date back to 2007. No country has been able to cut the number of males who are overweight or obese over the ten-year period. That said, there are some tentative signs that some countries have been able to stabilise or reduce the rate of increase for the most recent observations. The percentage of females who are overweight or obese has fallen in the most recent years in Estonia, Japan and Luxembourg. For males, the most recent data reveal a slight decline in countries such as Finland, Japan, Luxembourg, New Zealand and the United States.

Worrying patterns of smoking and obesity rates in some countries

Combining the information about smoking with information about overweight and obesity rates reveals that some countries are performing poorly for both indicators.

Table 2.6. Overweight and obesity rates among males and females: Country rankings and trends

	Females		Males	
	Rank	Trend	Rank	Trend
Australia	2011	2007-2011	2011	2007-2011
Austria	2006	-	2006	-
Belgium	2008	2001-2008	2008	2001-2008
Canada	2011	2001-2012	2011	2001-2012
Chile	2009	2003-2009	2009	2003-2009
Czech Republic	2010	2000-2010	2010	2000-2010
Denmark	2010	2000-2010	2010	2000-2010
Estonia	2012	2000-2012	2012	2000-2012
Finland	2011	2000-2012	2011	2000-2012
France	2012	2000-2012	2012	2000-2012
Germany	2009	1999-2009	2009	1999-2009
Greece	2008	2006-2008	2008	2006-2008
Hungary	2009	2000-2009	2009	2000-2009
Iceland	2010	-	2010	-
Ireland	2007	2002-2007	2007	2002-2007
Israel	2010	2002-2013	2010	2002-2013
Italy	2011	2001-2012	2011	2001-2012
Japan	2011	2000-2012	2011	2000-2012
Korea	2011	2001-2012	2011	2001-2012
Luxembourg	2011	2000-2013	2011	2000-2013
Mexico	2012	2000-2012	2012	2000-2012
Netherlands	2011	2000-2012	2011	2000-2012
New Zealand	2012	2003-2012	2012	2003-2012
Norway	2008	2002-2008	2008	2002-2008
Poland	2009	2004-2009	2009	2004-2009
Portugal	2006	1999-2006	2006	1999-2006
Slovak Republic	2008	-	2008	-
Slovenia	2012	2007-2012	2012	2007-2012
Spain	2011	2001-2011	2011	2001-2011
Sweden	2011	2000-2011	2011	2000-2011
Switzerland	2012	2002-2012	2012	2002-2012
Turkey	2012	2008-2012	2012	2008-2012
United Kingdom	2011	2000-2012	2011	2000-2012
United States	2012	2000-2012	2012	2000-2012

Best third | Middle third | Worst third

Rank females: Dark grey= overweight and obesity rates > 48%; Grey = between 48% and 41%; Light grey = less than 41%. **Trend females**: Dark grey = average annual percentage > 0.9%; Grey = average annual percentage between 0.5% and 0.9%; Light grey = average annual percentage < 0.5%; **Rank males**: Dark grey = overweight and obesity rates > 61.5%; Grey = between 61.5% and 55%; Light grey = less than 55%. **Trend males**: Dark grey = average annual percentage > 1.3%; Grey = average annual percentage between 0.7% and 1.3%; Light grey = average annual percentage < 0.7%.

Source: OECD Health Statistics 2013, http://dx.doi.org/10.1787/health-data-en.

Figure 2.7 compares each country's data with the OECD average for 2011 (or latest year). The intercept of the horizontal and vertical axes marks the OECD average for both smoking and weight. Countries to the right of the vertical axis record higher than OECD average smoking rates and those to the left have lower than average rates. Countries above the horizontal line have a higher percentage of people being overweight or obese compared to the OECD average, whereas countries below the line have lower than average rates. The figure illustrates that some countries have higher than average smoking rates and a higher than average percentage of people being overweight or obese (north-east quadrant). Countries that find themselves in the south-west quadrant have better than average lifestyles.

There are five countries that are consistently placed in in the north-east (higher than average) quadrant for both females and males (Chile, the Czech Republic, Germany, Greece and Hungary) and there are five countries that are consistently in the south-west quadrant (Canada, Finland, the Netherlands, Norway and Sweden). The figure also reveals substantial gender gaps in lifestyle behaviours, particularly in smoking. Female smoking rates in countries like Mexico, Japan and Korea are more than 5 percentage points below the OECD average, but for men, smoking rates are well above the OECD average in these countries.

Figure 2.7. **Countries compared to the OECD average in smoking and overweight and obesity rates**

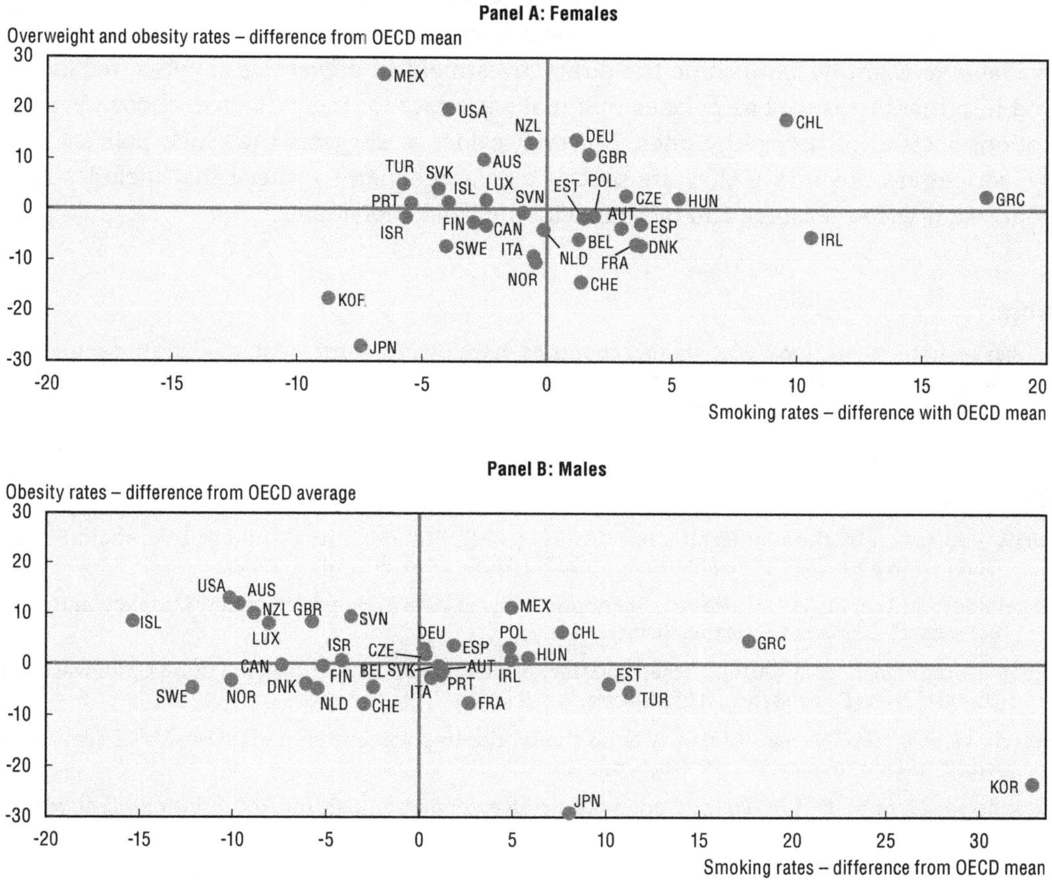

Source: *OECD Health Statistics 2013, http://dx.doi.org/10.1787/health-data-en.*

Summary

Unhealthy lifestyles are an important determinant of the burden of cardiovascular disease and diabetes across OECD countries. Smoking doubles the ten-year risk of a person experiencing a CVD event and obesity doubles the chances of diabetes and raises the likelihood of CVD by 30 to 40%. Unhealthy lifestyles also remain an important driver of cross-country variation in CVD and diabetes outcomes.

Countries have taken strong actions to reduce smoking rates, and these actions have born success, with smoking rates coming down in almost all countries over the last ten years. Nevertheless, there remains considerable variation in smoking patterns across OECD countries, and the potential is there to make even further gains in some countries. More comprehensive policies and stricter enforcement can deliver better outcomes.

The success achieved in reducing the percentage of people who smoke has not been replicated in obesity. The percentage of people who are either overweight or obese has continued to climb over the last ten years. OECD analysis indicates that a comprehensive strategy to reduce obesity can not only be effective but also highly cost-effective. However, strong policy action has been missing in many countries or has met substantial opposition from various stakeholders. That said, many countries have introduced (or have considered introducing) so-called "fat taxes". These fiscal policy instruments show some promise in terms of reducing the overall consumption of unhealthy foods, but their introduction has met widespread critique in some countries.

Governments must continue to play an active role in delivering policies that encourage individuals to make healthier choices. Governments have a range of policy instruments available to them which include the direct investment in preventive services, regulation and information, as well as policies that make it easier for individuals to choose healthy options instead of unhealthy ones. However, evidence suggests that such policies may deliver better outcomes if they are part of a comprehensive strategy that includes both population-wide measures and measures for high-risk individuals.

Note

1. Please note, that since 2010 many countries have made substantial modifications to their anti-tobacco policies but for the purposes of this analysis, the 2010 results are most appropriate as it covers the relevant observation period.

References

AIHW – Australia Institute of Health and Welfare (2014), "National Drug Strategy Household Survey Detailed Report: 2013", *Drug Statistics Series No. 28*, Cat. No. PHE 183, Canberra.

Ásgeirsdóttir, T.L. et al. (2013), "Was the Economic Crisis of 2008 Good for Icelanders? Impact on Health Behaviors", *Economics & Human Biology*.

Bibbins-Domingo, K. et al. (2010), "Projected Effect of Dietary Salt Reductions on Future Cardiovascular Disease", *New England Journal of Medicine*, Vol. 362, No. 7, pp. 590-599.

Brown, I.J. et al. (2009), "Salt Intakes Around the World: Implications for Public Health", *International Journal of Epidemiology*, Vol. 38, No. 3, pp. 791-813.

Cappuccio, F.P. et al. (2011), "Policy Options to Reduce Population Salt Intake", *British Medical Journal*, Vol. 343, London, p. 4995.

D'Agostino, R.B. et al. (2008), "General Cardiovascular Risk Profile for Use in Primary Care: The Framingham Heart Study", *Circulation*, Vol. 117, No. 6, pp. 743-753.

Freeman, B., S. Chapman and M. Rimmer (2008), "The Case for the Plain Packaging of Tobacco Products", *Addiction*, Vol. 103, No. 4, pp. 580-590.

He, F.J., J. Li and G.A. MacGregor (2013), "Effect of Longer Term Modest Salt Reduction on Blood Pressure: Cochrane Systematic Review and Meta-analysis of Randomised Trials", *British Medical Journal*, Vol. 346, London.

Henkel, D. (2011), "Unemployment and Substance Use: A Review of the Literature (1990-2010)", *Current Drug Abuse Reviews*, Vol. 4, No. 1, p. 4.

IHME – Institute for Health Metrics and Evaluation (2013), "The Global Burden of Disease: Generating Evidence, Guiding Policy", Institute for Health Metrics and Evaluation, Seattle.

Karppanen, H. and E. Mervaala (2006), "Sodium Intake and Hypertension", *Progress in Cardiovascular Diseases*, Vol. 49, No. 2, pp. 59-75.

Lim, S.S. et al. (2013), "A Comparative Risk Assessment of Burden of Disease and Injury Attributable to 67 Risk Factors and Risk Factor Clusters in 21 Regions, 1990-2010: A Systematic Analysis for the Global Burden of Disease Study 2010", *The Lancet*, Vol. 380, No. 9859, pp. 2224-2260.

Lindström, J. and J. Tuomilehto (2003), "The Diabetes Risk Score: A Practical Tool to Predict Type 2 Diabetes Risk", *Diabetes Care*, Vol. 26, No. 3, pp. 725-731.

Lundberg, M. and G. Shapirade (2014), "Determinants of Risky Behavior", *Risking Your Health: Causes, Consequences, and Interventions to Prevent Risky Behaviors*, World Bank, Washington, DC.

McClure, C.B. et al. (2012), "Economic Crisis and Smoking Behaviour: Prospective Cohort Study in Iceland", *British Medical Journal*, open, Vol. 2, No. 5.

Millett, C. et al. (2012), "Impacts of a National Strategy to Reduce Population Salt Intake in England: Serial Cross-sectional Study", *PloS one*, Vol. 7, No. 1, Cambridge, e29836.

NICE – National Institute for Health and Clinical Excellence (2010), "Prevention of Cardiovascular Disease at Population Level", *NICE Public Health Guidance*, Vol. 25, England.

OECD (2014a), "Obesity Update", OECD Publishing, Paris, *www.oecd.org/els/health-systems/Obesity-Update-2014.pdf*.

OECD (2012), "Obesity Update", OECD Publishing, Paris, *www.oecd.org/health/49716427.pdf*.

Pell, J.P. et al. (2008), "Smoke-free Legislation and Hospitalizations for Acute Coronary Syndrome", *New England Journal of Medicine*, Vol. 359, No. 5, pp. 482-491.

Rosenberg, M. et al. (2012), "Public Support for Tobacco Control Policy Extensions in Western Australia: A Cross-sectional Study", *British Medical Journal*, open, Vol. 2, No. 2.

Ruhm, C.J. (2005), "Healthy Living in Hard Times", *Journal of Health Economics*, Vol. 24, No. 2, pp. 341-363.

Sassi, F. (2010), *Obesity and the Economics of Prevention: Fit Not Fat*, OECD Publishing, Paris, *http://dx.doi.org/10.1787/9789264084865-en*.

Sassi, F., A. Belloni and C. Capobianco (2013), "The role of fiscal policies in health promotion", OECD Health Working Papers No. 66, OECD Publishing, Paris.

Takahashi, Y. et al. (2006), "Blood Pressure Change in a Free-living Population Based Dietary Modification Study in Japan", *Journal of Hypertension*, Vol. 24, pp. 451-458.

UK DOH – UK Department of Health (2014), *https://responsibilitydeal.dh.gov.uk/*.

WHO – World Health Organization (2012), *Guideline: Sodium Intake for Adults and Children*, World Health Organization, Geneva.

WHO (2011), "Global Atlas on Cardiovascular Disease Prevention and Control", S. Mendis, P. Puska and B. Norrving (eds.), World Health Organization, Geneva.

WHO (2010), "Global Health Observatory of the WHO", *www.who.int/gho/en/*.

Young, J.M. et al. (2014), "Association Between Tobacco Plain Packaging and Quitline Calls: A Population-based, Interrupted Time-series Analysis", *Medical Journal of Australia*, Vol. 200, No. 1, pp. 29-32.

ANNEX 2.A1

Tobacco control policies

Table 2.A1.1. **Tobacco policy categories by country: Higher scores indicate stricter policy**

	Protect	Help quit	Warn	Tax	Media campaigns	NTCP	Monitor
Australia	5	5	5	4	4	4	4
Austria	2	4	3	4	2	2	4
Belgium	1	5	4	5	2	3	4
Canada	5	5	4	4	2	4	4
Chile	3	3	5	5	2	3	2
Czech Republic	3	4	3	5	4	2	4
Denmark	2	4	3	4	5	3	4
Estonia	2	3	3	5	1	3	4
Finland	2	4	3	5	4	3	4
France	1	5	4	5	3	3	4
Germany	2	4	3	4	4	3	4
Greece	5	3	3	5	5	2	2
Hungary	2	4	3	5	3	3	2
Iceland	3	3	3	4	2	3	4
Ireland	5	5	3	5	5	4	4
Israel	2	5	3	5	4	1	4
Italy	1	4	3	5	4	2	4
Japan	2	4	3	4	2	4	4
Korea	2	5	3	4	1	3	4
Latvia	3	4	4	5	2	4	4
Luxembourg	3	4	3	4	1	1	4
Mexico	1	4	5	4	2	4	2
Netherlands	3	4	3	4	5	3	4
New Zealand	5	5	5	4	3	4	4
Norway	3	4	4	4	2	4	4
Poland	2	4	3	5	4	2	4
Portugal	3	4	3	5	2	3	4
Singapore	3	5	5	4	5	4	2
Slovak Republic	4	4	3	5	2	3	2
Slovenia	3	4	3	5	2	3	4
Spain	5	4	4	5	2	3	4
Sweden	2	4	3	4	5	3	4
Switzerland	2	4	3	4	4	4	4
Turkey	5	5	4	5	5	4	4
United Kingdom	5	5	4	5	5	3	4
United States	2	5	5	3	2	3	4

Note: See Box 2.1 for definitions.

Source: Global Health Observatory of the World Health Organization, 2010.

Cardiovascular Disease and Diabetes
Policies for Better Health and Quality of Care

Chapter 3

Improved control of cardiovascular disease risk factors and diabetes: The central role of primary care

The importance of primary care is increasing in managing cardiovascular disease (CVD) and diabetes. Chapter 3 focuses on the role of the primary care system and its ability to diagnose and control common CVD-related risk factors. It examines the strengths and weaknesses of primary care across countries by looking at the resources available, its accessibility, and quality. It includes data on prescribing patterns for diabetic patients and the rates of CVD and diabetes-related hospital admissions that are largely avoidable through proper primary care management. The chapter assesses country performance on the basis of its relative incidence of high blood pressure and cholesterol levels, avoidable hospital admissions, and quality prescribing and diabetes-related complications. It also examines primary care quality initiatives taking place across countries such as integrated and co-ordinated care, strengthening information systems for performance monitoring and pay-for-performance.

The statistical data for Israel are supplied by and under the responsibility of the relevant Israeli authorities. The use of such data by the OECD is without prejudice to the status of the Golan Heights, East Jerusalem and Israeli settlements in the West Bank under the terms of international law.

The ever increasing importance of primary care in managing cardiovascular disease and diabetes

The early diagnosis and control of cardiovascular risk factors and diabetes is of vital importance to improving health outcomes. Early diagnosis is an essential first step towards patients taking effective control, and limits the potential long-term damage that these risk factors can cause to the body. In many OECD countries, primary care is central to the diagnosis and management of risk factors. Not only are primary care providers the first point-of-contact with the health system for many patients, they also deliver a range of health care services. Primary care is uniquely positioned to identify individuals at risk of CVD, assess the need for interventions, as well as initiate, co-ordinate, and provide long-term follow-up for managing CVD risk factors as well as controlling diabetes (Perk et al., 2013).

The services delivered in the primary care setting are typically offered to individuals who have been assessed as high risk. Individually tailored services provide an important part of the overall package of prevention, diagnosis and management of both CVD and diabetes. The services provided in the primary care sector complement the population-wide strategies that were the focus of Chapter 2.

There is widespread evidence that the interventions delivered at the primary care level can be highly effective and cost-effective in the management of risk factors. This is true for both pharmacological and counselling interventions. Medications such as statins and antihypertensive that are prescribed in the primary care setting improve not only overall health outcomes but also produce cost-savings through fewer downstream hospitalisations (Krause et al., 2011; Taylor, 2014). Brief interventions to encourage smokers to quit in the primary care setting have also been found to be highly effective and cost-effective, and studies have also shown that behaviourally-based primary care interventions can moderately reduce weight and delay the onset of diabetes (NICE, 2008; Le Blanc, et al., 2011). The delivery of evidenced-based interventions in the primary care sector can therefore offer real opportunities for delivering value-for-money health care.

Primary care also remains the cornerstone for equitable delivery of health care. Many OECD countries have achieved good access to primary care even among those in lower socio-economic groups (Devaux and de Looper, 2012). Most individuals visit their general practitioner (GP) at least once a year and many have multiple visits. These regular contacts allow primary care practitioners to assess patient risk, monitor progress and deliver care for most individuals including hard-to-reach individuals, who often have higher health care needs and are at greater risk of developing CVD or diabetes (Peek et al., 2007). A strong primary care system has the capacity to generate greater equity of access and also deliver care to those who possibly stand to benefit most.

It is widely recognised that primary health care systems are likely to play an increasingly important role in health care delivery. The demographic change that is occurring in OECD countries is also driving changes in health care needs. As discussed in Chapter 1, alongside the ageing population there is a corresponding rise in the prevalence of long term conditions with many patients suffering complex multi-morbidities. Elderly patients are more likely to be suffering from multiple morbidities, may be more fragile and require multiple health and social services to deliver best-practice care. Such changing health needs have required reconfiguration of health care delivery models, including more effective co-ordination of care and greater continuity of care (OECD, 2011). In addition, technological changes have placed greater onus on primary care providers to deliver care in the community setting. As more patients survive CVD events such as heart attacks, primary care providers are charged with ensuring that patients receive proper follow-up care in the community setting. Delivering the health care needs for an increasingly older and sicker population will place greater pressure on existing primary health care resources. A key challenge for health care systems across OECD countries is to realign health delivery systems with the evolving needs of the ageing population.

A recent Scottish study, using electronic clinical record systems, examined the prevalence of multiple morbidities for patients presenting to a general practice (Guthrie et al., 2011). The study found that from age 65, over half the population have two or more chronic conditions. From age 75 the majority of people with any chronic condition have three or more conditions. Table 3.1 presents information on the type of multiple morbidities that patients suffered. Not surprisingly, there is a high degree of multiple comorbidities among patients with diabetes and CHD. For example, 54% of patients with diabetes also had hypertension and 23% had CHD. However, many patients who suffered from CVD or diabetes had also been diagnosed with chronic obstructive pulmonary disease (COPD) and mental illnesses. More than one in five patients with dementia also had coronary heart disease and 18% had a stroke or transient ischaemic attack (TIA). People with multiple morbidities are at greater risk of care co-ordination problems, ineffective or unsafe combinations of prescriptions and receiving unsafe care (Guthrie et al., 2011).

Multiple morbidities raise some important issues for CVD and diabetes care. These include the need to broaden clinical evidence to make it more relevant for patients with multiple morbidities, as well as make clinical guidelines recommendations more suitable for people with complex needs. There are also health care implications to improve continuity through better information flows between providers. Such complex patients require primary care health systems to be centre-stage in the effort to provide not only the care that patients need, but also deliver cost-effective health care.

This chapter focuses on the central role of primary care in managing risk factors for CVD and diabetes. It starts by examining the importance of risk factors such as high blood pressure and high cholesterol and diabetes that are typically managed in the primary care setting. This chapter looks at the existing resources available for primary care, and the degree of access that patients have to primary care providers. It will also report on a number of primary care quality indicators by examining prescribing rates and avoidable hospitalisations. Finally, this chapter will describe some of the innovative steps countries have taken to improve primary care quality and draw out specific lessons for countries to learn from each other.

Table 3.1. **Patients with CVD and diabetes often have multiple conditions**

Patients who suffer from this condition... / ... also suffer from these conditions	CHD	Hypertension	Heart failure	Stroke/TIA	Diabetes	COPD	Cancer	Painful condition	Depression	Schizophernia or bipolar	Dementia	Any other condition
	%	%	%	%	%	%	%	%	%	%	%	%
CHD		52	14	13	22	13	8	24	17	1	3	71
Hypertension	18		5	10	18	8	7	19	14	1	2	61
Heart failure	59	57		16	23	18	9	23	17	1	4	81
Stroke/TIA	29	61	8		19	12	8	22	21	1	5	63
Diabetes	23	54	6	9		8	6	21	18	2	2	63
COPD	19	33	6	8	11		7	23	18	1	2	70
Cancer	14	34	4	7	10	8		19	14	1	2	60
Painful condition	16	36	3	6	13	10	7		31	2	3	70
Depression	10	23	2	5	9	7	4	27		4	2	64
Schizophernia or bipolar	6	16	2	4	9	6	3	15	45		3	75
Dementia	21	41	6	18	13	9	8	19	32	3		83
Any other condition	11	27	2	5	9	7	5	17	17	1	1	

Note: COPD = Chronic Obstructive Pulmonary Disease; TIA = TIA, or Transient Ischemic Attack, or "mini-stroke".

Source: Guthrie, B. et al. (2011), "Multicomorbidity: The Impact on Health Systems and their Development", Chapter 6 in *Health Reform: Meeting the Challenge of Ageing and Multiple Morbidities*, OECD Publishing, Paris, *http://dx.doi.org/10.1787/9789264122314-en*.

Opportunities to reduce cardiovascular risk in primary care

Risk factors such as high blood pressure, high blood cholesterol and diabetes greatly increase the likelihood of suffering a CVD event. The well-known Framingham Study estimated the role of risk factors in predicting the likelihood of suffering a CVD event such as coronary death, heart attack, coronary insufficiency and angina as well as stroke and heart failure (D'Agostino et al., 2008). Table 3.2 reports the chances of a person experiencing a CVD event over a ten year period, based on estimates from the Framingham study. The risks have been calculated on the basis of a 60-year-old non-smoker, not being treated for high blood pressure.[1] For example, a 60-year-old female diabetic with a mean total cholesterol[2] of 215 mg/dl and mean untreated systolic blood pressure (SBP) of 126 mm Hg has a 5% chance of suffering CVD event in the next ten years. Independent of other risk factors, diabetics have a substantially higher risk of suffering a CVD event. For males, for example, the presence of diabetes increases the ten-year risk from 1.8% to 8.2% for those with mean total cholesterol and SBP levels. A one-standard-deviation increase in total cholesterol (44 mg/dl) increase CVD likelihood by between 10% and 70%, depending on the presence of other risk factors. According to the Framingham risk scores, elevated SBP substantially raises CVD risk. A one-standard-deviation increase in SBP (20 mm Hg), more than doubles the likelihood of CVD in the presence of other raised risk factors such as diabetes and cholesterol.

The ten-year risk of a CVD event can be substantially reduced if cholesterol levels and blood pressure can be lowered and effectively controlled. Similarly, there is widespread evidence that good glycaemic control has been shown to prevent CVD events in diabetic individuals if instituted soon after the diagnosis of diabetes (Holman et al., 2008). Indeed, proper management of diabetes, particularly blood glucose levels, can reduce the incidence of complications including myocardial infarctions by 17% (Ray et al., 2009).

Primary care guideline recommendations for optimal treatment take into account a patient's overall level of CVD risk estimated on the basis of calculators such as the one shown in Table 3.2 as well as the specific values for individual risk factors (e.g. Woods et al., 2005).

For example, the New Zealand primary care guidelines recommend the commencement of drug therapy if total cholesterol levels are greater than eight mmol/l or if CVD risk is greater than 20% and cholesterol levels are greater than 4 mmol/l. For blood pressure, patients with readings greater than 170/100 mm Hg should have drug treatment as well as specific lifestyle advice. For those with systolic blood pressure greater than 140 mm Hg treatment recommendations depend on the patient's overall level of CVD risk (NZ Guideline Group, 2012).

Table 3.2. **Predicting the ten-year likelihood of a CVD event: Diabetes, cholesterol and blood pressure**

	Females		Males	
	Non-diabetic %	Diabetic %	Non-diabetic %	Diabetic %
Total cholesterol = 215 mg/dl				
SBP = 126 mm Hg	1.6	5.0	1.8	8.2
SBP = 146 mm Hg	10.5	13.6	15.6	21.1
Total cholesterol = 259 mg/dl				
SBP = 126 mm Hg	2.8	6.1	4.2	10.4
SBP = 146 mm Hg	11.5	14.6	17.7	23.0

Note: SBP = systolic blood pressure. Predicted risk scores have been calculated on the basis of a 60 year old person who is a non-smoker, was not being treated for high blood pressure and has HDL-C of 57.6 mg/dl.

Source: Based on estimates from D'Agostino, R.B. et al. (2008), "General Cardiovascular Risk Profile for Use in Primary Care: The Framingham Heart Study", *Circulation*, Vol. 117, No. 6, pp. 743-753.

It should be noted that some of the main clinical guidelines have undergone some important recent changes (Kaposi et al., 2014). The 2012 European Society of Cardiology (ESC) set treatment goals for systolic blood pressure to be lowered to 140 mmHg (and diastolic blood pressure to less than 90 mmHg). For cholesterol, recommended treatment goals for total plasma cholesterol should be less than 5 mmol/L and LDL cholesterol should be less than 3 mmol/L, although in subjects with higher CVD risk, the treatment goals should be lower (Perk et al., 2012). In the United States, the 8th Joint National Committee increased the systolic/diastolic BP goal to 150/90 mmHg for those older than 60 years of age (James et al., 2014). For cholesterol, the new American College of Cardiology/American Heart Association (ACC/AHA) guidelines do not set treatment targets but have expanded the population for whom treatment is recommended. Indeed, Kavousi et al. (2014) estimate that under the new ACC/AHA guidelines around 96% of men and 66% of women aged 55 and over would be recommended to take cholesterol lowering medications. Under ESC guidelines, 66% of men and 39% of women would be recommended to initiate cholesterol lowering medication.

The potential expansion in the number of patients recommended to be on medication can have important consequences for health care resources, particularly pharmaceutical budgets. The revised guidelines in the United States move away from the notion that they should set out strict treatment criteria and options for some risk factors and patient groups. Instead, there is greater recognition of the persistent uncertainties over some aspects of the evidence-base as well as the need for clinical judgements that place due emphasis on patient characteristics and preferences. This renewed focus may have important policy implications. With greater clinical flexibility and accounting for patient heterogeneity, it may become more difficult to measure primary care performance or implement quality-based payment mechanisms that are based on simple measures (Krumholz, 2014). Performance measurement of primary care, particularly in relation to

CVD risk factors, may need to become more nuanced to support the implementation of such guidelines.

Figure 3.1 shows the percentage of the population with high cholesterol and high blood pressure in OECD countries. These data come from the World Health Organization's (WHO) Global Health Observatory and are generally drawn from household surveys and have been age-standardised. The high cholesterol data indicates the percentage of the population aged 25 and over with total cholesterol level greater or equal to 6.2 mmol/l. The indicator for high blood pressure shows the percentage of the population aged 25 years and over with systolic blood pressure ≥ 140 mm Hg or diastolic blood pressure ≥ 90. Both indicators are derived through clinical measurements observed in 2008.

Figure 3.1. **High cholesterol and high blood pressure prevalence in OECD countries, 2008**

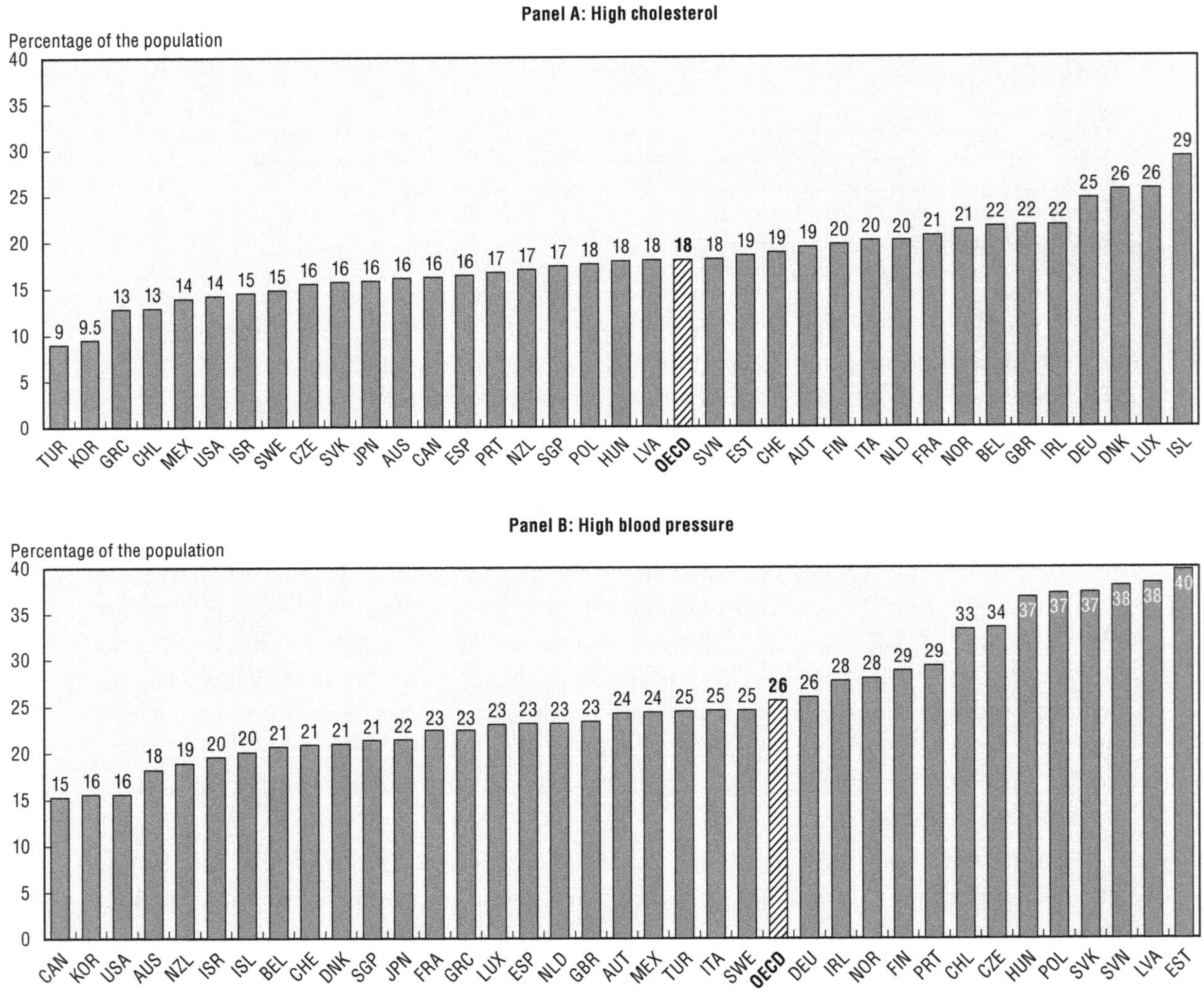

Source: Global Health Observatory of the World Health Organization, 2008.

Across OECD countries around 18% of adults have high cholesterol levels. In Iceland, Luxembourg and Denmark this percentage is over 25% whereas Turkey and Korea have a prevalence rate of less than 10%. In terms of high blood pressure, 26% of adults across OECD countries have high blood pressure, although there is considerable variation between countries. The percentage of adults with high blood pressure is 16% or less in the United States, Korea and Canada but exceeds 35% in many Central and Eastern European Countries including Estonia, Latvia, Slovenia, the Slovak Republic, Poland and Hungary. Note that Panel B in Figure 3.1 does not include those who are successfully using their hypertension medication to control their blood pressure.

There are many potential underlying reasons for the degree of variation between countries. While the figures have been age- and sex-standardised to account for different demographic profiles, there may be other important determinants that are outside of the control of the health care system. For example, genetic and ethnic factors may make some communities more susceptible to high blood pressure to others (ICBPGWAS, 2011; Agyemang et al., 2005; Fryar et al., 2005). Nevertheless, the widespread variation in prevalence rates for both high cholesterol and blood pressure may also provide some indication that countries can reduce these two CVD risk factors which, in turn, has the potential to reduce the CVD mortality and morbidity burden.

Despite the recent increase in the use of medications over recent decades, many patients remain well below their target goals. The EUROSPIRE III survey of over 4 000 patients in 12 European countries (including eight OECD countries) revealed that only 26% and 31% of patients on medications achieved their blood pressure or cholesterol goals, respectively (Kotseva et al., 2010).

With the slow onset of symptoms, Type 2 diabetes may remain undetected for many years, during which time unmanaged elevated blood glucose can lead to serious and irreversible development of cardiovascular complications as well as microvascular complications such as retinopathy (damage to the retina). In many instances, patients are diagnosed once symptoms and complications have already occurred, leading to worse health outcomes (Fowler, 2011). It has long been suspected that the rate of undiagnosed diabetes is high but there has been paucity of evidence. More population-based studies are now undertaking clinical measurements to diagnose diabetes and ask respondents whether they have known-diabetes. Such studies use either oral glucose tolerance test (OGTT) or fasting blood glucose (FBG) test, with the former considered the gold standard for population-wide studies (Beagley et al., 2014).

Figure 3.2 summarises the results from the systematic review by Beagley et al. (2014) to identify the prevalence of undiagnosed diabetes. The review found studies in 13 OECD countries as well as Singapore. The data refer to the percentage of clinically diagnosed diabetics, who were unaware that they had the condition. For example, in Poland, 28% of those who were diagnosed during the study did not know that they had diabetes. The figure demonstrates that the results may be highly dependent on the type of test that is used to diagnose diabetes, with the OGTT detecting a far higher percentage of people with undiagnosed diabetes. On average, studies showed an average of 24% and 45% undiagnosed rates employing the FGB and OGTT, respectively. Among studies using the FGB test, Korea had the highest percentage of undiagnosed diabetes. It should be noted that the percentage of undiagnosed diabetes in Korea fell considerably between 1998 and 2005 (Choi et al., 2009). The Finnish study showed the highest percentage of undiagnosed diabetes among OGTT studies in OECD countries, with over 60% of the sampled population with diabetes unaware of their condition. Spain has the lowest rate of undiagnosed diabetes among the studies using OGTT.

The results of the 14 studies shown in Figure 3.2 confirm that the number of undiagnosed diabetes is very high suggesting that further efforts to screen for type-2 diabetes may be warranted. However, population-wide screening programmes have not been universally recommended because the overall benefits remain unclear (IDF, 2012). Screening programmes in community settings have uniformly demonstrated low yield and poor follow-up. An analysis of over 50 diabetes-related interventions showed that population-wide screening interventions were among the least cost-effective programmes considered (Li et al., 2010). Instead, the CDC as well as numerous other organisations advocates for periodic screening of high-risk individuals as part of ongoing medical care.

Primary care is central to the early detection of diabetes. Indeed, several countries have put in place measures to improve primary care screening on both the supply and demand side. In Singapore, for example, diabetes screening is included in a raft of primary care performance measures and under their Community Health Assist Scheme patients can receive additional subsidies for outpatient treatments for chronic conditions such as diabetes. In Japan, a population-wide screening programme was introduced in 2008 that targets metabolic syndrome (collective term that includes diabetes, hypertension and hyperlipidemia). Health screening is offered to 52.8 million Japanese residents aged 40-74. Those who are found to be at risk of metabolic syndrome are offered health guidance to help modify unhealthy lifestyles. The evaluation of the first five years identified the screening rate of 46.3% and 1.34% reduction of metabolic syndrome compared with the starting year of 2008 after age-sex adjustment (Ministry of Health, Labour and Welfare, 2012).

While a number of countries encourage general health checks on healthy individuals, a recent Cochrane Review concluded that these do not necessarily improve overall health outcomes (Krogsbøll et al., 2012). While this finding is consistent with previous reviews, local circumstances may be different to the clinical trial settings upon which these conclusions are based (Boulware et al., 2007). This is why the Cochrane Library suggests that practitioners continue investigating patients with symptoms as well as focus on tests that are targeted to the patient's age, sex, and specific risk factors (Thompson et al., 2012).

Figure 3.2. **Undiagnosed diabetes – percentage of diabetics unaware of their condition**

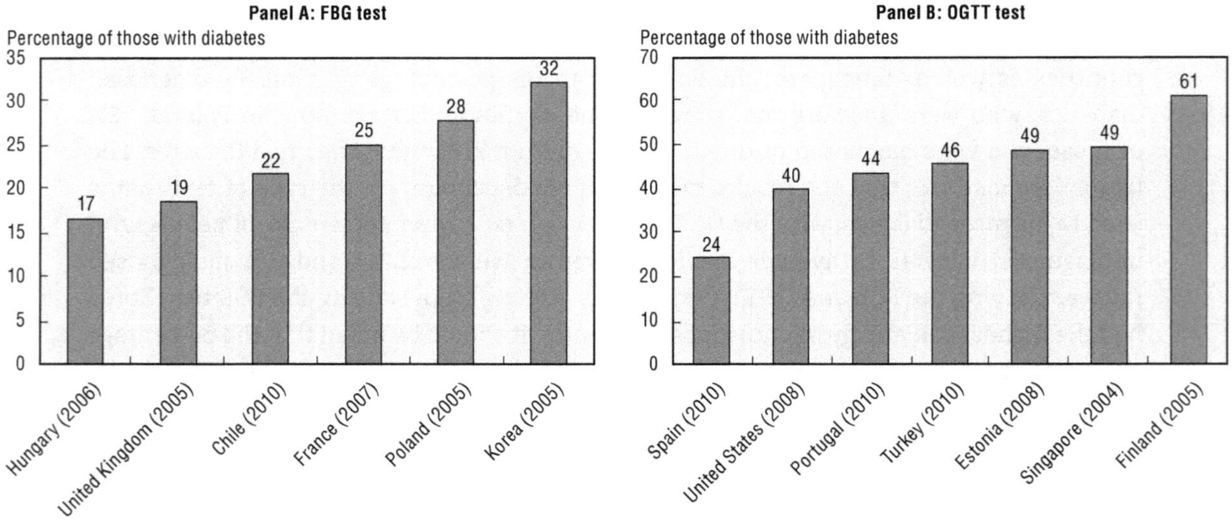

Source: Adapted from Beagley, J. et al. (2014), "Global Estimates of Undiagnosed Diabetes in Adults", *Diabetes Research and Clinical Practice*, Vol. 103, No. 2, pp. 150-160.

In addition to the issue of undiagnosed diabetes, poor control among those whose diabetes status is known remains a fact of life. The EUROSPIRE III survey revealed that patients with self-reported diabetes, 40% achieved their blood glucose level goal (Hab1c < 6.1%) and only 13% reach their blood pressure target (Kotseva et al., 2010). These figures reveal that the majority of patients do not attain their clinical goals as recommended in guidelines (Perk, 2012; James, 2014).

Towards a better understanding of primary care quality in OECD countries

Ensuring that patients have access to high quality primary care has become an important policy priority. Nevertheless, preventing and managing chronic conditions remains suboptimal. Many health systems continue to face the challenge of helping high-risk patients achieve healthier lifestyles in the primary care setting and to effectively manage CVD risk factors and diabetes (Ghandehary et al. 2008; Kotseva et al., 2010; Hajjar and Kotchen. 2003). For example, a cross-country study of over 58 000 people residing in ten European countries revealed that after 15 months of follow-up 60% of patients did not attain their cholesterol lowering goal (van Ganse et al., 2005). Importantly, only 16% of patients had their drug regimens adjusted, suggesting that for the majority of patients drug regimens were not adjusted even though they were not attaining their target.

Although governments and professional organisations have invested substantial resources in the development and dissemination of clinical practice guidelines, there remains a substantial gap between recommended care and actual care. An important underlying reason for this quality gap is that much of the structure of today's health care systems was developed in an era where the main concern was on the treatment of acute illnesses rather than the prevention and management of chronic conditions (OECD, 2011). In the acute care era, the health system's focus was on providing short and intense treatments that were most often provided in a hospital setting. In the chronic disease era, care has become more complex and requires frequent multidisciplinary interventions over long periods of time and across different health care settings. Proper care of chronic conditions requires continuous monitoring, treatment adjustments and a stronger emphasis on prevention.

Many countries have implemented reforms to improve the alignment between health services delivery and health needs. These reforms have aimed to improve the management of chronic diseases by delivering the right care at the right time in the most effective and efficient setting. This has meant a renewed focus on the quality of primary care including its role in preventing and managing risk factors. Box 3.1 provides a summary of key primary care strengths that have recently been identified and tested as part of the Primary Health Care Activity Monitor project. As part of the focus on strengthening primary health care there have been concerted efforts to improve the measurement of primary care quality at both the national and international levels. This section reports the latest available international data as well as examines innovative national efforts to improve the measurement of primary care quality relating to diabetes and CVD care. Where possible, new insights into primary care quality are provided through the adjustment of some of indicators, collected as part of the OECD's Health Care Quality Indicators (HCQI) project.

Box 3.1. **Defining strong primary care systems**

The Primary Health Care Activity Monitor for Europe project has identified a core set of five primary care characteristics (and associated indicators) to measure the strength of primary care:

- *Structure*: Characterised by the existence of primary care policies and regulations (e.g. population coverage for primary care services, resourcing and funding, policies to reduce mal-distribution of primary care providers and facilities; workforce development and training for primary care.
- *Accessibility*: Characterised by the ease of access to primary care services (e.g. national and geographic supply of primary care services; the way access is organised including appointment systems and access to after- hours care as well as the affordability and acceptability of services as perceived by patients).
- *Continuity*: Characterised by the set of conditions put in place to develop enduring doctor-patient relationships (e.g. patient registration systems, electronic health records, indicators of the doctor-patient relationship).
- *Co-ordination*: Reflects the ability of primary care providers to co-ordinate patients' use of other parts of the health care system (e.g. the existence of a gatekeeping system, the skill-mix of primary care providers, collaboration with other providers, and the integration of public health functions).
- *Comprehensiveness*: Characterised by the breadth of services available in primary care (e.g. procedures and certain preventive services).

Source : Kringos, D.S. et al. (2013), "Europe's Strong Primary Care Systems Are Linked to Better Population Health but Also to Higher Health Spending", Health Affairs, Vol. 32, No. 4, pp. 686-694.

Prescribing rates reveal consistent patterns of pharmaceuticals use to control CVD risk factors

In dealing with CVD risk factors, primary care physicians have a number of options available to them on how best to treat these conditions. The decision to start antihypertensive or cholesterol lowering treatments will depend on a patient's clinical measures and total cardiovascular risk. For those with mild to moderate risk, a primary care physician can recommend non-pharmacological strategies such as lifestyle changes to reduce smoking, salt, and excessive alcohol consumption, as well as improve nutrition, reduce weight and increase physical activity. However, for those at higher risk, or for those where lifestyle changes have not succeeded, pharmacological treatments may be recommended.

Figure 3.3 present data on the number of defined daily doses (DDD) of antihypertensive and cholesterol lowering medication consumed. The figures take into account the prevalence of elevated blood pressure and cholesterol within each country – based on 2008 data reported by WHO as shown in Figure 3.1. DDDs are the assumed average maintenance dose per day for a drug used for its main indication in adults. The volume of hypertension drugs consumption is the sum of five drug categories which can all be prescribed against hypertension. These are antihypertensive, diuretic, beta-blockers, calcium channel blockers and agents acting on the renin-angiotensin system. The data presented in Figure 3.3 generally refer to outpatient consumption only although it also includes hospital consumption for the Czech Republic, Estonia, Italy and Sweden.

On average, patients with elevated blood pressure are prescribed 0.8 DDD of antihypertensive medications. This ranges from 0.5 per patient in Korea to the 1.2 in Germany (Panel A). While these data cannot inform debate about what is the correct number of DDDs, they do highlight the extent to which countries rely on pharmaceutical interventions to control CVD risk factors, the level of access, as well as the prescribing patterns of doctors. For cholesterol, the reliance on medication is remarkably similar in a large number of countries. In 18 out of 23 countries, the number of DDD is between 0.3 and 0.5 per person with high cholesterol. In Chile and Estonia there are lower levels of consumption (0.1 DDD), whereas in Australia and Hungary there is a greater reliance on medication. In Chile, public coverage for the main cholesterol lowering medication (statin) commenced in 2000 which is somewhat later than many other OECD countries. However, the consumption of statins may increase in many OECD countries if the revised ACC/AHA[3] recommendations become more widely implemented.

There is a weak association between the drug consumption patterns for both CVD risk factors. In general, countries with high consumption in one drug tend to be high users of the other. Nevertheless, there is considerable variation within some countries. Germany, for example, is a relatively high prescriber of hypertension drugs but a low consumer of cholesterol lowering drugs.

Figure 3.3. **Pharmaceutical consumption per patient with elevated CVD risk factor, defined daily doses 2008**

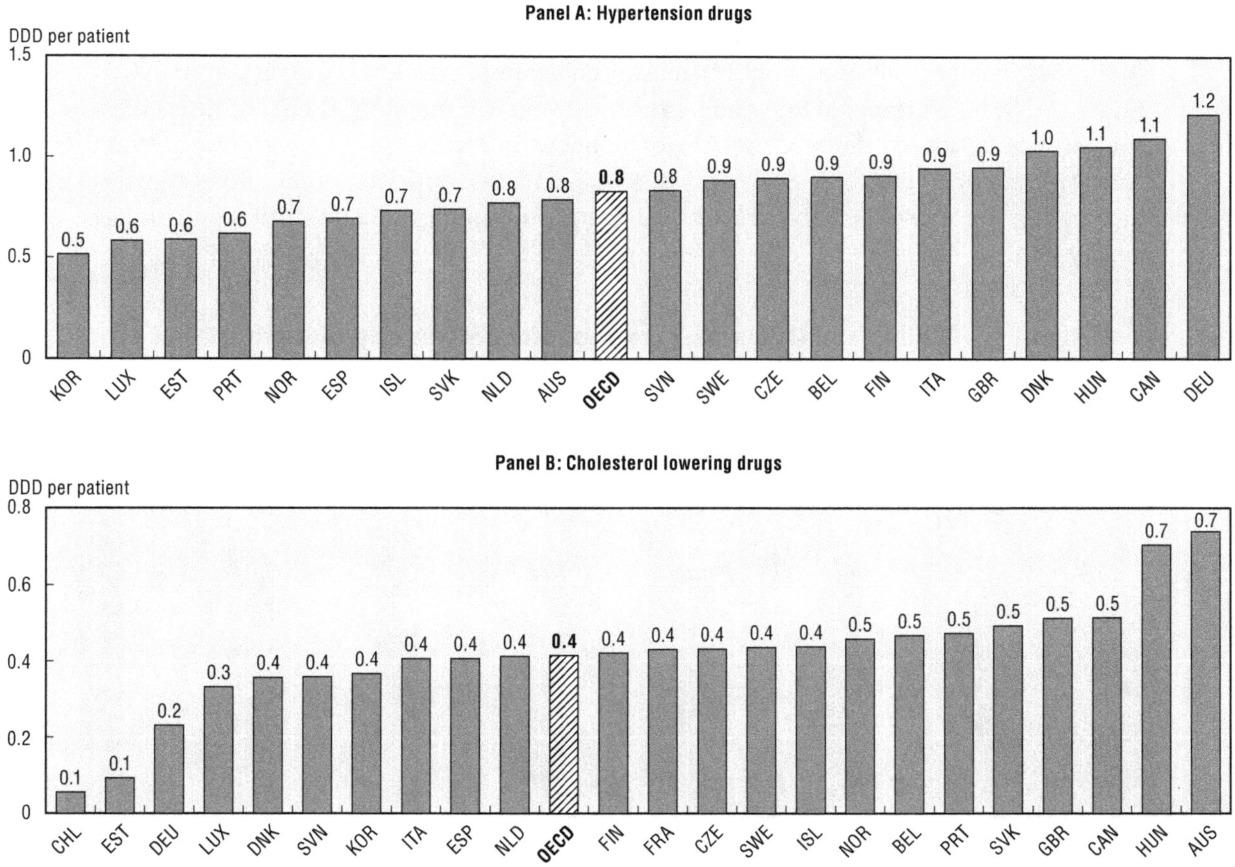

Note: The DDD data for Canada relate to Manitoba and Saskatchewan. The data for Spain refer to outpatient consumption for prescribed drugs covered by the National Health System.

Source: *OECD Health Statistics 2013* and Global Health Observatory of the World Health Organization, 2008.

The OECD's HCQI project has recently undertaking a pilot study to test the feasibility of gathering international comparable data on prescribing. These prescribing indicators are intended to expand the set of currently available quality measures for primary care. Two of these indicators involve measurement of prescribing patterns for patients with diabetes. The first indicator examines the proportion of diabetic patients who are prescribed cholesterol lowering drugs. The second indicator looks at the number of diabetic patients who are prescribed first choice antihypertensive agents,[4] as a proportion of diabetic patients who are prescribed any type of antihypertensive agent.

Patients with diabetes are at greater risk of suffering CVD morbidity and mortality. The management of CVD risk factors is particularly pertinent in this population group in order to reduce the excess risk that diabetes patients face (Sidorenkov et al., 2013). When it comes to managing CVD risk factors, clinical guidelines typically recommend earlier instigation of pharmacological treatment and lower treatment goals for diabetic patients (Perk et al., 2012; Wood et al., 2005).

Figure 3.4 presents the results from the pilot-study that included eight countries/regions that were able to provide data for these indicators. The percentage of diabetic patients receiving cholesterol lowering medication ranges between 46% (Germany) and 77% (Netherlands), with the other six countries/regions prescribing cholesterol lowering medication to between 60% and 70% of diabetic patients. The low percentage in Germany is in line with low level of consumption shown in Figure 3.3 (Panel B), as well as with previous results found in the literature (Walley et al., 2005). It should be noted that a proportion of diabetes patients may need statin treatments, although guidelines suggest that most diabetes patients would benefit if cholesterol was lowered (Perk et al., 2012; ACC/AHA, 2014). In terms of first choice antihypertensive treatment there is considerable consistency between the countries/regions shown in Figure 3.4. In seven out of eight countries/regions, between 81% and 86% of diabetes patients on antihypertensive medication are prescribed the first choice agents, although in Belgium this percentage is only 73%.

Figure 3.4. **The use of CVD risk-factor medication among diabetics, 2012**

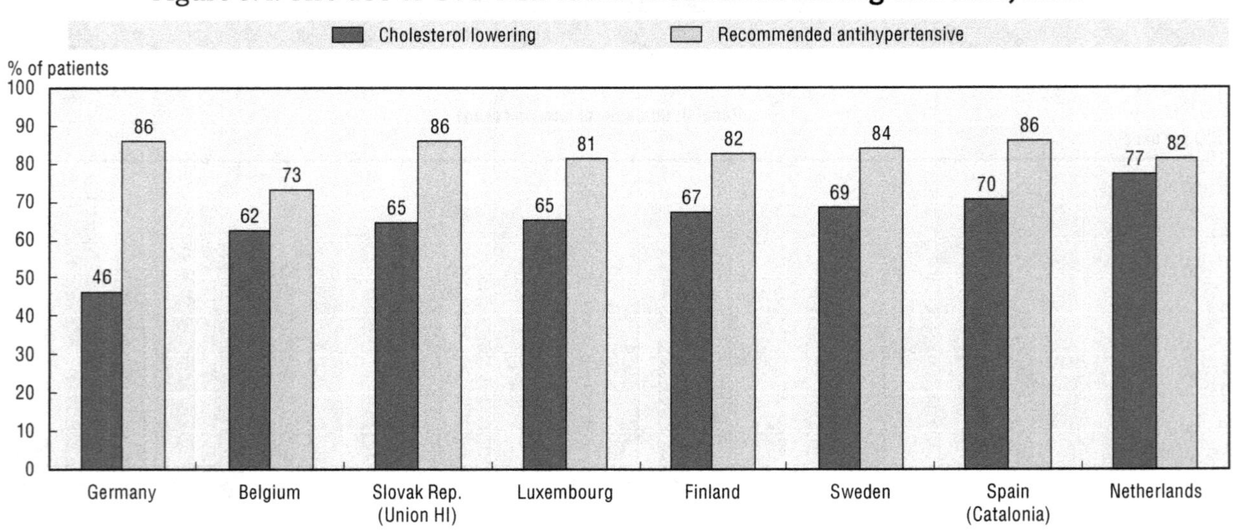

Source: OECD pilot study on prescription data, 2013.

Primary care can be strengthened to reduce avoidable admissions

Diabetes-related avoidable admissions

Numerous countries have used hospital admission records for selected conditions as a proxy to measure the quality of their primary care sector (Purdy et al., 2009). Even though these indicators are based on hospital inpatient data, some types of hospital admissions can provide insights into primary care quality. Organisations such as the United States Agency for Healthcare Research and Quality (AHRQ) has identified a set of "ambulatory care sensitive conditions" for which good outpatient care can potentially prevent the need for hospitalisation or for which early intervention can prevent complications or more severe disease. A commonly used example of an ambulatory care sensitive condition are admissions for patients with diabetes who may receive inpatient care if their condition is not adequately managed in the primary care setting. With high-quality primary care, hospitalisation for these illnesses often can be avoided.

Figure 3.5 shows the number of diabetes-related hospitalisations across OECD countries. Here, diabetes admissions relate to admissions for short-term and long-term complications as well as for uncontrolled diabetes hospitalisations without complications. The number of admissions shown in Figure 3.5 has been adjusted to account of the prevalence of diabetes in each country, based on data from the International Diabetes Federation. Thus, the figure reports the number of diabetes-related admissions per 1 000 diabetes patients. Across the OECD, for every 1 000 diabetic patients there are 24 diabetes-related hospitalisations per year. In Hungary and Germany this rate exceeds 50 hospitalisations whereas in Spain and Mexico there are fewer than ten. Adjusting the data to account for diabetes prevalence makes an important difference to interpretation of the data. In the case of Mexico, for example, the number of diabetes-related hospitalisation is one of the highest in the OECD on a per population basis but is the lowest when the high level of diabetes prevalence is taken into account.

Figure 3.5. **Diabetes admissions per 1 000 patients with diabetes, 2011 (or nearest year)**

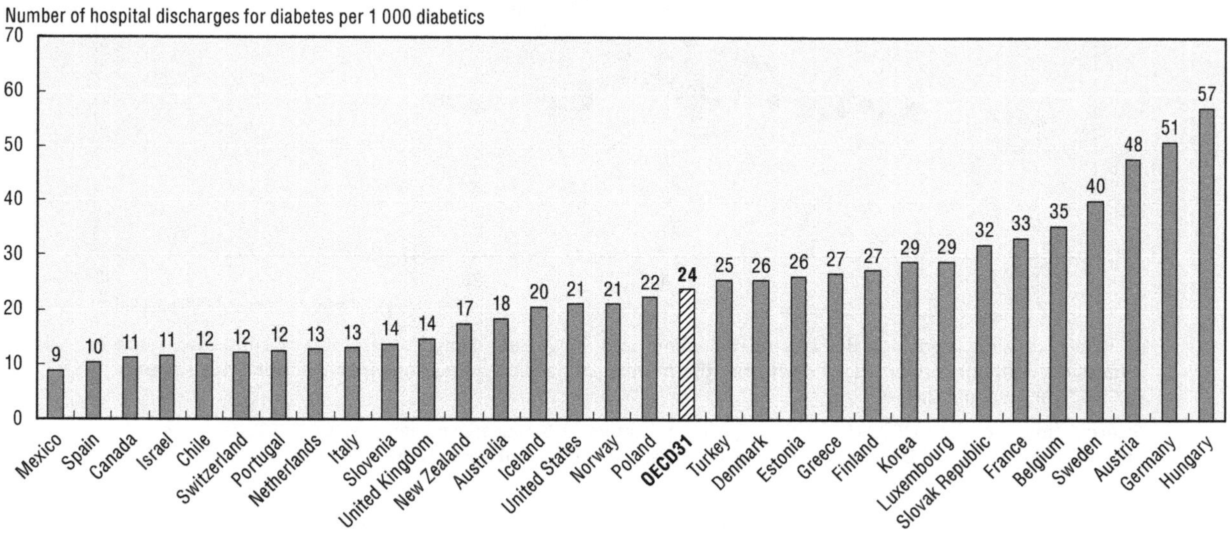

Source: Admissions data: *OECD Health Statistics 2013*; Diabetes prevalence: IDF (2013), *IDF Diabetes Atlas, 6th Edition*, International Diabetes Federation, Brussels, *www.idf.org/diabetesatlas/previouseditions*.

While the hospitalisation rate for ambulatory care sensitive conditions provides an indication of primary care quality, there are a number of other factors that influence these indicators which are outside the direct control of the primary health care system. These include environmental factors, disease prevalence and the age profile. Importantly, especially in relation to international comparisons, hospitalisation rates are also a measure of the access and role that hospitals play in the overall health care system. In some countries, access to hospitals is restricted due to financial or physical barriers. For example, Mexico, Chile and Turkey have fewer than three hospital beds per 1 000 population compared to an OECD average of 4.9. In other countries, hospitals remain the predominant institution within which health care is provided. This is the case in many Central and Eastern European Countries such as Hungary, Austria and Germany.

To further explain the variation across countries in avoidable hospital admissions for diabetes, Figure 3.6 looks at the access and use of hospital care for the general population. It shows that there is a strong positive relationship between hospital admissions for the general population and diabetes-related hospital admissions among diabetic patients. This provides some indication that high access and use of hospitals in the general population may also play a role in explaining high use of hospitals among the diabetic population. However, there are a number of countries where diabetes-related hospitalisations go beyond that which can be explained by the general use of hospitals. Countries such as Hungary, Sweden, Belgium, France and Korea have particularly high rates of hospitalisation, even after controlling for general hospital use. On the other hand, diabetic patients in countries such Israel, Slovenia and Switzerland have fewer diabetes-related hospitalisations.

Figure 3.6. **Comparing diabetes-related admissions and overall admissions across OECD countries**

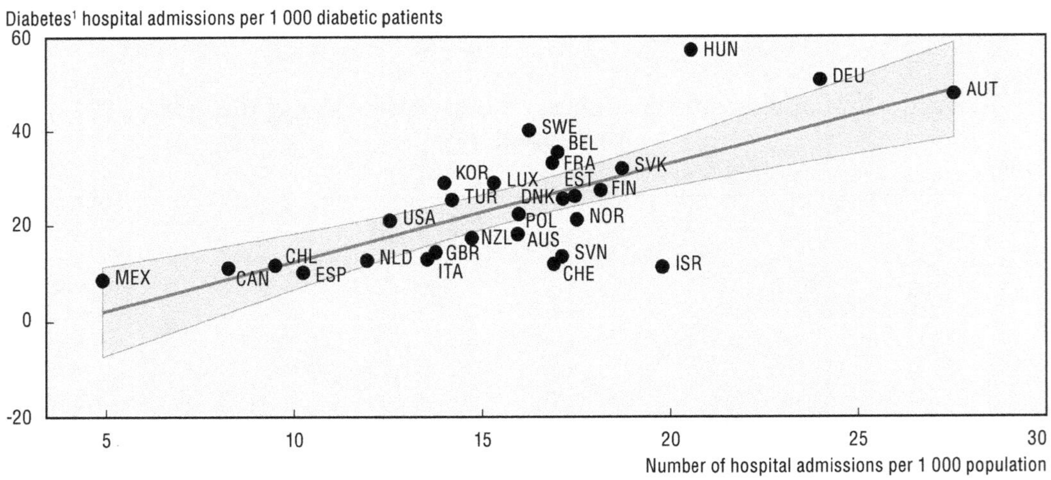

1. Refers to admissions for diabetes-related short and long-term complications and uncontrolled diabetes admissions without complications. Note that the number of hospital admissions includes same-day separations in SVK, TUR, USA and CHL.

Source: Admissions data: OECD Health Care Quality Indicators 2013; Diabetes prevalence: IDF (2013), *IDF Diabetes Atlas, 6th Edition*, International Diabetes Federation, Brussels, *www.idf.org/diabetesatlas/previouseditions*.

The adjustments made in Figures 3.5 and 3.6 provide some additional insights into the comparison of diabetes-related avoidable hospital admissions. However, a number of limitations associated with such indicators remain. In particular, there are widespread differences in hospital coding practices across countries. Countries that commonly code multiple diagnoses in their hospital administrative records are likely to pick-up more diabetes-related hospitalisations than those where the usual practice is to record only a small number of diagnostic codes. Such differences between countries may be systematic, particularly if funding arrangements are tied to the coding practices in some countries and not in others. For this reason the OECD's HCQI project continues to work on the research and development of these indicators to enhance further international comparability.

Heart failure avoidable admissions:

Similar to the previous discussion on diabetes, hospital admissions related to heart failure are regarded as ambulatory care sensitive conditions, and many could be avoided with proper management in the primary care sector. Figure 3.7 shows the number of heart failure admissions across OECD countries for 2011. Unfortunately, there are no international comparable data on the incidence of heart failure. Hence, the numbers shown in Figure 3.7 are based on the number of admissions per 100 000 population, rather than the number of admissions per person with heart failure.

Heart failure accounts for a substantial number of admissions. In 2011, there were 2.4 hospital admissions due to heart failure for every 1 000 people. This represents around 2% of all hospital admissions. The number of heart failure admissions is virtually double the OECD average in Hungary and almost three times as high in Poland. In the United Kingdom, Korea, Mexico and Slovenia the rates are less than half the OECD average. However, as was the case with the diabetes data, this indicator may be influenced by a range of factors which are outside of the control of the primary care system. For example, the incidence of heart failure may vary across countries which are likely to be an important determinant of hospital admissions. Indeed there is evidence that some of the rise in heart failure cases is due to the success that many countries have had in reducing mortality following a heart attack. Heart failure can occur after a heart attack where there is damage to the heart muscle.

Figure 3.7. **Heart failure admissions per 1 000 population, 2011 (or nearest year)**

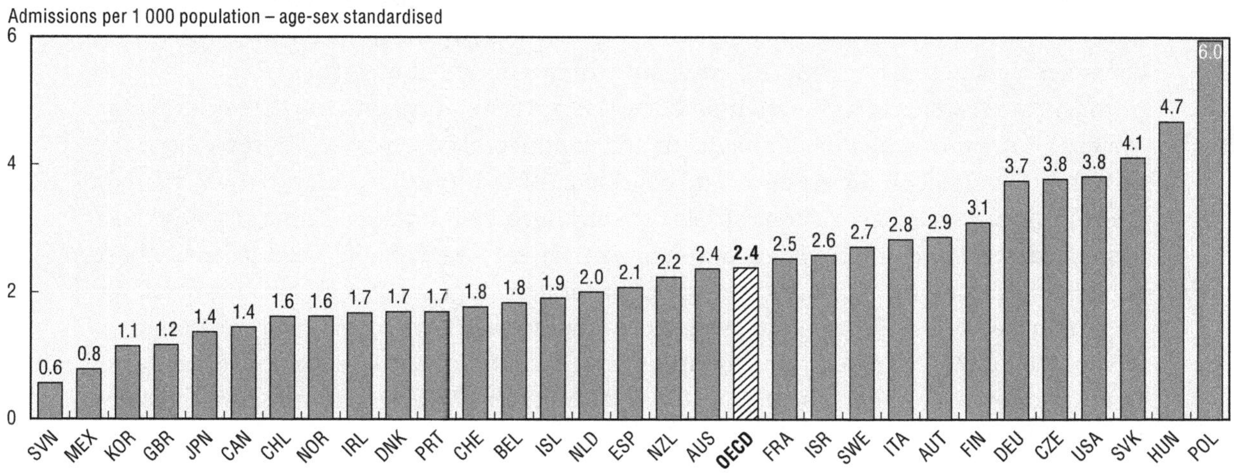

Source: OECD Health Care Quality Indicators 2013.

Some of the variation in heart failure admissions may also be influenced by the access and role of the hospital sector across countries. Figure 3.8 examines the relationship between overall hospital admissions and heart failure admissions. There is a strong positive relationship between overall admissions and heart failure hospitalisations. However, there remains substantial heterogeneity between countries even after controlling for overall hospital use, as indicated by the shaded area. The graph reiterates that many Central and Eastern European Countries have high number of admissions that are potentially avoidable. Slovenia, however, has comparatively few admissions for both heart failure and diabetes. While there may be multiple reasons for this, it is noteworthy that Slovenia's primary care system is highly accessible (Figure 3.8) and comparatively well-resourced compared to many of its Central and Eastern European Neighbours.

Figure 3.8. **Comparing heart failure admissions and overall admissions across OECD countries**

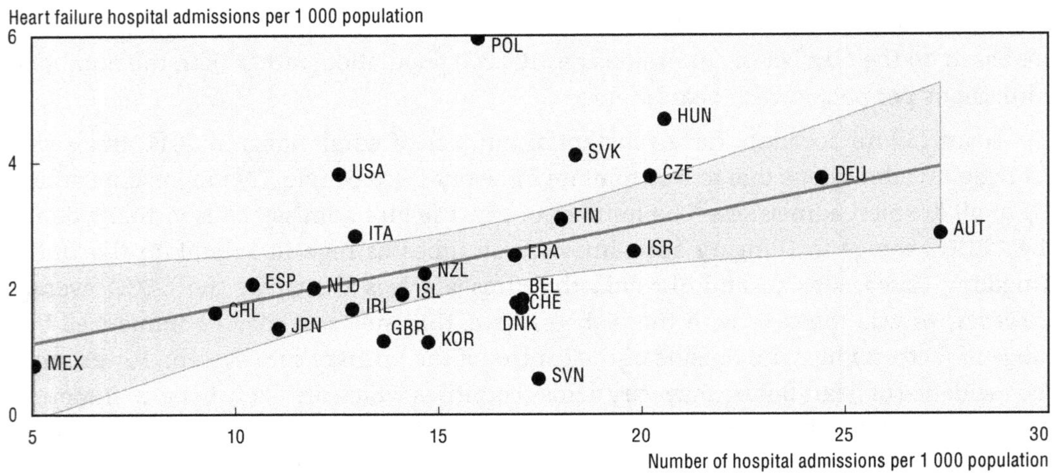

Source: OECD Health Care Quality Indicators 2013.

Strengthening national and international comparability of primary care quality

Designing international indicators to measure quality in primary care is not an easy task. Primary care systems encompass a myriad of activities and its functions differ considerably across countries. The availability of international measures of the quality of primary care systems is further hampered by the current state of primary care information systems. Differences in provider payment and contractual schemes across countries have an important effect on the scope of data collected. For example, countries that pay primary care physicians on a fee-for-service basis typically have well-developed administrative data systems designed to pay providers or reimburse patients. As a result, these countries have good data on the primary care the number of services (e.g. number of consultations) but there may be far less information available on the types of care provided or the outcomes of care (OECD, 2010). In addition, countries have different laws in place about the use of that information for analysis (OECD, 2013a). As a result, the ability to measure the same thing across health systems is hampered.

As a result, the OECD's HCQI project has thus far relied on administrative hospital records on avoidable admissions as a proxy for primary care quality. These indicators have their merits but they are not direct measures of primary care quality. For this reason, OECD countries have been investigating the feasibility of using prescribing data to complement the existing suit of primary care performance measures. Two indicators that related to diabetes care and were part of the feasibility study are reported above. The OECD's HCQI project will continue with the research and development of these prescription indicators as a potential source for quality data.

Furthermore, significant progress is being made across a number of OECD countries. Benchmarking and monitoring activities of primary care are becoming more common place as are pay-for-performance systems. These activities require better information systems and a number of countries have invested (OECD, 2013a). For example, the Scottish Care Information – Diabetes Collaboration (SCI-DC) dataset forms an electronic, population-based register of over 99% of people with a diagnosis of diabetes. It is routinely linked to other databases, such as hospital admissions and deaths (OECD, Forthcoming). The data collected is used for epidemiological research providing key information to help develop and plan services, benchmark performance at a regional level, and improve outcomes for people living with diabetes across Scotland. The 2012 report showed that more people had an HbA1c recorded, are accessing retinopathy screening, and had good blood pressure. The data also identified continuing challenges including the growing number of people with diabetes, poor glycaemic control particularly among Type 1 diabetics as well as substantial geographic variation in the outcomes achieved (SDMSG, 2013). Data on SCI-Diabetes can also be viewed by GP practices and hospitals as well as the "My Diabetes My Way" website (*www.mydiabetesmyway.scot.nhs.uk*) so that people who have registered can review their own data to support them self-management.

These efforts, as well as those planned in other countries, are likely to increase the number of countries that can monitor the quality of their primary care systems. Nevertheless, many countries may face challenges in reaching the goal of strengthening their health information infrastructure to improve health care quality, as well as ensure privacy-respectful uses of data. Alongside these national developments, there are opportunities to improve the international comparability of performance measures, particularly in the area of primary care that can deliver better analysis and benchmarking across OECD countries. One example of such international collaboration is the European Best Information through Regional Outcomes in Diabetes (EUBIROD) project. This project has worked towards compiling diabetes data available in EU countries and made a significant contribution towards developing technical platforms for internationally comparable data (EUBIROD Consortium, 2009).

Most countries provide good access to primary care but there are some important challenges

OECD countries invest substantial resources into primary care including the professional fees paid to physicians as well as the pharmaceuticals. On average, OECD countries spent around USD 690 per capita on ambulatory care (in constant USD PPP). The United States is by far the biggest spender on ambulatory care, mostly reflecting the higher prices that are paid for services there (Figure 3.9). Turkey, on the other hand, spent around one-seventh of the OECD average. Similar to other aspects of health care, national income is closely linked to ambulatory care expenditure; as incomes rise so do ambulatory care expenditures.

Figure 3.9. **Per capita ambulatory care expenditure, 2011 (or nearest year)**

Constant USD PPP

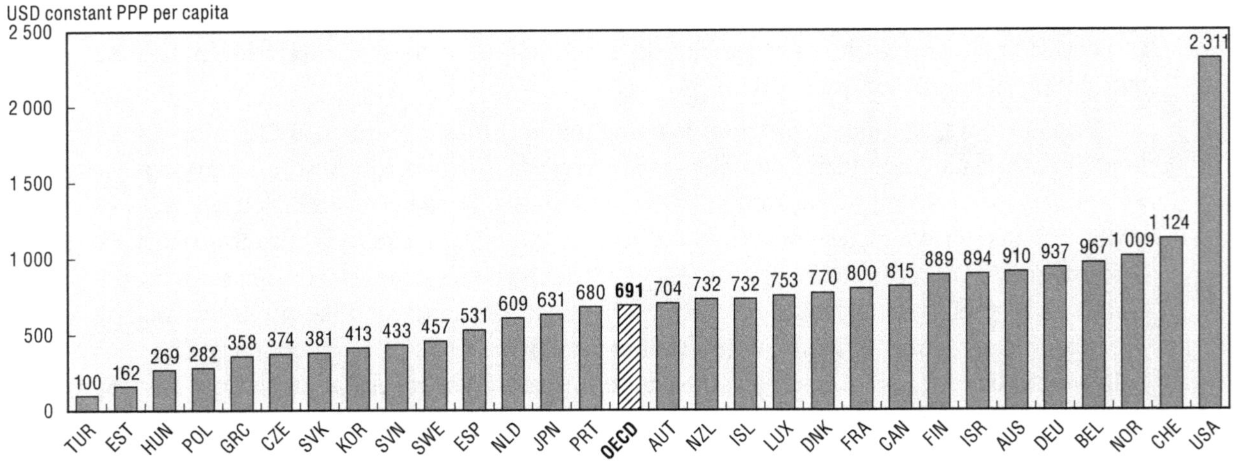

Note: Data based on the value of payments made to health care professionals primarily engaged in delivering health care services directly to out-patients visiting the health professional's office. Expenditure on dentist's visits has been excluded but the figures can include treatment of day-cases and the delivery of home care services.

Source: OECD Health Statistics 2013, http://dx.doi.org/10.1787/health-data-en.

Figure 3.10 shows the main sources of finance for ambulatory care (Panel A) and prescription drug expenditure (Panel B). In most OECD countries, the two main ambulatory care financing sources are government and patient out-of-pocket (OOP) costs with a relatively small contribution through private sources such as private health insurance. Only in the United States, Turkey and Israel, for instance, do private sources account for 20% or more of ambulatory care expenditure. On average, government finances around 72% and patients contribute around 19% of ambulatory care expenditure through OOP costs. All countries shown in Figure 3.10 use a mix of financing sources to fund ambulatory care, although there is substantial variation between countries in the importance placed on some sources. For example, OOP costs account for less than 10% of ambulatory care expenditure in countries such as Estonia, Luxembourg and France but exceeds 40% in Turkey, Greece and Hungary.

There is greater reliance on OOP costs to finance prescription medicines (Figure 3.10, Panel B). Across OECD countries, 22% of prescription medicines are paid by patients directly and in 15 OECD countries OOP costs contribute more than 20% of overall prescription drug expenditure. Private health insurance plays a relatively small role in financing prescription drugs in most countries, with the exception of Canada and Slovenia. Private health insurance also plays an important role in financing prescriptions in the United States, although *OECD Health Statistics* cannot distinguish between private health and OOP costs financing. In some countries such as Hungary and the Slovak Republic, the patient contribution for both ambulatory care and prescription drugs is relatively high. Other countries use OOP costs as a major form of financing for one sector but not in the other. In Estonia, for example, OOP costs play a minor role in financing ambulatory care (5%) but patients directly finance 43% of their prescription drug cost. In Switzerland, patients appear to enjoy greater financial protection for their prescription drugs than their ambulatory care costs, with patients directly contributing 14% and 29% of expenditure, respectively. The figures reveal that there are widespread differences between and within countries on the degree of financial protection given to patients.

Figure 3.10. **Financing sources for ambulatory care and prescription drugs**

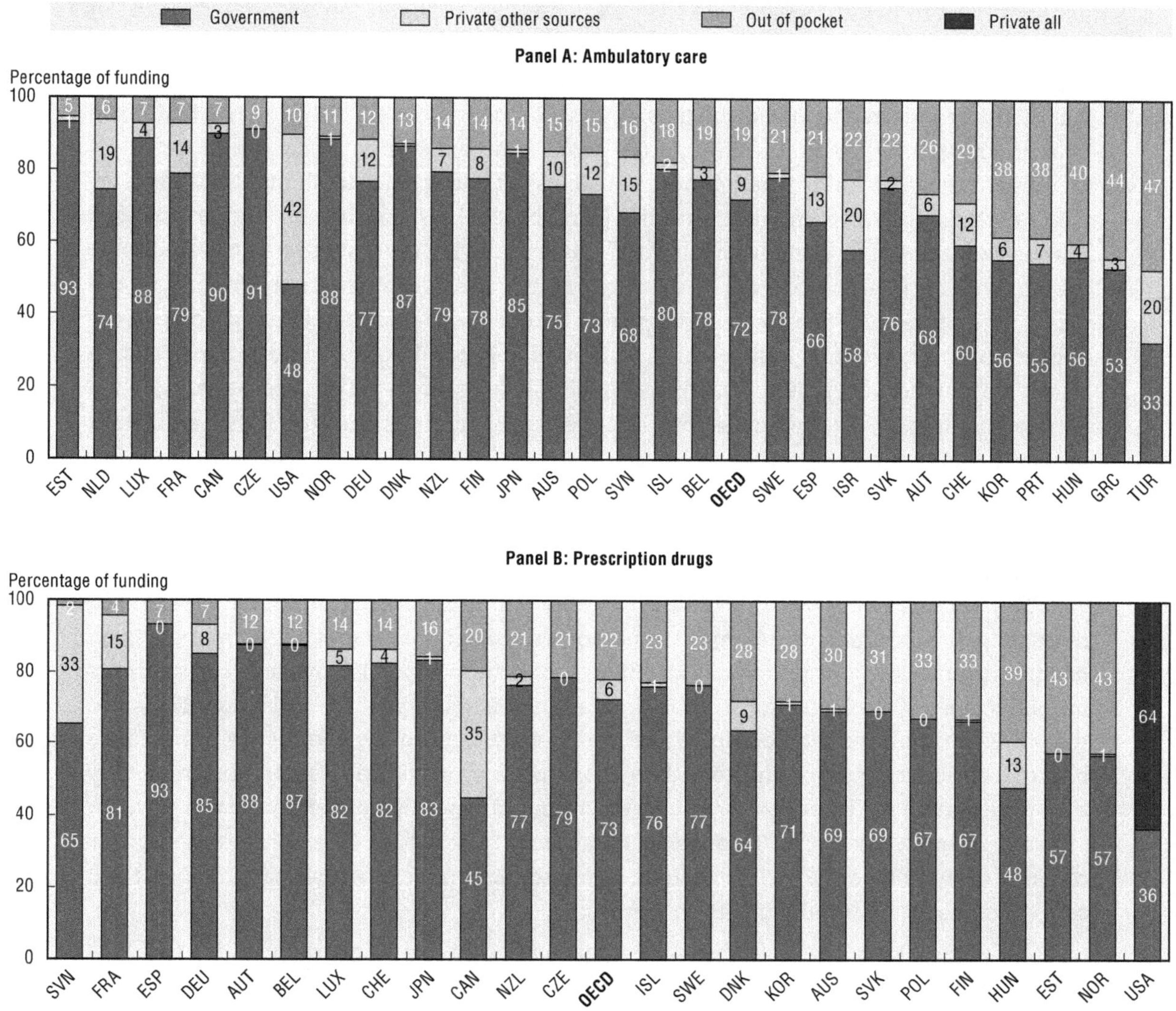

Source: OECD Health Statistics 2013, http://dx.doi.org/10.1787/health-data-en.

While Figure 3.10 illustrates the overall distribution of financing, a number of countries have put in place additional measures to protect people with chronic diseases from high OOP costs. In Chile, for example, both diabetes and CVD risk factors are part of eighty health conditions that are guaranteed by law. This means that patients diagnosed with these conditions receive 100% reimbursement for a range of health care services and products used to treat these conditions. Similarly, countries such as Portugal, France and Mexico, provide additional coverage for specific treatments for identified diseases including diabetes and CVD. In a number of OECD countries such as Ireland and Australia patients obtain additional coverage on the basis of income, age as well as high use. Nevertheless, chronic diseases such as CVD and diabetes remain a source of high OOP cost burden and can impose strong barriers of access in some countries. In Mexico, patients pay more than 50% of the total health care costs for their diabetes-related treatment (Arrendondo and Reyes, 2013). In the United States, almost one in four diabetic patients face high OOP costs, although this number has fallen over the last ten years (Li et al., 2014). With the recent reforms and additional insurance coverage in the United States, this proportion may fall even further.

The method by which care is financed has enormous implications on the access that patients have to health care. While OOP costs are by no means the only determinant of access, numerous studies have shown that demand for medical care has a significant and negative relationship with OOP costs (Cutler and Zeckhauser, 2000; Zweifel and Manning, 2000; Remler and Greene, 2009). The most famous of these is the US RAND Health Insurance Experiment conducted in the 1970s and 1980s. This experiment concluded that a 1% increase in the price paid by patients leads to 0.2% fall in the quantity demanded (Manning et al., 1987). Longer-term follow-up studies from the Health Insurance Experiment showed that despite the reduced medical care for those with high OOP costs there appeared to be little impact on health. However, there were two notable exceptions to this finding: i) the very poor (bottom 20% of income earners); and ii) those with prior health conditions. These two groups improved their health status for a number of conditions including hypertension if they did not face any OOP costs. This result should be interpreted with some caution due to small sample sizes (Newhouse and the Insurance Experiment Group, 1993; Tamblyn et al., 2001).

Several other studies collaborate the finding of the Health Insurance Experiment and find that higher OOP costs can have detrimental equity implications as well as health outcomes, particularly for ambulatory-sensitive conditions (Atella et al., 2006; Trivedi et al., 2010). Chandra et al. (2010) examine not only the direct impact of an increase in OOP costs on pharmaceutical consumption and doctor visits, but also downstream impacts on hospitalisation. Using longitudinal data, they exploit the staggered increase in co-payments for public employees in California to estimate the policy's impact on utilisation. They find that OOP costs for prescription drugs and doctor visits caused the chronically ill to reduce pharmaceutical consumption more than those without such illnesses. Importantly, they also find that those in poorer health with chronic illness also experienced the greatest increase in hospitalisations. This leads the authors to conclude that an increase in OOP costs for drugs and doctor visits may have a subsequent impact on other parts of the health care system and potentially health outcomes.

While insurance coverage through either public or private means provides financial access, patients also require easy physical access to primary care providers. Such physical access encompasses several factors including waiting times, transaction costs such as travel expenses and time, and availability of out-of-hours care. One proxy of such physical access is the number of doctors practicing within the health care sector. Figure 3.11 presents information on the number of generalist physicians per 1 000 population. In most countries, the data refer to practising generalist doctors, including general practitioners/family doctors and other generalist (non-specialist) medical practitioners.[5] On average, there is one generalist practitioner per 1 000 population. Though Ireland has the highest number of generalists, most of these are not GPs ("family doctors") but rather non-specialist doctors working in hospitals and other settings (OECD, 2013b). Furthermore, the number of practising generalist doctors in Ireland has declined since 2009, following the start of the financial crisis. In 2008, there were 3.26 generalist doctors per 1 000 population compared to 2.48 in 2012. While Greece has the lowest number of generalist doctors, the country has the highest number of physicians overall. This is explained by the fact that generalist doctors make a very low proportion of the medical workforce in Greece. This is also true for a number of other countries such as the United States and Hungary, where the specialist medical workforce account for a greater proportion of physicians.

Figure 3.11. **Number of generalist doctors per 1 000 population, 2011 (or nearest year)**

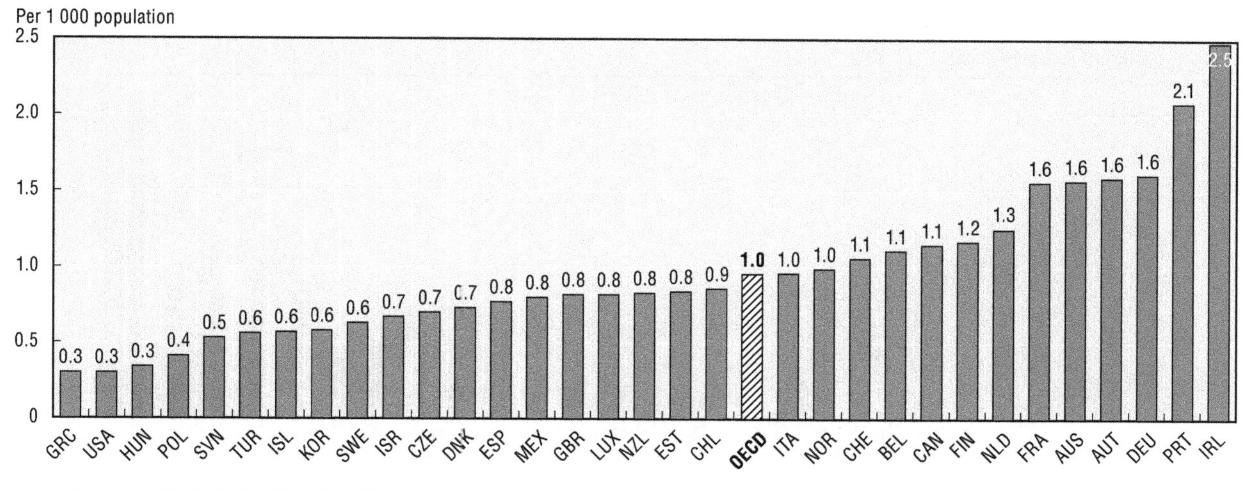

Source: OECD Health Statistics 2013, http://dx.doi.org/10.1787/health-data-en.

The increasing levels of specialisation of the medical workforce indicate a growing imbalance in a number of OECD countries, raising concerns about access to primary care. The higher remuneration of specialists compared to general practitioners may be factor in this imbalance. In 19 out of the 22 OECD countries for which data is available, specialists earn more than their general practitioner counterparts, particularly if the specialist is self-employed. In countries such as Australia, Belgium, Canada, France, and the Netherlands, specialist average wages are more than 50% higher than their GP counterparts. Furthermore, the remuneration gap appears to be growing in favour of specialists (OECD, 2013c). While remuneration is not the only determinant, it can play an important role in a medical graduate's to pursue a career in primary care.

Physical and financial barriers to access can also be measured by the extent to which people forego medical consultations. Unmet health care needs, as reported in surveys such as the European Statistics of Income and Living Conditions (EU-SILC), provide data on the proportion of people who reported that at least once in the previous 12 months they felt they needed medical care and did not receive it either because 1) it was too expensive; 2) they had to wait; or 3) it was too far away. Figure 3.12 reports unmet needs for the population as well as for low and high socio-economic groups; defined on the basis of household income. The low income group represents those whose income belongs to the bottom 20% of income earners in their respective country, whereas the highest income group belong to the top 20% of income earners. Across the European OECD countries in which the EU-SILC is implemented, the percentage of people with unmet needs is 3%. However, in many countries this percentage is less than 1% indicating a high degree of access. In countries such as Greece, Estonia, Poland and Latvia the percentage of the population reporting an unmet need was in excess of 8%. In all countries, people with low incomes are more likely to report unmet care needs than people with high incomes. On average, individuals in poor income household were three times more likely to report unmet needs compared to those in high income households. The gap between low and high incomes was particularly large in Latvia, Italy, Greece, Hungary and Poland.

Figure 3.12. **Unmet care needs for medical examination by income, European countries, 2012 (or nearest year)**

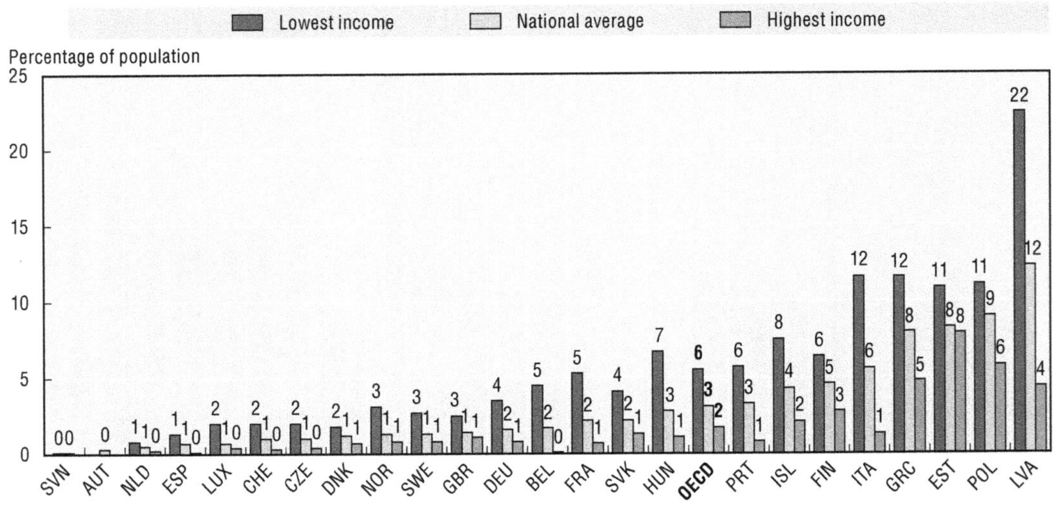

Source: EU-SILC 2012.

In health systems where OOP costs are an important financing source, the use of health care is driven by the willingness and ability to pay by patients. The greater the reliance on OOP costs to finance health care, the greater is the purchasing powers of wealthier sections of the community. This, in turn, provides important market signals to the suppliers of health care. Such a system can generate a wedge between the type of health care that is supplied and what is needed by those who are sick. This is particularly true when, as is often observed, those with the lowest ability to pay also have the highest health care needs.

By contrast, health systems with a greater reliance on insurance to fund care not only provide greater financial protection to the sick, it also gives them a stronger economic voice to influence the supply of health care. The greater purchasing power of the sick in insurance-based systems provide important market signals to health care providers to deliver care that is attuned to those who need care most. Health care financing arrangements can therefore not only influence the amount of care that is consumed by patients but also the type of health care supplied. The introduction of Medicare in the 1960s is an example of such an effect, where the increase in insurance coverage had a significant impact on the number of new hospitals entering the market (Finkelstein, 2007).

Good access to primary care is a cornerstone to effective diagnosis and management of CVD risk factors and diabetes. Barriers to access can lead to greater unmet needs, which in turn may lead to worse health outcomes and higher costs through the increased likelihood of cardiovascular events and diabetes complications. While good access is a necessity for effective management, the primary care system must also provide high quality services in order to minimise the burden of CVD and diabetes.

Examining primary care quality initiatives

The quality of care agenda is now firmly embedded in OECD countries. Governments have introduced substantive reforms and invested significant resources to explicitly improve the quality of care provided to patients. The instruments by which governments can try to influence quality of care are summarised in Table 3.3. Broadly, the four main mechanisms through which governments have introduced quality care reforms can be described as: 1) ensuring that high quality health care inputs that includes workforce measures and technology assessment activities; 2) ensuring that systems of responsibility for the quality of care are in place; 3) setting standards of care and having the capacity to monitor quality; and 4) establishing incentives to improve the quality of care which may include the removal of disincentives for quality. For each of these main policy instruments, this section looks at some of the main policy initiatives that have been directed at the quality of primary care, with a particular focus on policies designed to improve CVD or diabetes care.

Table 3.3. **Policies to improve quality of care in primary care**

Policy type	Examples
Health system inputs (professionals, organisations, technologies)	Accreditation and certification of health care institutes. Professional licensing including GPs and specialised nurses (e.g. diabetes or heart failure) and credentialing. Assessment and control of pharmaceutical products.
Health system design (allocation of responsibilities)	Accountability requirements at the primary care level. Quality governance structures in recognition of shifting focus of CVD and diabetes care towards primary care and social care. Quality as part of contracting and patient choice.
Monitoring (standards and information systems)	National standards and guidelines. Regulation on public reporting (including policies and support for registries, use of administrative databases, electronic health records, data sharing across health sectors, and patient surveys). Audit studies. Integrated guidelines on chronic diseases
Improvement (incentive structures and programmes)	Financial incentives such as pay-for-performance, care bundling, patient self-management. Programmes on patient safety and quality improvement.

Source: Adapted from OECD (2010), *Improving Value in Health Care: Measuring Quality*, OECD Publishing, Paris, *http://dx.doi.org/10.1787/9789264094819-en*.

Many OECD countries are recognising the need to transform their health care systems and place greater focus on primary care and its role in managing complex patients (Anderson, 2011). As part of this transformation, policy makers face the challenging task of making their health system more responsive to their population's health needs. This entails, in part, shaping the health care workforce, its institutions as well as the co-ordination of care around the health care needs of patients with multiple chronic diseases (Plochg et al., 2011).

Integrated and co-ordinated care

The proper management of patients with long-term diseases such as diabetes and CVD poses challenges to the organisation of health care delivery. In particular, fragmented health care systems between primary and specialist care have led to a number of structural barriers that prevent strong continuity of care and care co-ordination between providers (Glasby et al., 2006). Countries have responded to this challenge by developing new models of care. While there is no one unique model of care, the initiatives can be characterised by some key elements which include the scope and depth of integration among providers, development of performance indicators, governance arrangements, the use of financial incentives, and emphasis on patient-centred care. Furthermore, in most OECD countries, primary-care providers act to some degree as care co-ordinators, particularly in the case of referrals from hospitals back to primary care providers (Hofmarcher et al., 2007). The main aim is to develop a model of health care that is co-ordinated between providers rather than providing fragmented care (Strandberg-Larsen and Krasnik, 2009).

Most integrated care programmes had a positive impact on patient functional status and outcomes (Ouwens, 2005). Integrated care also showed a positive impact on process outcomes, such as guideline adherence. However, with the exception of one study, the ability for integrated care to affect mortality remains unclear. Whilst almost all studies concluded that integrated care reduced the number of hospitalisations, these did not result in overall cost savings. Most reviews found mixed or insignificant evidence on the effects of integrated care on health care cost.

More recent studies confirm that interventions aimed at co-ordinating care are more likely to produce positive patient health outcomes and an increase in patient satisfaction than produce cost savings (Davies et al., 2008). In fact, a review of 15 randomised trials among Medicare beneficiaries found that costs were higher for patients enrolled in the co-ordination arm of the trial compared to patients in the control arm. In most instances these differences were not statistically significant, leading the authors to conclude that care co-ordination can improve some patient outcomes and be cost neutral (Peikes et al., 2009; Nelson, 2012).

A study of the evaluation methods used on disease management programmes in 13 European countries found that the lack of an overarching definition of integrated care complicates policy analysis. Due to this lack of clarity, a large and diverse number of initiatives can fall under this term making it difficult to assess the added value of each activity (RAND Europe and Ernst and Young, 2012). Nevertheless, there appear to be some common elements. The majority of countries tend to focus on care models for populations with defined conditions (most frequently diabetes type 2) and involve some form of GP-led care co-ordination. Furthermore, nurse-led approaches are becoming more common and many models are being implemented in selected geographical regions. Whilst some form of patient self-management support is frequently offered, the overall use of clinical information systems for chronic disease management is the least developed strategy in many integrated care initiatives (RAND Europe and Ernst and Young, 2012).

Better information systems to monitor performance

The use of information technology is becoming an important tool for performance management in primary care. A number of countries are making better use of electronic patient records to automatically derive information that can be used to improve patient care as well as measure performance within and outside the practice.

The Danish General Practice Quality Unit (DAK-E) was established in 2007 and provides a good example of a performance measurement system aimed at monitoring and improving the quality of Danish General Practice. As part of its mandate, the DAK-E has introduced a system of automatic data capture from primary care records to monitor quality. The data include diagnoses, procedures, prescribed drugs and laboratory results. Since April 2011 every practice has become obliged to participate in the data capture system. The system provides a platform through which GPs can access quality reports from their own practice for the management of chronic diseases including diabetes and heart failure, as well as other clinical areas of primary care practice. The system enables easy identification of individual patients who are treated sub-optimally and also allows them to benchmark their practice against other practices. Recent evidence shows that more effective use of the quality reports could be made (OECD, 2013d). Nevertheless, recent analysis examining the quality of diabetes primary care reported significant improvements in the proportion of diabetics on antidiabetic, antihypertensive and lipid-lowering medications (Schroll, 2012; Guldberg, 2011).

Israel has a sophisticated programme for collecting data and monitoring the quality of primary care (OECD, 2012). The National Programme for Quality Indicators in Community Healthcare (QICH) is a voluntary programme and provides information to policy makers and the public on the quality of community health care provided across Israel's four health insurance plans (often referred to as Health Maintenance Organisations – HMOs). The QICH draws on data collected by health insurance plans across six key topic areas including CVD and diabetes. The programme captures more than 35 measures of quality of care on preventive measures, use of recommended care and the effectiveness of care. The data are available for almost the entire population according to age, sex and a proxy for socio-economic status.

The QICH is an important resource for quality improvement activities undertaken by the four HMOs in Israel. They draw on the QICH data to benchmark their own performance and identify potential shortfalls. A survey of HMO managers suggests that the information collected as part of the QICH brings a management focus on improving the quality of care (Rosen and Nissanholtz-Gannot, 2010). It suggests that the existence of good and comparable data has promoted informed discussions about quality of care alongside other operational considerations (OECD, 2012). HMOs have developed innovative programmes including patient education and empowerment initiatives and have also developed targeted programmes to deliver greater access to high quality care specific patient groups. The success of the QICH programme is in large measure due to the support and co-operation of Israel's four HMOs and provides a positive example of a scientific, systematic and ongoing scheme for monitoring and improving the quality of primary care.

QICH data, published annually at the national level, have recorded some notable improvements in primary care, particularly on process indicators relating to cardiovascular risk factors and diabetes. For instance, the percentage of individuals with diabetes mellitus with a record of HbA1c in the past year reached 92.3% in the past year and 90.4% of individuals with diabetes had a record of an LDL-cholesterol test during the measurement year. Other measures such as glycaemic control are proving more difficult, with the percentage of patients with good blood glucose control staying relatively stable over recent years (OECD, 2012).

Pay-for-performance

Over the last 20 years, pay-for-performance schemes have become an increasingly common method for paying primary care providers in OECD countries. Pay-for-performance schemes operate in around half of all OECD countries, focusing mainly on preventive care and care for chronic disease. While the design of these schemes varies considerably across countries, the central tenant is to make some element of provider reimbursement conditional on the quality of care delivered. All schemes include a common set of four basic elements: 1) performance domains and measures; 2) basis for reward; 3) reward; and 4) data reporting and verification (Cashin, forthcoming).

A recent systematic review found that pay-for-performance schemes have led to a 5% improvement in performance of incentivised aspects of care (Eijkenaar et al., 2013). The effects were generally stronger in primary care than in secondary care. The results suggest that pay-for-performance schemes appear to have had a small positive impact on the quality of care for diabetes but not for heart disease in the United Kingdom and the United States. However, the review also concluded that there was considerable heterogeneity in the impact of pay-for-performance schemes, reflecting perhaps not only differences in study design but also that their impact may be highly context specific.

One of the more studied pay-for-performance schemes is the United Kingdom's Quality Outcomes Framework (QOF). The QOF was established in 2004 and rewards points to GP for the proper management of some of the most common chronic diseases (e.g. diabetes), how well the practice is organised and how patients view their experience at the surgery. In 2012/13, the QOF measured achievement against 148 indicators; practices scored points on the basis of achievement against each indicator, up to a maximum of 1 000 points. The value of one QOF point for 2013/14 is around GBP 133 (Scotland) to GBP 157 (England). A systematic review of 124 QOF-related studies reports that quality of care for those conditions where incentives have been put in place improved at a faster rate than prior to QOF initially. However, subsequent evaluations show that the rate of improvement has returned to their pre-QOF levels (Gillam et al., 2012). Given the cost of QOF (an extra GBP 1 billion per year) there has been much debate about the scheme's cost-effectiveness.

Pay-for-performance schemes can potentially form a useful part of a blended payment system, particularly if it promotes development and measurement of quality indicators in primary care. It can be part of an important move toward better purchasing arrangements where the quality of care delivered plays a more prominent role. However, it is becoming increasingly recognised that such schemes are highly context-specific, suggesting that there are other conditions that need to be met in order for pay-for-performance to have a positive impact on outcomes.

The growing recognition of empowering patients to take effective control of their chronic diseases

Patient self-management is key component for the effective control of chronic diseases such as diabetes. Self-management is about patients being actively involved in their care and empowering them to make informed choices about the management of their disease. The American Association of Diabetes Educators (AADE) describes seven essential self-care behaviours that are strongly associated with better health outcomes including good glycemic control, reduction of complications and improvement in quality of life. The behaviours are: healthy eating, being physically active, monitoring of blood sugar, compliant with medications, good problem-solving and coping skills and risk-reduction behaviours (AADE, 2008). Despite the potential benefits of these behaviours, compliance to these activities has been found to be low (Cramer et al., 2008).

A number of programmes have been developed and implemented that aim to reduce barriers to self-care and facilitate greater adherence to recommended treatments and behaviours. Structured patient education programmes for patients with type 2 diabetes can help identify their health risks and set goals by developing diabetes management skills (Davies, 2008; Deakin, 2006). General patient self-management programmes are also available for people with diabetes. The chronic disease self-management programme (CDSMP), for example, provides series of workshops to patients in community settings. Patients are taught a variety of techniques to deal with problems, exercise and eat well, appropriately use medications, and communicate effectively with family, friends, and health professionals. Participants also receive educational materials. CDSMP has been implemented in 25 countries including Australia, Canada, Denmark, Japan, Spain, the United Kingdom and the United States (Lorig, 2001; EDLF, 2012).

The importance of supporting self-management is being increasingly recognised. A number of countries have invested directly in self-management programmes. For example, the Danish National Board of Health, The Danish Committee for Health Education and the Danish municipalities have collaborated successfully to implement the aforementioned CDSMP in 78 out of 98 Danish municipalities, with the majority of those established within three years of the programme's commencement in 2006 (EDLF, 2012). Diabetes self-management education has been found to be effective over the short and long run if regular follow-up is provided (Gary et al., 2003; Deakin et al., 2005; Norris et al., 2001; Renders et al., 2001 ; Polonsky et al., 2003). Programmes adapted to specific cultural background and age groups are also considered to improve outcomes (Brown et al., 2005, 1999; Anderson et al., 2005; Sarkisian et al., 2003; Chodosh et al., 2005). Evaluations of the CDSMP model have shown positive effects on quality of life, physical activity, social support, and use of strategies to manage symptoms (EDLF, 2012). In the United States, a recent national study of over 1 100 participants has shown significant reductions in emergency department visits, hospitalisations, equating to net savings of USD 364 per participant after taking program costs into account (Ahn et al., 2013).

Active self-care participation depends not only on the willingness and ability of patients but also on the capacity of health care professionals to support their efforts. This requires some important attributes of the provider-patient relationship including visits that have a stronger emphasis on education, take more time, and involve multiple health care providers, including allied health and educational staff. A number of countries have used incentives that are targeted at providers to encourage them to promote self-management, rather than reward them for repeated encounters with the health care system. For example, contracts for general practitioners in the United Kingdom, bundled payments in the Netherlands and pay-for-performance within Medicare in the United States (Rijken et al., 2008).

At the same time, there is a need to enhance the skills of the health professionals to support patients in their self-management. In the United Kingdom, for example, the Skills for Health Organisation was established to help create a skilled and flexible health care workforce by developing national workforce competency frameworks which includes case managers and community matrons to improve the scope and capacity of health professionals to support the chronic disease agenda, including better self-care (Nolte et al., 2008). Over time, new technologies are likely to play a more important role in a patient's ability to manage their disease. Information and communication technologies including telecare, home monitoring devices and phone apps are advancing the scope of self-management tasks that can be undertaken at home or in the community, including the patient's capacity to track their progress over time. These development underscore the potential benefits that such technologies can have in a system where self-management is an important part of the chronic disease management model. As noted by Rijken et al. (2008), the challenge for policy makers is to ensure that systems, organisations, individual professionals and the community all facilitate the patient to self-manage successfully.

Summary

Good access to primary care remains the foundation of the health care system, and is key to the effective management of CVD and diabetes together with health promotion and prevention as described in Chapter 2. It is integral to the early diagnosis of CVD risk factors and diabetes. Most countries have achieved good access to primary care and this must be maintained or, in the case of some countries, strengthened even further. This involves not only comprehensive insurance coverage of the primary services but also of drugs and medical goods typically prescribed for CVD and diabetes. It is becoming evident that poor access to primary care leads to adverse long-term health consequences and increased health care costs if CVD risk factors and diabetes are not managed properly at their early stage.

While access remains the foundation, more countries are placing a stronger emphasis on improving the quality of primary care. Countries are using a variety of policy instrument to improve the quality of services including the strengthening of primary care governance, financial incentives to deliver better care and outcomes, benchmarking and setting of targets, training and accreditation. At the heart of these efforts sits a greater need for performance monitoring. A number of countries have invested significant resources to enable better measurement of primary care activities, particularly around processes of care and, to a lesser extent, health outcomes. While some countries have made substantial progress in this field, measuring primary care quality remains a complex task. In many health care systems, primary care is characterised by thousands of independent practises which makes system-wide changes more difficult. This, in part, explains why countries have also invested time and effort into developing better governance structures for primary care.

More countries are looking towards expanding the role of primary care CVD and diabetes management including the co-ordination of care across health sectors and further integration of multidisciplinary care. This is warranted because the reliance on the acute sector remains very strong in many countries. Such efforts can also encompass a greater focus on CVD and diabetes prevention in primary care, although this may require further strengthening and integration of primary care systems with health promotion and public health activities.

Primary care also faces a number of substantial challenges in the management of CVD, diabetes and other chronic diseases. The ageing population will generate not only greater demand for primary health care services, they will also change the health care needs of the population. More patients will suffer multiple morbidities and require more complex consultations from a wider field of primary care providers, and they will need those services more often. Recent changes to clinical guidelines are recognising these changes by placing greater emphasis on the heterogeneous nature of a patient's needs. These challenges should be met by strengthening the evidence base for real-world clinical care that takes a broader view of patient needs beyond single diseases or risk factors.

In an era of cost constraint, the primary care sector can play an important role in the delivery of highly cost-effective services, as well as improve long-term health outcomes for patients with CVD and diabetes. This is increasingly being recognised in OECD countries with greater emphasis on the role that high quality primary care services can play in preventing, managing and controlling disease.

Notes

1. Hypertension (high blood pressure) puts a strain on the heart and arteries. People with hypertension are at greater risk of suffering from coronary heart disease, stroke, heart failure, peripheral vascular disease and kidney failure.
2. High cholesterol means having an excessively high level of lipids (cholesterol) in the blood. Cholesterol is a fatty substance which the body produces naturally but levels are also influenced by diet and being overweight. When someone has high cholesterol, fatty deposits can build up in their

blood vessels, making it harder for the blood to flow through. This increases their risk of having a heart attack or stroke.

3. American College of Cardiology/American Heart Association.
4. Angiotensin converting enzyme inhibitors (ACE-I) or angiotensin receptor blockers (ARB) are first-choice antihypertensives when treating diabetes patients because of their beneficial effectiveness for both cardiovascular and renal outcome.
5. In many countries, the numbers include interns and residents (doctors in training). The numbers are based on head counts. Several countries also include doctors who are active in the health sector even though they may not provide direct care to patients. Portugal reports the number of physicians entitled to practice (resulting in an over-estimation). Data for Spain (2010) include dentists, while data for Belgium include stomatologists (also resulting in a slight over-estimation).

References

AADE – American Association of Diabetes Educators (2008), "AADE7 Self-Care Behaviors", *The Diabetes Educator*, Vol. 34, pp. 445-449.

Agyemang, C. et al. (2005), "Prevalence, Awareness, Treatment, and Control of Hypertension among Black Surinamese, South Asian Surinamese and White Dutch in Amsterdam, The Netherlands: The SUNSET Study", *Journal of Hypertension*, Vol. 23, No. 11, pp. 1971-1977.

Ahn, S. et al. (2013), "The Impact of Chronic Disease Self-management Programs: Healthcare Savings through a Community-based Intervention", *BMC Public Health*, Vol. 13, No. 1, p. 1141.

Anderson, R.M. et al. (2005), "Evaluating a Problem Based Empowerment Program for African Americans with Diabetes: Results of a Randomized Controlled Trial", *Ethnicity and Disease*, Vol. 15, pp. 671-678.

Arredondo, A. and G. Reyes (2013), "Health Disparities from Economic Burden of Diabetes in Middle-Income Countries: Evidence from Mexico", *PloS one*, Vol. 8, No. 7, e68443.

Atella, V. et al. (2006), "Drug Compliance, Co-payment and Health Outcomes: Evidence from a Panel of Italian Patients", *Health Economics*, Vol. 15, No. 9, pp. 875-892.

Beagley, J. et al. (2014), "Global Estimates of Undiagnosed Diabetes in Adults", *Diabetes Research and Clinical Practice*, Vol. 103, No. 2, pp. 150-160.

BIRO – Best Information through Regional Outcomes Consortium (2009), *Best Information through Regional Outcomes: A Shared European Diabetes Information System for Policy and Practice*, University of Perugia, Italy

Boulware, L.E. et al. (2007), "Systematic Review: The Value of the Periodic Health Evaluation", *Annals of Internal Medicine*, Vol. 146, No. 4, pp. 289-300.

Brown, S.A. et al. (2005), "Dosage Effects of Diabetes Self-management Education for Mexican Americans", *Diabetes Care*, Vol. 28, pp. 527-532.

Cashin, C. et al. (2014), *Paying for Performance in Health Care: Implications for Health System Performance and Accountability*, McGraw-Hill Education, United Kingdom.

Chandra, A., J. Gruber and R. McKnight (2010), "Patient Cost-Sharing and Hospitalization Offsets in the Elderly", *American Economic Review*, Vol. 100, No. 1, pp. 193-213.

Chodosh, J. et al. (2005), "Meta-analysis: Chronic Disease Self-management Programs for Older Adults", *Annals of Internal Medicine*, Vol. 143, pp. 427-438.

Choi, Y.J. et al. (2009), "Prevalence and Management of Diabetes in Korean Adults Korea National Health and Nutrition Examination Surveys 1998-2005", *Diabetes Care*, Vol. 32, No. 11, pp. 2016-2020.

Cramer, J.A. et al. (2008), "The Significance of Compliance and Persistence in the Treatment of Diabetes, Hypertension and Dyslipidaemia: A Review", *International Journal of Clinical Practice*, Vol. 62, No. 1, pp. 76-87.

Cutler, D. and R. Zeckhauser (2000), "The Anatomy of Health Insurance", in A. Culyer and J. Newhouse (eds.), *Handbook of Health Economics*, Vol. 1A, Handbooks in Economics, Elsevier, Amsterdam.

D'Agostino, R.B. et al. (2008), "General Cardiovascular Risk Profile for Use in Primary Care: The Framingham Heart Study", *Circulation*, Vol. 117, No. 6, pp. 743-753.

Davies, M.J. et al. (2008), "Effectiveness of the Diabetes Education and Self-Management for Ongoing and Newly Diagnosed (DESMOND) Programme for People with Newly Diagnosed Type 2 Diabetes: Cluster Randomised Controlled Trial", *British Medical Journal*, Vol. 336, No. 7642, pp. 491-495.

Deakin, T.A. et al. (2006), "Structured Patient Education: The Diabetes X-PERT Programme Makes a Difference", *Diabetic Medicine*, Vol. 23, No. 9, pp. 944-954.

Deakin, T. et al. (2005), "Review: Group Based Education in Self-management Strategies Improves Outcomes in Type 2 Diabetes Mellitus", *Cochrane Database Systematic Review*, Vol. 2, CD003417.

EDLF – European Diabetes Leadership Forum (2012), "Copenhagen Catalogue of Good Practices in Diabetes", *www.idf.org/sites/default/files/Copenhagen%20Catalogue.pdf*.

Eijkenaar, F. et al. (2013), "Effects of Pay for Performance in Health Care: A Systematic Review of Systematic Reviews", *Health Policy*, Vol. 110, No. 2, pp. 115-130.

Finkelstein, A. (2007), "The Aggregate Effects of Health Insurance: Evidence from the Introduction of Medicare", *Quarterly Journal of Economics*, Vol. 122, No. 1, pp. 1-37.

Fowler, M.J. (2011), "Microvascular and Macrovascular Complications of Diabetes", *Clinical Diabetes*, Vol. 29, No. 3, pp. 116-122.

Fryar, C.D. et al. (2010), "Hypertension, High Serum Total Cholesterol, and Diabetes: Racial and Ethnic Prevalence Differences in US Adults, 1999-2006", *National Center for Health Statistics data brief*, Vol. 36, pp. 1-8.

Gardette Correia, et al. (2012), *Diabetes: Facts and Numbers 2012, Annual Report of the National Diabetes Observatory Portugal*, *www.spd.pt*.

Gary, T.L. et al. (2003), "Meta-analysis of Randomized Educational and Behavioral Interventions in Type 2 Diabetes", *Diabetes Educator*, Vol. 29, pp. 488-501.

Ghandehary, H., S. Kamal-Bahl and N.D. Wong (2008), "Prevalence and Extent of Dyslipidaemia and Recommended Lipid Levels in US Adults with and without Cardiovascular Comorbidities: The National Health and Nutrition Examination Survey 2003-2004", *American Heart Journal*, Vol. 156, pp. 112-119.

Gillam, S.J., A.N. Siriwardena and N. Steel (2012), "Pay-for-performance in the United Kingdom: Impact of the Quality and Outcomes Framework – A Systematic Review", *Annals of Family Medicine*, Vol. 10, No. 5, pp. 461-468.

Glasby, J., H. Dickinson and E. Peck (2006), "Guest Editorial: Partnership Working in Health and Social Care", *Health & Social Care in the Community*, Vol. 14, No. 5, pp. 373-374.

Guldberg, T.L. et al. (2011), "Improved Quality of Type 2 Diabetes Care Following Electronic Feedback of Treatment Status to General Practitioners: A Cluster Randomized Controlled Trial", *Diabetic Medicine*, Vol. 28, No. 3, pp. 325-332.

Guthrie, B. et al. (2011), "Multicomorbidity: The Impact on Health Systems and their Development", Chapter 6 in *Health Reform: Meeting the Challenge of Ageing and Multiple Morbidities*, OECD Publishing, Paris, *http://dx.doi.org/10.1787/9789264122314-en*.

Hajjar, I. and T.A. Kotchen (2003), "Trends in Prevalence, Awareness, Treatment, and Control of Hypertension in the United States, 1988-2000", *Journal of the American Medical Association*, Vol. 290, pp. 199-206.

Hoffmarcher, M.M., H. Oxley and E. Rusticelli (2007), "Improved Health System Performance through Better Care Coordination", *Health Working Paper No. 30*, OECD Publishing, Paris, *http://dx.doi.org/10.1787/246446201766*.

Holman, R.R. et al. (2008), "10-year Follow-up of Intensive Glucose Control in Type 2 Diabetes", *New England Journal of Medicine*, Vol. 359, No. 15, pp. 1577-1589.

ICBPGWAS – International Consortium for Blood Pressure Genome-Wide Association Studies (2011), "Genetic Variants in Novel Pathways Influence Blood Pressure and Cardiovascular Disease Risk", *Nature*, Vol. 478, No. 7367, pp. 103-109.

IDF – International Diabetes Federation (2013), *IDF Diabetes Atlas, 6th Edition*, International Diabetes Federation, Brussels, *www.idf.org/diabetesatlas/previouseditions*.

IDF (2012), *Clinical Guidelines Task Force: Global Guideline for Type 2 Diabetes*, Brussels, *www.idf.org/sites/default/files/IDF-Guideline-for-Type-2-Diabetes.pdf*.

James, P.A. et al. (2014), "Evidence-based Guideline for the Management of High Blood Pressure in Adults: Report from the Panel Members Appointed to the Eighth Joint National Committee (JNC 8)", *Journal of the American Medical Association*, Vol. 311, No. 5, pp. 507-520.

Kavousi, M. et al. (2014), "Comparison of Application of the ACC/AHA Guidelines, Adult Treatment Panel III Guidelines, and European Society of Cardiology Guidelines for Cardiovascular Disease Prevention in a European Cohort", *Journal of the American Medical Association*, Vol. 311, No. 14.

Keeler, E.B. (1992), "Effects of Cost Sharing on Use of Medical Services and Health", *Medical Practice Management*, Vol. Summer, pp. 317-321.

Kotseva, K. et al. (2010), "EUROASPIRE III. Management of Cardiovascular Risk Factors in Asymptomatic High-risk Patients in General Practice: Cross-sectional Survey in 12 European Countries", *European Journal of Cardiovascular Prevention & Rehabilitation*, Vol. 17, No. 5, pp. 530-540.

Krause, T. et al. (2011), "Management of Hypertension: Summary of NICE Guidance", *British Medical Journal*, Vol. 343, d4891.

Kringos, D.S. et al. (2013), "Europe's Strong Primary Care Systems Are Linked to Better Population Health but Also to Higher Health Spending", *Health Affairs*, Vol. 32, No. 4, pp. 686-694.

Krogsbøll, L.T. et al. (2012), "General Health Checks in Adults for Reducing Morbidity and Mortality from Disease", *Cochrane Database of Systematic Reviews*, Oct. 17, Vol. 10, CD009009.

Krumholz, H.M. (2014), "The New Cholesterol and Blood Pressure Guidelines: Perspective on the Path Forward", *Journal of the American Medical Association*, Vol. 311, No. 14, pp. 1403-1405.

LeBlanc, E.S. et al. (2011), "Effectiveness of Primary Care-relevant Treatments for Obesity in Adults: A Systematic Evidence Review for the US Preventive Services Task Force", *Annals of Internal Medicine*, Vol. 155, No. 7, pp. 434-447.

Li, R. et al. (2014), "Changes Over Time in High Out-of-Pocket Health-Care Burden in US Adults With Diabetes, 2001–2011", *Diabetes Care*, Vol. 37, No 6, pp. 1629-1635.

Li, R. et al. (2010), "Cost-effectiveness of Interventions to Prevent and Control Diabetes Mellitus: A Systematic Review", *Diabetes Care*, Vol. 33, No. 8, pp. 1872-1894.

Lorig, K.R. et al. (2001), "Chronic Disease Self-management Program: 2-year Health Status and Health Care Utilization Outcomes", *Medical Care*, Vol. 39, No. 11, pp. 1217-1223.

Manning, W.G. et al. (1987), "Health Insurance and the Demand for Medical Care: Evidence from a Randomized Experiment", *American Economic Review*, Vol. 77, No. 3, pp. 251-277.

Ministry of Health, Labour and Welfare (2012), *Implementation of Health Check-up and Guidance in 2012*, Japan, *www.mhlw.go.jp/bunya/shakaihosho/iryouseido01/dl/info03_h24_00.pdf.*

Nelson, L. (2012), "Lessons from Medicare's Demonstration Projects on Disease Management and Care Coordination", *Working Paper No. 2012-01*, Congressional Budget Office, Washington, DC.

Newhouse, J.P. and the Insurance Experiment Group (1993), *Free for All? Lessons from the RAND Health Insurance Experiment*, Harvard University Press, Cambridge.

New Zealand Guidelines Group (2012), *New Zealand Primary Care Handbook 2012, 3rd ed.*, New Zealand Guidelines Group, Wellington.

NICE – National Institute for Health and Clinical Excellence (2008), "NICE Public Health Guidance 10. Smoking Cessation Services in Primary Care, Pharmacies, Local Authorities and Workplaces, Particularly for Manual Working Groups, Pregnant Women and Hard to Reach Communities", *www.nice.org.uk/nicemedia/pdf/PH010guidance.pdf.*

Nolte, E., C. Knai and M. McKee (eds.) (2008), *Managing Chronic Conditions: Experience in Eight Countries* (No. 15), WHO Regional Office Europe.

Norris, S.L. (2002), "Self-management Education for Adults with Type 2 Diabetes: A Meta-analysis on the Effect on Glycemic Control", *Diabetes Care*, Vol. 25, pp. 1159-1171.

Norris, S.L. et al. (2001), "Effectiveness of Self-Management Training in Type 2 Diabetes: A Systematic Review of Randomized Controlled Trials", *Diabetes Care*, Vol. 24, No. 3, pp. 561-587.

OECD (forthcoming), *Strengthening the Information Infrastructure: Findings and Recommendations of the Advisory Panel of Experts on Health Information Infrastructure*, OECD, Paris.

OECD (2013a), *Strengthening Health Information Infrastructure for Health Care Quality Governance: Good Practices, New Opportunities and Data Privacy Protection Challenges*, OECD Health Policy Studies, OECD Publishing, Paris, doi: *http://dx.doi.org/10.1787/9789264193505-en.*

OECD (2013b), *OECD Health Statistics*, OECD Publishing, Paris, *http://dx.doi.org/10.1787/health-data-en*.

OECD (2013c), *Health at a Glance 2013: OECD Indicators*, OECD Publishing, Paris, *http://dx.doi.org/10.1787/health_glance-2013-en*.

OECD (2013d), *OECD Reviews of Health Care Quality: Denmark 2013 – Raising Standards*, OECD Publishing, Paris, *http://dx.doi.org/10.1787/9789264191136-en*.

OECD (2012), *OECD Reviews of Health Care Quality: Israel 2012 – Raising Standards*, OECD Publishing, Paris, *http://dx.doi.org/10.1787/9789264029941-en*.

OECD (2011), *Health Reform: Meeting the Challenge of Ageing and Multiple Morbidities*, OECD Publishing, Paris, *http://dx.doi.org/10.1787/9789264122314-en*.

OECD (2010), *Improving Value in Health Care: Measuring Quality*, OECD Publishing, Paris, *http://dx.doi.org/10.1787/9789264094819-en*.

Ouwens, M. et al. (2005), "Integrated Care Programmes for Chronically Ill Patients: A Review of Systematic Reviews", *International Journal of Quality in Health Care*, Vol. 17, No. 2, pp. 141-146.

Peek, M.E., A. Cargill and E.S. Huang (2007), "Diabetes Health Disparities: A Systematic Review of Health Care Interventions", *Medical Care Research and Review*, Vol. 64, Suppl. 5, pp. 101S-156S.

Peikes, D. et al. (2009), "Effects of Care Coordination on Hospitalization, Quality of Care, and Health Care Expenditures Among Medicare Beneficiaries", *Journal of the American Medical Association*, Vol. 301, No. 6, pp. 603-618.

Perk, J. et al. (2012), "European Guidelines on Cardiovascular Disease Prevention in Clinical Practice (version 2012)", *European Heart Journal*, Vol. 33, No. 13, pp. 1635-1701.

Plochg, T. et al. (2011), "Reconfiguring Health Professions in Times of Multi-morbidity: Eight Recommendations for Change", *Health Reform: Meeting the Challenge of Ageing and Multiple Morbidities*, OECD publishing, Paris, *http://dx.doi.org/10.1787/9789264122314-en*.

Polonsky, W.H. et al. (2003), "Integrating Medical Management with Diabetes Self-management Training: A Randomized Control Trial of the Diabetes Outpatient Intensive Treatment Program", *Diabetes Care*, Vol. 26, pp. 3094-3053.

Powell-Davies, G. et al. (2008), "Coordinating Primary Health Care: An Analysis of the Outcomes of a Systematic Review", *Medical Journal of Australia*, Vol. 188, No. 8, p. 65.

Purdy, S. et al. (2009), "Ambulatory Care Sensitive Conditions: Terminology and Disease Coding Need to Be More Specific to Aid Policy Makers and Clinicians", *Public Health*, Vol. 123, No. 2, pp. 169-173.

RAND Europe, Ernst and Young LLP (2012), *National Evaluation of the Department of Health's Integrated Care Pilots*, RAND Europe, Cambridge.

Ray, K.K. et al. (2009), "Effect of Intensive Control of Glucose on Cardiovascular Outcomes and Death in Patients with Diabetes Mellitus: A Meta-analysis of Randomised Controlled Trials", *The Lancet*, Vol. 373, No. 9677, pp. 1765-1772.

Remler, D.K. and J. Greene (2009), "Cost-Sharing: A blunt instrument", *Annual Review of Public Health*, Vol. 30, pp. 293-311.

Renders, C.M. et al. (2001), "Interventions to Improve the Management of Diabetes in Primary Care, Outpatient, and Community Settings: A Systematic Review", *Diabetes Care*, Vol. 24, pp. 1821-1833.

Rijken, M. et al. (2008), "Supporting Self-management", *Caring for People with Chronic Conditions: A Health System Perspective*, McGraw-Hill International.

Rosen, B. and R. Nissanhotz-Ganot (2010), *From Quality Information to Quality Improvements – Interim Report: Summary and Analysis of Interviews with Health-Plan Managers*, Myers-JDC-Brookdale Institute, Jerusalem.

Sarkisian, C.A. et al. (2003), "A Systematic Review of Diabetes Self-care Interventions for Older, African American or Latino Adults", *Diabetes Educator*, Vol. 28, pp. 467-479.

Schroll, H. et al. (2012), "The Danish Model for Improvement of Diabetes Care in General Practice: Impact of Automated Collection and Feedback of Patient Data", *International Journal of Family Medicine*.

SDMSG – Scottish Diabetes Monitoring Study Group (2013), *Scottish Diabetes Survey 2013*, NHS, *www.sci-diabetes.scot.nhs.uk/*.

Sidorenkov, G. et al. (2013), "Treatment Quality Indicators Predict Short-term Outcomes in Patients with Diabetes: A Prospective Cohort Study Using the GIANTT Database", *British Medical Journal Quality and Safety*, Vol. 22, No. 4, pp. 339-347.

Siu, A.L. et al. (1986), "Inappropriate Use of Hospitals in a Randomized Trial of Health Insurance Plans", *New England Journal of Medicine*, Vol. 315, No. 20, pp. 1259-1266.

Strandberg-Larsen, M. and A. Krasnik (2009), "Measurement of Integrated Healthcare Delivery: A Systematic Review of Methods and Future Research Directions", *International Journal of Integrated Care*, Vol. 9.

Tamblyn, R. et al. (2001), "Adverse Events Associated with Prescription Drug Cost-sharing among Poor and Elderly Persons", *Journal of the American Medical Association*, Vol. 285, No. 4, pp. 421-429.

Taylor, F. et al. (2013), "For the Primary Prevention of Cardiovascular Disease", *Cochrane Database of Systematic Reviews*, Vol. 1, Art. No. CD004816.

Thompson, S. and M. Tonelli (2012), "General Health Checks in Adults for Reducing Morbidity and Mortality from Disease [editorial]", *Cochrane Database of Systematic Reviews*, 17 Oct, 10:ED000047, *www.thecochranelibrary.com/details/editorial/2723031/General-health-checks-in-adults-for-reducing-morbidity-and-mortality-from-diseas.html* (accessed 28 March 2014).

Trivedi, A.N. ,W. Rakowski and J.Z. Ayanian (2008), "Effect of Cost Sharing on Screening Mammography in Medicare Health Plans", *New England Journal of Medicine*, Vol. 358, No. 4, pp. 375-383.

Van Ganse, E.V. et al. (2005), "Lipid-modifying Therapy and Attainment of Cholesterol Goals in Europe: The Return on Expenditure Achieved for Lipid Therapy (REALITY) Study", *Current Medical Research and Opinion*, Vol. 21, No. 9, pp. 1389-1399.

Walley, T. et al. (2005), "Trends in Prescribing and Utilization of Statins and Other Lipid Lowering Drugs across Europe 1997-2003", *British Journal of Clinical Pharmacology*, Vol. 60, No. 5, pp. 543-551.

Wolf-Maier, K. et al. (2004), "Hypertension Treatment and Control in Five European Countries, Canada, and the United States", *Hypertension*, Vol. 43, pp. 10-17.

Wood, D. et al. (2005), "JBS 2: Joint British Societies' Guidelines on Prevention of Cardiovascular Disease in Clinical Practice", *Heart*, Vol. 91.

Zweifel, P. and W.G. Manning (2000), "Moral Hazard and Consumer Incentives in Health Care", *Handbook of Health Economics*, Vol. 1A, Handbooks in Economics, Elsevier, Amsterdam.

Cardiovascular Disease and Diabetes
Policies for Better Health and Quality of Care

Chapter 4

Improving acute cardiovascular care quality and access

Even with the best efforts in cardiovascular disease (CVD) prevention and risk-factor management through primary care, many people will still require immediate medical attention or hospitalisation to treat an acute CVD event or diabetes complication including strokes, heart attacks and cardiac arrests. Chapter 4 describes advancement in acute treatment of people with a CVD event, and cross-country variation in available resources and accessibility to timely and specialised treatments for acute CVD episodes and diabetes complications. It examines the use of procedures such as bypass surgery and other coronary interventions and also shows recent trends in acute care quality for stroke and heart attack. It then highlights some of the major reforms that countries have put in place at both national and local levels to improve the full pathway of acute care services by bringing care into line with best practice standards in CVD treatment.

The statistical data for Israel are supplied by and under the responsibility of the relevant Israeli authorities. The use of such data by the OECD is without prejudice to the status of the Golan Heights, East Jerusalem and Israeli settlements in the West Bank under the terms of international law.

Advances in acute care treatments are improving CVD outcomes

Even with the best efforts in cardiovascular disease (CVD) prevention and risk-factor management, many people will still require hospitalisation to treat an acute CVD event or diabetes complication. The American Heart Association estimates that around one in six healthy 40-year-old males will suffer a stroke at some stage in their life and for women this risk is one in five. In the United States alone, there were approximately 785 000 new coronary attacks in 2010, and a further 470 000 patients were likely to have a recurrent attack (Lloyd-Jones et al., 2010). In OECD countries, 13% of all hospitalisations are due to CVD, or around 22.4 million admissions. Acute myocardial infarctions, or heart attacks, lead to around 1.8 million hospitalisations in OECD countries and account for 8% of all CVD-related admissions.

Recent decades have witnessed substantial innovations in the acute treatment of patients. The 1960s saw important breakthroughs in revascularisation procedures to restore blood flow to the heart muscle. In 1970 the first vein bypass surgery was performed, involving sophisticated diagnostic procedures to locate blockages where the flow of blood to the heart is impeded. The first angioplasty was carried out in 1978, involving the insertion of a balloon inside the artery to diminish or obliterate the blockage. Since their introduction, both angioplasty procedures and bypass surgery methods have undergone significant innovations to make their use safer and more effective (Weisfeldt and Zieman, 2007).

For ischemic stroke care, clinical trials have demonstrated the benefits of thrombolytic treatment (Hacke et al., 1998; NINDS, 1995). Thrombolytic therapy can dissolve acute blocks in brain arteries and surgical procedures, including angioplasty-stents, can also be used. In the case of haemorrhagic stroke, more surgical options have become available to stop bleeding in the brain. Due to the dangers of prescribing the wrong treatment, accurate diagnosis of the type of stroke is of vital importance in deciding the right treatments and requires specialised equipment and skills (Kramer, 2013).

These technological advancements have lifted the health care system's capacity to treat acute cases of CVD. To take maximum advantage of these innovations, however, health care systems have had to reorganise the way in which hospital services are delivered. From the moment a CVD emergency event takes place, a complex chain of processes (sometimes referred to as the chain of rescue) needs to be put in place to maximise a patient's chances of immediate survival and improve their longer-term health outcomes. See Box 4.1 for further details of the acute care interventions and services used in the treatment of heart attack, cardiac arrest and stroke.

In this chapter special attention is paid to conditions that are acute in nature and require immediate medical attention, including strokes, heart attacks and cardiac arrests. It will first highlight some of the important recommendations that flow from recent clinical evidence on how to maximise patient outcomes. The focus is on the impact that these recommendations may have on the delivery of acute health care services. It then looks at some of the links in the CVD acute care chain, starting with pre-hospital emergency services, timeliness of diagnosis and care, access to treatments and specialised care, as well as the available hospital resources to deliver high-quality care. It will look at some of the main performance measures used to monitor various aspects of the acute care CVD treatment pathway. In doing so, this chapter will highlight some of the major reforms that countries have put in place at both national and local levels to improve acute care services by bringing care into line with best practice standards in CVD treatment.

Box 4.1. **Common CVD interventions and services in the acute care sector**

Reperfusion involves restoring blood flow and oxygen to heart muscle (in the case of heart attack) or to the brain (in the case of ischemic stroke) that has been deprived of circulation. Some of the main reperfusion techniques are:

- *Percutaneous coronary intervention (PCI):* Is performed to open blocked coronary arteries and restore arterial blood flow to the heart tissue, without the need for open-heart surgery. PCI usually involves the combination of two procedures:
  - Angioplasty: A procedure used to widen blocked or narrowed coronary arteries. The procedure involves using a balloon to stretch open a narrowed or blocked artery.
  - Stent: In modern angioplasty procedures, a stent (a short wire-mesh) is inserted into the artery. The stent is left in place permanently to allow blood to flow more freely.
- *Primary percutaneous coronary intervention (primary PCI):* Also often referred to as a primary angioplasty. This treatment involves re-opening a blocked coronary artery while someone is still having a heart attack.
- *Thrombolysis:* Thrombolysis is a treatment used to dissolve blood clots so that blood flow can resume. It involves administering a "clot-busting" medicine to a patient suffering from an ischemic stroke or heart attack.

Automated external defibrillator (AED): Is a portable machine that delivers an electric shock to the heart of someone who is having a cardiac arrest, with the aim of restoring the heart's normal rhythm.

Cardiac catherisation/cath lab: Cardiac catherisation is an invasive procedure to examine how well a heart is functioning. The procedure is carried out in a hospital cardiac catheterisation lab (cath lab). It usually involves inserting a catheter into a blood vessel that leads to the heart, and taking x-ray images of the coronary arteries.

Implantable Cardioverter Defibrillator (ICD): An ICD is a battery-powered device that keeps track of someone's heart rate. The device is placed under the skin and connected to the heart by thin wires. If the ICD detects an abnormal heart rhythm, it delivers an electric shock to restore a normal heartbeat.

Specialised coronary care unit (CCU) or intensive cardiac care unit (ICCU): A hospital ward that specialises in the care of patients with heart attacks and other cardiac conditions that require continuous monitoring and treatment.

Specialised stroke unit: A specially organised in-hospital facility that is entirely (or almost entirely) devoted to care for patients with stroke. It is staffed by a multidisciplinary team with special knowledge in stroke care and is concerned with the immediate mobilisation and early rehabilitation after stroke.

The evidence on optimum acute treatments has widespread implications for health service delivery models

There are well-established guidelines for the treatment of patients suffering a CVD event such as a stroke or acute myocardial infarction (AMI). Professional organisations such as the European Society of Cardiology, the American Society of Cardiology and the American Heart Association routinely synthesise and assess the available evidence to set out clear treatment recommendations (Jauch et al., 2013; Steg et al., 2012; Tamis-Holland et al., 2014). Such guidelines are frequently updated in accordance with the latest studies and have been widely disseminated and adopted across countries.

Treatment recommendations for AMI depend on whether the patient is suffering from a ST-segment elevation myocardial infarction (STEMI) or a non-STEMI. The former is a type of heart attack where a coronary artery is completely blocked and parts of the heart muscle are unable to receive blood. A non-STEMI occurs when the coronary artery blockages are partial or temporary. In the case of a STEMI, reperfusion therapy to restore blood flow through blocked arteries should take place as soon as possible. This therapy can be achieved through either thrombolytic drugs designed to remove blood clots or percutaneous catheter intervention (PCI), a mechanical procedure that unblocks narrowed coronary arteries.

PCI is the preferred reperfusion strategy in patients with STEMI, provided it can be performed expeditiously and by an experienced team that includes interventional cardiologists and skilled support staff. Importantly, the European Society of Cardiology (ESC) guidelines recommend that PCI should only be undertaken in hospitals with an established interventional cardiology programme that is available 24/7. In settings where PCI cannot be performed by an experienced team and within 120 minutes of first medical contact, thrombolytic therapy is recommended (Steg et al., 2012). Reperfusion therapy for STEMI patients involves a complex set of processes involving the activation of emergency medical services, use of sophisticated diagnostic technologies and specialised procedures, and concluding with the provision of therapies for residual ischemia (Tamis-Holland and O'Gara, 2013).

In the case of acute ischemic stroke, thrombolytic therapy is the treatment of choice. There is strong evidence that ischemic stroke patients receiving intravenous thrombolysis with recombinant tissue plasminogen activator (rt-PA) have better survival and lower disability compared to patients receiving placebo (Jauch et al., 2013). Similar to the AMI reperfusion therapy, the benefit of treatment is time dependent. Patients are more likely to survive their stroke and acquire less disability if treatment is initiated early (Meretoja et al., 2014). Treatment initiated within 90 minutes of symptom onset more than doubles the chances of favourable outcome at three months compared with placebo (odds ratio = 2.11). For treatments initiated between 90 and 180 minutes, the odds of a favourable outcome were still higher compared to placebo, but were much lower than for patients who received thrombolytic therapy in less than 90 minutes (odds ratio = 1.69) (Marler et al. 2000). Several large-scale studies in both the trial and community setting have corroborated the finding that faster treatment improves outcomes (Wardlaw et al., 2003; Fonarow et al., 2011).

Innovations in hospital care are not just restricted to new technologies. In the case of stroke, there is strong evidence that the type of facility in which stroke care is provided has a major influence on patient outcomes (Seenan et al., 2007). Both clinical trial and observational studies have shown that patients treated in facilities with dedicated stroke resources had increased rates of intravenous thrombolytic administration, shorter time intervals and better patient outcomes compared to patients treated in community hospitals without specialised stroke care (Meretoja et al., 2010; Smith et al., 2010). A relatively small number of economic evaluations have also shown that stroke units are a highly cost-effective form of care (e.g Launois et al., 2004; Karla et al., 2005; Moodie et al., 2006; Saka et al., 2009).

The evidence on what constitutes optimum acute care is continuously improving and it is becoming increasingly clear that patient access to evidence-based technologies is only part of the treatment pathway. In order to derive maximum benefit from these innovations, access to care must be swift, available at all times, and delivered in high-quality facilities. In this way, the clinical evidence has enormous implications on the way that health care services are delivered. This includes the way that services are organised and co-ordinated, the resources available, the timeliness of care and the processes by which quality of care is monitored.

This complex pathway is sometimes referred to as the *chain of survival* in recognition of the importance of each link in the pathway from the moment a person suffers a CVD event. A well-functioning chain is one where: patients or bystanders recognise symptoms; bystanders know how they can help; first medical responders are on the scene in the fastest possible time, able to provide appropriate diagnosis and care as well as transport patients to the most the suitable acute care facility; and the right care is provided at the right time by the right clinical staff.

As will be highlighted in this chapter, OECD health systems have struggled to consistently deliver recommended care. Health care services have faced significant challenges in implementing all the links in the chain of survival. Nevertheless, there are many impressive successes that have had a real impact on the delivery of care and, most importantly, on patient outcomes. The next sections of this chapter will focus on the health system's capacity to provide access to high-quality acute care for CVD patients. The chapter will examine some of the leading indicators of CVD acute care processes, and describe some of the remarkable efforts that have been put in place across OECD countries.

Out-of-hospital survival for some CVD events is low and could be improved

The speed at which a person receives emergency care after suffering a CVD event can often mean the difference between life and death. In the case of cardiac arrest, for example, there is a 10% decrease in the likelihood of survival for every minute that defibrillation[1] is delayed. In a systematic review of 67 studies, Berdowski et al. (2010) found that survival after an out-of-hospital cardiac arrest ranged from 1.2% for studies conducted in Asian regions to 12.8% for studies conducted in Australian cities. European and North American studies recorded survival rates of 10% and 6.8%, respectively. These rates are based on the percentage of patients who survive to be discharged from hospital. Some of the studies used in this analysis date back to 1990 and it is possible that survival rates may have changed since then. The most recent figure for the United States, for example, shows that survival after cardiac arrest is 9.5% (Go et al., 2013).

Of note is that most of the studies are based on data at the regional level, suggesting that many OECD countries lack an overall national picture. This is important because recent findings from the United Kingdom suggest that there may be considerable within-country variation, with cardiac arrest survival ranging from 2% to 12% depending on the place of residence (Perkins and Cooke, 2012). This implies that a study based on a select number of regional data may not be representative of the overall national situation.

The variation in cardiac arrest survival that was found across studies may reflect differences in study methodology, case definitions, and patient clinical characteristics, as well as true differences in emergency medical service systems and hospital treatment. Nevertheless, the extensive variability in survival found by Berdowski at al. (2010) suggests that there may also be opportunities to improve survival. In particular, the resources and organisation of emergency services as well as the ability of bystanders to respond can have large effects on survival (Neumar et al., 2011; Rea et al., 2010; Holdenberg, 2005).

A recent meta-analysis concluded that the overall rate of survival following an out-of-hospital cardiac arrest has been fairly stable over the last 30 years (Sasson et al., 2010). Nevertheless, many emergency services have witnessed substantial improvements in patient outcomes.

The links in the out-of-hospital survival chain that many jurisdictions have sought to strengthen include 1) raising public awareness and education about recognising the symptoms of heart attack and stroke; 2) the ability of bystanders to respond, which includes calling emergency services and providing cardiopulmonary resuscitation (CPR); 3) greater access to automated external defibrillators (AEDs) (see Box 4.1) in public spaces and in workplaces; 4) a high-functioning ambulance system that provides fast response times, ability to accurately diagnose, and a professional workforce able to deliver an appropriate first response; 5) a high level of integration between emergency services and acute care facilities. This last point encompasses a high level of communication between specialised CVD facilities and emergency services so that the patient can be transported to the right place straight away, and specialised acute care services are forewarned about the imminent arrival of a patient.

Experiences in London and Seattle have shown remarkable improvements in CVD survival and may provide important lessons for others to follow (Malhotra and Rakhit, 2013). In particular, both emergency service systems have sought to make continuous improvements along the complex chain of survival from the moment a person goes into cardiac arrest.

In London, survival from out-of-hospital cardiac arrest has increased from 12% to 32% in a short five-year period (Fothergill et al., 2013). This improvement has been attributed to an extensive list of initiatives implemented by the London Ambulance Service between 2007 and 2012. Some of the main initiatives include: 1) implementing new guidelines on continuing resuscitation on scene; 2) delivery of a structured education programme for personnel to enhance the quality of medical services provided on scene; 3) improved pre-arrival instructions and assistance provided to emergency service callers; 4) training 30 000 members of the public to recognise cardiac arrest and deliver bystander interventions; 5) raising public awareness through media campaigns directed at improving bystander CPR rates; 6) implementing a pathway for patients to be conveyed directly to a specialised cardiac care unit; and 7) increasing the number of fast response units and reducing call to arrival at scene intervals from an average of 7 to 6 minutes.

Seattle and King County in Washington State have the highest reported survival rates in the world for out-of-hospital cardiac arrest (Malhotra and Rakhit, 2013). This area has a long history of working with leading physicians and community leaders to create a fire department-based system to deliver care quickly to victims. According to the consensus recommendations from the American Heart Association (Neumar et al., 2011), one of the driving features of the Seattle/King County model has been its focus on continuous improvement. Quality of care reviews are routine in the Seattle model, including recording of the emergency calls to determine if the cardiac arrest was identified at the time of the initial call and if CPR was delivered to the victim. Physicians will review any deviations from optimal care, and feedback is provided to help firefighters improve their response to the next event. Hospitals are also provided with reports on the profile of care that they delivered to surviving patients to encourage best practices. The systems have set in place important accountability structures that include measurement of process and outcome indicators that are reported publicly each year and reviewed by public officials (EMS Division, 2013). The availability of resources has also been noted as an important feature of the Seattle/King County model. Under the model, firefighters are trained as emergency medical technicians and are equipped with automated external defibrillators. For every 100 000 residents in King County, there are 15 full-time paramedics dedicated to treating serious emergency conditions.

There are many other examples from around the world of improvements to out-of-hospital cardiac care. These efforts include raising general awareness and skills among the general public to recognise symptoms and provide appropriate first responses. As of January 2014, for example, the Canadian province of Manitoba has implemented The Defibrillator Public Access Act, which mandates that all public places have AEDs, including gyms, arenas, community centres, golf courses, schools and airports. The Act also requires for these machines to be registered so that emergency responders can inform those trying to care for a cardiac arrest victim to find the nearest AED and advise them on its proper use.

Many OECD countries are investing significant resources into their emergency medical services. According to the OECD CVD and Diabetes Survey conducted for this project, the installation of defibrillators that can provide an electric shock to the heart to restore a normal rhythm is becoming more common. In countries such as Canada,[2] Germany, Japan, Ireland, Israel, Poland and Singapore, almost all ambulances carry this device. Although use of defibrillators is expanding, coverage in countries such as the Czech Republic, Korea, Slovakia and Spain is not complete. Some countries have also enhanced the capabilities of their ambulances to reduce the time to hospital treatment. In a small number of countries, for example, ambulances are equipped with additional diagnostic and communication equipment that can help with the accurate diagnoses of STEMI, and send these reports to specialised coronary units for assessment. A recent study in the United States showed that pre-hospital diagnoses allowed more patients to bypass the emergency department and be transported directly to the catheterisation laboratory of a PCI-capable hospital. This practice cut the time to reperfusion by 20 minutes and lowered mortality rates (Bagai et al., 2013). Such innovations warrant close examination as they can potentially save precious minutes and help ensure that the right patient goes to the right hospital at the right time.

A number of jurisdictions have attempted highly innovative approaches to improving emergency response times and care for stroke. Examples of these include improving the ability of emergency services to diagnose and communicate patient details (for rapid evaluation), and initiate stroke treatment. However, some evaluations have shown that these technologies can be cumbersome and expensive; they suggest that further large-scale randomised trials are needed to determine whether pre-hospital stroke diagnosis and treatment, using some of these innovative approaches, can deliver better outcomes for patients (Hölscher et al., 2013).

In many OECD countries, emergency services are the responsibility of local government or regionally based health services. As a result, there are substantial differences in emergency services' resources and organisation both within and across countries. For example, many emergency medical services use locally created protocols to determine whether and when to cease treatment efforts. There is also substantial variation in the skills and training of first responders: some communities provide their first responders with basic life support training and an automated external defibrillator; others rely on paramedics trained to provide advanced life support; and some communities routinely employ nurses or physicians in pre-hospital settings (Sasson et al., 2010). It is not clear to what extent these differences can help explain the widespread heterogeneity between survival rates across studies. Nevertheless, experiences from both London and Seattle suggest that greater focus on pre-hospital quality care can deliver substantial benefits in patient outcomes.

The decentralised nature of emergency medical services in many OECD countries limits the ability to report comparative national data in many OECD countries. Most studies conducted in this field are on a regional basis and show considerable heterogeneity in not only patient outcomes, but also processes of care, emergency services, resources and organisation. Some of this variation may be attributed to variations in study design and baseline patient characteristics; however, there is evidence that the way emergency services are organised, as well as the resources which are available, can also have an important effect on outcomes. The findings reported here suggest that a stronger role for policy makers may be warranted. The establishment of a national policy framework for the measurement, benchmarking and continuous quality improvement of emergency services could lift overall standards and reduce heterogeneity within countries. In addition, some initiatives, including raising public awareness, training and communication networks, require strong national leadership and co-ordination across regional jurisdictions.

Much of this section has focused on emergency medical services in relation to cardiac arrest. This focus is warranted not only because of the prominent role of these services in measuring emergency quality in jurisdictions, but also because of the magnitude of cardiac arrests that occur each year. There are an estimated 359 000 out-of-hospital cardiac arrests each year in the United States, and approximately 275 000 in Europe (Go et al., 2013; Atwood et al., 2005). On the basis of these numbers alone, health systems have a strong motivation to improve the quality, responsiveness and accessibility of emergency services. Nevertheless, improving the performance of emergency medical services will have even wider ramifications with the potential for improving AMI and stroke outcomes as well.

Timeliness of care: Evidence of variation across countries, but there is room for optimism

As noted previously, there is strong evidence that shorter time intervals between the onset of CVD events and treatment can greatly enhance health outcomes (Marler, 2000; Leupker et al., 2000). In the case of ischemic stroke, a number of guidelines recommend that the time from emergency room arrival to initiation of thrombolysis should be 60 minutes or less (ESO, 2008; Jauch et al., 2013). This is often referred to as the "door-to-needle" time. In the case of AMI, the preferred time frame has generally been set at less than 60 or 90 minutes, depending on whether a patient arrives at a centre that can safely perform primary PCI (Steg et al., 2012). In the case of an angioplasty following a heart attack, the measure is known as the "door-to-balloon" time.

As part of the OECD's CVD and Diabetes Survey, a number of countries were able to report their average door-to-needle and door-to-balloon times. Table 4.1 reports the results for nine countries. Four countries achieved an average door-to-needle time that corresponds to the recommended guidelines. Two countries (the Czech Republic and Poland) reported having reduced their door-to-balloon time to 30 minutes, and a further three countries were under the 90 minute benchmark. It should be noted that these are average times and do not mean that all patients were treated within the recommended time frame. The American Heart Foundation provides another measure of treatment delays by reporting on the percentage of patients who receive timely access to treatment. Their latest results show that for 33.8% of ischemic stroke patients, the door-to-needle time was less than or equal to 60 minutes. In the United States' Veteran Health Association System, the door-to-balloon time for 69% of patients was within 90 minutes. This figure was over 90% for patients treated in hospitals that were part of HIQR or ACTION-GWTG programmes[3] (Go et al., 2013).

Table 4.1. **Treatment times (measured in minutes) for ischemic stroke and heart attacks, 2012 (or nearest year)**

	Door-to-needle time (ischemic stroke)	Door-to-balloon time (heart attacks)
Canada	72[1]	
Czech Republic	60	30
Israel		68
Korea	66	66
Poland	60	30
Singapore	104	79
Slovak Republic	60	102[1]
Sweden	61	170
United Kingdom (England)	55	

1. Median.

Source: OECD Cardiovascular Disease and Diabetes Health System Characteristics Survey, 2014, unpublished.

A number of countries have shown substantial improvements in the timeliness of care over recent years. In Poland and the Czech Republic, average door-to-needle time fell from 90 to 60 minutes between 2005 and 2012, and in the Slovak Republic it fell from 120 minutes to 60 minutes. In Korea, average door-to-needle times fell from 79.5 to 66.2 minutes in the space of one year and door-to-balloon time fell from 72.3 to 65.8 minutes. While the Swedish door-to-balloon time fell substantially from 200 minutes in 2004 to 170 minutes in 2011, its average time remained outside the 60 or 90 minute benchmark recommended by clinical guidelines.

Given the importance of timeliness in delivering acute care, a number of health systems have established process indicators that measure the time it takes to deliver care. These include:

- Ambulance response times for CVD events measure the time from the first call to the arrival of first medical responders.
- Call-to-door time measures the ambulance response plus the time it takes for the patient to be brought to the hospital door.
- Door-to-needle/balloon time (as discussed above) focuses on measuring the time it takes for a patient to receive treatment from the moment they arrive at the hospital door.

These measures have become part of the suite of quality indicators used in some countries to monitor hospital performance,[4] as they provide good measures of an evidence-based process that can have a direct effect on patient outcomes and are, to a large degree, within the health system's realm of control. A broader measure is the "onset-to-needle/

balloon time", which reflects the time it takes from the first sign of AMI or stroke symptoms to treatment. This indicator captures the entire chain of survival time. Although it can be argued that some aspects of this indicator are outside the control of the health care system, it does recognise the importance of early recognition of symptoms by patients or bystanders.

Numerous studies in the literature have shown how targeted strategies have successfully reduced the time to treatments. In the United States, following the establishment of the national "Door-to-Balloon (D2B) Alliance", treatment times fell substantially in participating hospitals. In the space of three years, the percentage of patients with door-to-balloon times of less than 90 minutes increased from around 25% to 75% (Bradley et al., 2009). The alliance was managed and sponsored by the American College of Cardiology but included 38 partner organisations composed of professional associations, private insurers, hospital groups and health care quality organisations. The strategy was set out in four distinct phases (Krumholz et al., 2008):

- *Planning phase:* Involved developing evidence-based tools, setting out plans that would foster commitments towards the alliance's goals, creating award credits for recertification and continuing medical education, and establishing an evaluation plan to assess the overall impact of the effort.
- *Participation phase:* Aimed to enrol as many primary PCI hospitals as possible in the D2B Alliance. The launch gained widespread media coverage and used the endorsement of senior leadership and the local chapters of the American College of Cardiology to encourage participation. Many of the partners also participated in actively communicating with clinicians and hospitals to encourage enrolment. The public release of the list of participating hospitals and the use of deadlines were also employed as strategies to boost enrolment. Around 1 000 hospitals joined the D2B Alliance including some outside of the United States.
- *Intervention phase*: Included disseminating a kit with a description of the project and tools (made available on the D2B Alliance website); conducting educational sessions; establishing an online community to provide a venue for the exchange of information; conducting a baseline survey; providing hospital-specific action plans to each participating hospital on the basis of the survey data; and numerous locally initiated strategies.
- *Evaluation phase:* Included an assessment of the initiative impact, as well as generate knowledge about how best to disseminate and translate the model into practice. The evaluation sought to analyse: changes in the use of the evidence-based strategies; changes in D2B times; hospital views on the D2B Alliance's role; and remaining barriers to improving D2B times.

The success of the D2B Alliance has stimulated further action. The American Heart Association/American Stroke Association's "Target: Stroke" initiative aims to build on programmes such as the D2B Alliance and the "Get with the Guidelines" project to improve door-to-needle times for ischemic stroke (Fonarow et al., 2011). While a number of successful programmes have reduced treatment times, initiatives such as the D2B Alliance provide a good example of a national plan that was evidence-based, well-coordinated, and that has had a positive effect on outcomes.

Access to revascularisation procedures has improved, but some countries are lagging behind

Since the mid-1980s, PCI has been promoted as an alternative to a coronary artery bypass graft (CABG), and recent decades have seen the rate of CABG falling while PCI procedures have been rising. Nevertheless, CABG remains the recommended treatment option for patients with multiple-vessel obstruction, diabetes and other conditions (Deb et al., 2013). The uptake and diffusion of procedures such as CABG and PCI have varied considerably across OECD countries. There are several reasons for this, including the available economic resources, patient needs, regulatory and financial arrangements, as well as organisational features such as the skills and expertise of the medical workforce (OECD, 2005).

While CABG and PCI have now become standard procedures in many OECD countries, they do require highly skilled professionals who are supported by sophisticated diagnostic technologies and facilities. Such expertise and infrastructure are not always widely available, particularly when the technology first becomes available. It is therefore highly appropriate that sophisticated procedures like CABG and PCI are only undertaken if they can be performed safely and are diffused more widely once the professional skills and facilities are upgraded. This means that countries, with their widely varying resources and capabilities, will have widely varying diffusion paths (Laut et al., 2013).

Over time, however, it may be reasonable to expect that the uptake and diffusion of technologies start to converge across countries. As the evidence gathers, costs fall, and skills are developed, countries that may have been late starters have the ability to catch up to the early adopters. Figure 4.1 provides some evidence of this phenomenon; however, it also reveals that some 30 years after the first use of percutaneous transluminal coronary angioplasty (PTCA), and 40 years since the introduction of CABG, there remains wide-ranging variation in the use of these procedures.

The horizontal axes of Figure 4.1 show the number of CABG and PCI procedures per 100 000 population in Panels A and B, respectively. The vertical axes indicate the annual rate of growth in the number of procedures based on data observed between 2000 and 2011. Panel A shows that the average number of CABG procedures across OECD countries is around 40 per 100 000 population and ranges from less than 4 (Mexico) to 68 (Germany). It should be noted that there has been considerable growth in the number of CABG surgeries in Mexico, albeit coming off a very low base. In around 70% of countries, the rate is between 30 and 60 CABG surgeries per 100 000 population. The number of CABG per head of population has been declining or has been steady in most countries, with the biggest falls witnessed in Hungary. Panel B provides comparative data on the rate of PCI procedures (with or without insertion of stent). In 2011, the average number of PCI procedures was 181 per 100 000 population. Most countries provide between 150 and 250 PCI procedures per 100 000 population, although the rate in Germany has reached 350, whereas in Mexico the procedure is rarely performed.

Over the 2000 to 2011 period, most countries increased the use of PCI. In Canada, Greece, Belgium and the Czech Republic there were small declines, although it should be noted that the growth rates for these countries were calculated after 2005. In the case of Greece, the data only showed a drop in PCI between 2006 and 2008 and then a rise in 2009. The lower growth rates observed in more recent years may be explained by the wider diffusion of drug-eluting stents in some countries. Drug-eluting stents should reduce the need for subsequent PCI procedures (Epstein et al., 2011). Although PCI and CABG are to some extent substitutes for each other, countries that reported the biggest rises in PCI procedures also witnessed smaller falls in CABG surgeries. This suggests that greater access and higher needs may be driving some of the changing patterns in treatment.

Figure 4.1. **Bypass surgery and percutaneous coronary interventions per 100 000 population, 2011 (or nearest year)**

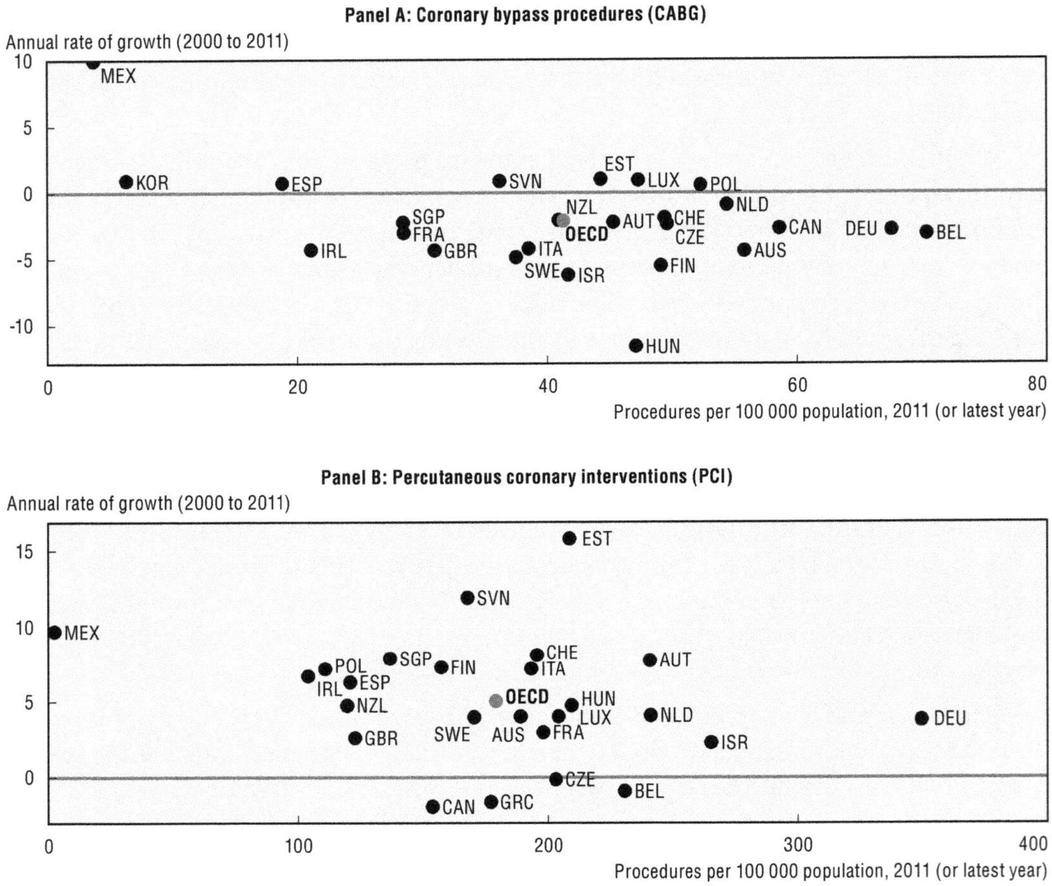

Source: OECD Health Statistics 2013, http://dx.doi.org/10.1787/health-data-en.

The widespread disparity in PCI procedures across countries has led to programmes such as the European "Stent 4 Life" initiative. This initiative, launched in 2008, aims to improve the delivery of care and patient access to primary PCI and is based on a partnership between professional associations, government representatives, industry partners and patient groups. It supports the implementation of ESC guidelines on the management of STEMI heart attacks, helps identify barriers to the implementation of guidelines, and defines actions to improve access to PCI in Europe. The objectives of "Stent 4 Life" include increasing the use of primary PCI to more than 70% among all STEMI patients and ensuring access 24/7.[5]

A recent survey revealed that primary PCI use increased dramatically in countries that had been participating in the "Stent for Life" initiative since its start. Between 2007 and 2011, primary PCI use among STEMI AMI patients increased from 33% to 64% in France, 9% to 32% in Greece, 30% to 50% in Spain, and 8% to 78% in Turkey (Kristensen et al., 2014).

According to these results, other countries such as the Czech Republic, Italy, Portugal and the United Kingdom have also seen substantial increases.

The widespread variation in the uptake of PCI provides an instructive case study of the importance of aligning the health system's capacity and the delivery evidence-based care. As noted previously, the first PCI was undertaken in 1978, but it took another ten years for clinical trials to demonstrate that it was superior to thrombolysis in the treatment of STEMI AMI, and then a further ten years before it was recommended by the main professional associations (Widemski and Kristensen, 2012). Now, some 40 years after its first introduction, there remains widespread variation in its use and severely limited access in some countries. A number of health system barriers have been identified as potential reasons for the variation, including resources and skills, financial (dis)incentives to deliver PCI, and the lack of networks in some countries that enable easy and fast transfer of patients to PCI centres (Laut et al., 2011).

Care in specialised facilities improves outcomes but access remains limited in some countries

Stroke units

Numerous studies have demonstrated the benefits of providing care in specialised stroke units. Specialised facilities have been shown to standardise integrated stroke pathways and improve adherence to best practices. Evidence shows that stroke units can reduce both mortality and morbidity over the short and long term (Jauch et al., 2013). In fact, the benefit of stroke units is comparable to the effects achieved with intravenous administration of rtPA (Gilligan et al., 2005).

The first systematic review that showed the benefits of stroke units was published in 1993 (see Langhorne et al., 1993). Yet the implementation and adoption of stroke units has been slow. A 2006 survey of over 800 European hospitals that treated stroke patients showed that less than 10% had optimal facilities; and in 40% of hospitals, even the minimum level care was not available (Leys et al., 2007). The authors concluded that those countries with a higher proportion of small hospitals (treating fewer than 50 stroke patients per year) also had a higher proportion of facilities without minimum levels of care.

Figure 4.2 indicates the percentage of patients who are treated in stroke units across 11 OECD countries. The data relate to the most recent year available, although it should be noted that, for Canada, France and Germany, this relates back to pre-2009. In the United Kingdom (England), 93% of stroke patients are treated in dedicated facilities. This represents a nearly four-fold increase since the early 2000s, and reflects a concerted effort to improve care in the United Kingdom under its National Stroke Strategy. The high percentage in Sweden is consistent with previous reports suggesting that patients in Scandinavian countries have had high access to specialised stroke unit care. Access in countries such as France and Canada is below 30%, although there are efforts in both countries to expand the number of stroke unit facilities. The Calgary Stroke Programme has shown that stroke units can save lives, reduce morbidity and are cost-effective (Zhu et al., 2009). The positive experiences in Calgary have armed the Canadian Stroke Network with the evidence and knowledge to develop a set of recommendations on how to establish a successful stroke care programme.

Figure 4.2. **Percentage of patients treated in stroke units, 2011 (or latest year)**

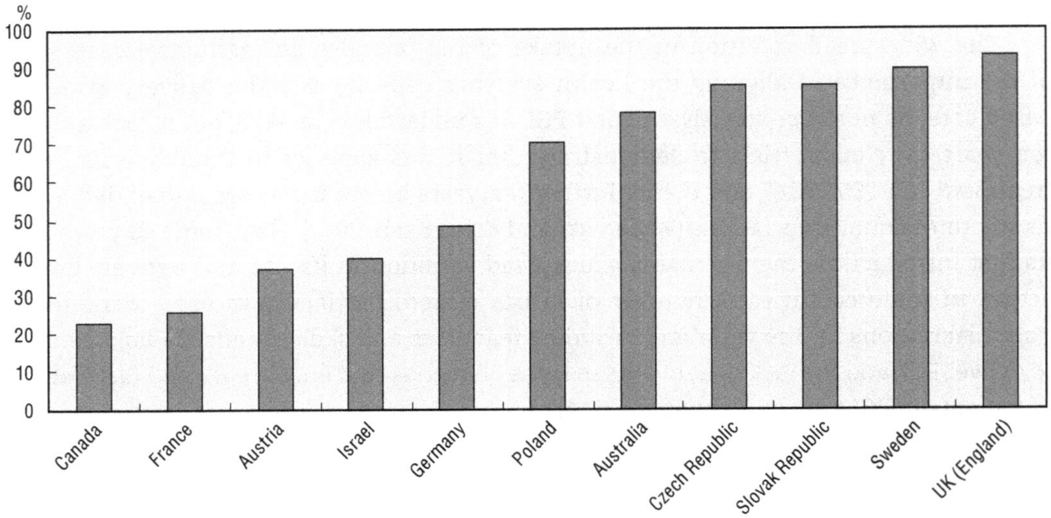

Note: The Canadian figures were derived from an audit report of selected hospitals which may not reflect overall figures.

Source: OECD Cardiovascular Disease and Diabetes Health System Characteristics Survey, 2014, unpublished.

A number of professional organisations have established evidence-based criteria around the definition of specialised care (ESO, 2008; Jauch et al., 2013; Schwamm et al., 2005). The European Stroke Organisation (ESO), for example, has set up a Stroke Unit Certification Committee to define the requirements and criteria for official certification for ESO stroke care facilities. The ESO Committee has established two levels of certification levels consisting of (Ringelstein et al., 2013):

- ESO Stroke Units must meet a minimum set of criteria to provide evidence-based care for stroke patients: 1) to ensure vital functions; 2) to provide early diagnostic investigations; 3) to allow basic surveillance and 4) stroke-specific therapeutic interventions; 5) to perform general therapeutic and diagnostic interventions; 6) to start secondary prevention; and 7) to combine this with multi-professional early mobilisation and rehabilitation procedures.
- ESO Stroke Centres must meet all the requirements of an ESO Stroke Unit and have more advanced equipment, higher staffing, and more diversified resources. They can serve as primary treatment centres in their catchment area, but additionally provide more advanced diagnostic and therapeutic equipment and expertise on rare or complex stroke subtypes.

One of the success stories has been the Czech Republic's recent efforts in establishing a network of specialised stroke care facilities. Financial support from the European Union was used as the basis for developing a network of stroke units and centres across the country. There are now 34 stroke units that can provide thrombolysis as well as 13 stroke centres that can deliver more specialised treatments, including neurosurgery; collectively, these serve a population of around 10.5 million people. Hospitals and emergency departments have direct access to, and support from, specialised staff in stroke facilities who can give advice about individual patients. A strong culture of data collection and reporting has been developed within the network that includes regular analysis of stroke care performance. Stroke facilities are required to send data every six months, which are then analysed by the Ministry of Health to identify areas for quality improvement. A committee made up of representatives from the ministry, health insurers, patients and professional groups provide oversight of the network, including performance monitoring. Stroke facilities are provided with reports that indicate their performance on both process and outcome measures. In the case of underperformance, facilities will be asked to identify reasons and develop plans to improve care. Facilities risk losing their stroke care certification if performance remains unsatisfactory. The 30-day case-fatality rates for ischemic stroke fell by 41% between 2001 and 2011 in the Czech Republic compared to an average decline of 24% across OECD countries.

PCI centres

According to a 2005 policy statement by the ESC, the role of specialised coronary care units is to monitor and support failing vital functions in acute and/or critically ill cardiac patients in order to perform diagnostic measures followed by medical and invasive therapies (Hasin et al., 2005). The ESC's statement provides a set of guidelines on the necessary requirements for a properly functioning coronary care unit that includes the equipment, beds and staffing levels. Nevertheless, it is recognised that there is a lack of evidence on the proper structure and functioning of coronary care units. The authors of the policy statement call for more research on issues such as the number of ICCU beds required for a given population size, specific equipment and required personnel (Hasin et al., 2005).

The delivery of primary PCI requires appropriate cardiac catheterisation laboratories with specialised and experienced staff. There is evidence that patient outcomes are related to appropriate staff education and specialisation, as well as a sufficient volume of procedures. Furthermore, studies have shown that patients who have a heart attack on the weekend or out-of-hours have a higher risk of adverse outcomes, indicating the need for 24/7 access to coronary care units that are capable of performing PCI (Steg et al., 2013).

Figure 4.3 provides an overview of the number of PCI-capable centres in 13 OECD countries. These data are based on those reported by Kristensen et al. (2014) and Widemski et al. (2010). To improve reliability and comparability across years, only those countries where the data are derived from national or regional registries covering at least 90% of the population are shown in Figure 4.3. It should be noted that these figures do not reflect the size of each PCI centre. Germany reportedly has 521 PCI-capable centres, which translates to 6.4 centres per one million population. The figure shows considerable cross-country variation, with Denmark, the Netherlands and the United Kingdom all having fewer than two centres per million population. The variation may reflect the lack of evidence-based standards on determining the right number of centres based on demographic, geographic and resource factors (Hassin et al., 2005).

All countries either increased or held steady the number of PCI capable centres over the three years to 2011. Combining the data shown in Figure 4.3 with OECD Health Statistics reveals that there is a strong positive correlation between the number of PCI centres and the number of PCI procedures performed. This relationship holds true when the increase in the number of centres and the number of PCI procedures are compared within a country. While this cannot explain all the variation in PCI procedures across countries, it does suggest that greater resourcing for PCI centres could be an important determinant of access.

The increase in the number of PCI centres was particularly big in Poland, where the number of centres rose from 95 to 137 over the three-year period. The most recent figures suggest that the number of centres has continued to increase, with 151 centres that provide

PCI 24/7. The significant investment in PCI resources resulted in a near doubling of the number of PCI between 2005 and 2011 (Jaworski et al., 2012). This expansion coincided with substantial changes in the Polish health care system to monitor performance. In 2004 and 2005, Poland implemented a number of cardiovascular registries including the National Registry of acute coronary syndromes and the National Registry of cardiac surgical procedures. Under the auspices of the Polish Cardiac Society, hospitals are monitored at a regional level. This well-established information infrastructure is an important link in the setting of the acute care targets in Poland: delivering reperfusion therapy in over 90% of patients with STEMI, providing access to mechanical reperfusion in 90 minutes from first medical contact, and hospital mortality of less than 5%.

Figure 4.3. **The number of PCI capable centres per million population**

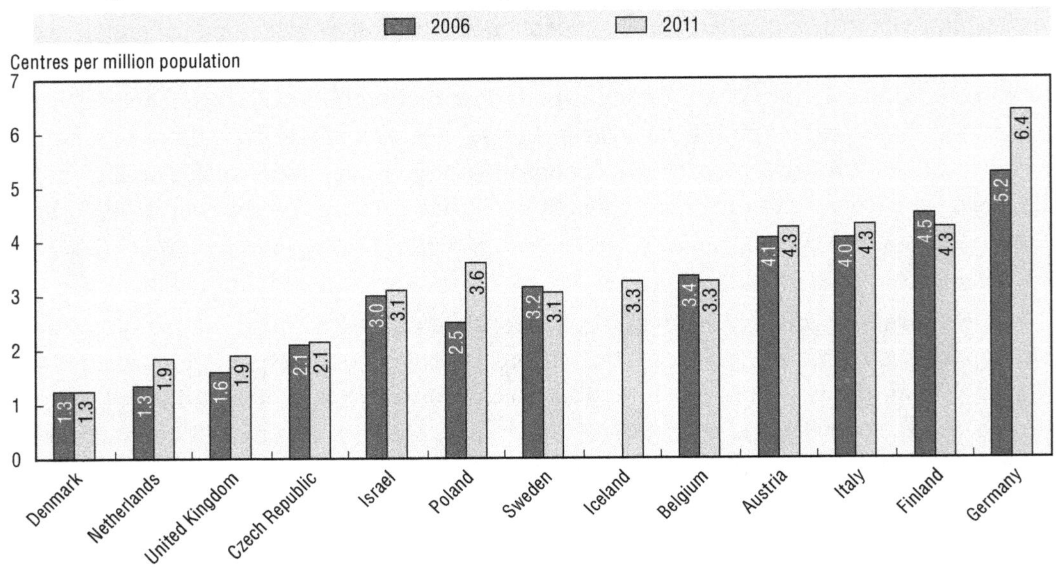

Source: Kristensen, S.D. et al. (2014), "Reperfusion Therapy for ST Elevation Acute Myocardial Infarction 2010/2011: Current Status in 37 ESC Countries", *European Heart Journal*, eht529; Widimsky, P. et al. (2010), "Reperfusion Therapy for ST Elevation Acute Myocardial Infarction in Europe: Description of the Current Situation in 30 Countries", *European Heart Journal*, Vol. 31, No. 8, pp. 943-957.

Though many health systems have aimed to provide widespread geographic access, there are important resource and staffing constraints that may restrict the expansion of PCI-capable centres. Importantly, there are also quality considerations. Evidence suggests that facilities with a low number of cases may provide less than optimum care (Steg et al., 2012; Jauch et al., 2013). With an increasing number of PCI-capable centres in a country, the number of procedures per centre may fall to a level where the quality of care could be compromised.

Whether or not low-volume centres should continue to perform primary PCI is controversial and suggests that countries face a delicate trade-off in their desire to expand PCI capabilities and at the same time ensure high-quality care. This is one of the motivating factors behind the establishment of national and regional PCI networks. Networks between primary and tertiary hospitals with good co-operation and clear care pathways can play an important role in delivering good access and high-quality care.

Certain regions have already shown that it is possible to achieve at least 75% of STEMI patients receiving reperfusion therapy within the shortest possible time, particularly through well-organised networks (Bassand et al., 2005). A programme in Minnesota demonstrated that a regional network of 30 hospitals located up to 300 kilometres away from a PCI-capable centre is not only feasible but also safe. In North Carolina a state-wide network was designed and implemented to overcome barriers that impede comprehensive and timely access to PCI. As part of this programme PCI-capable hospitals agreed to provide single-call catheterisation laboratory activation by emergency medical personnel, accept patients regardless of bed availability, and improve STEMI care for the entire region regardless of hospital affiliation (Jollis et al., 2007). Following implementation, median reperfusion times significantly improved from 165 to 128; although non-reperfusion rates were unchanged (15%) in non-PCI hospitals and decreased from 23% to 11% in the PCI hospitals.

The establishment of an overarching coronary network also provides opportunities to monitor quality and develop quality improvement programmes. The Ontario Cardiac Care Network, for example, works with hospitals to provide cardiac services. It develops strategies to improve management of cardiovascular disease including strategies to prevent acute hospital readmissions, decrease demand on emergency departments and decrease the need for initial and repeat procedures.

Hospital care resources

Specialised workforce

Aside from the financial resources, access to health care is also determined by its physical resources. The specialist workforce is an important indicator of availability of health care services, including interventional treatments. Figure 4.4 presents data on the number of cardiologists and neurologists involved in the treatment of coronary heart disease and stroke, respectively. The role and functions of the specialist workforce will vary by country, making it difficult to get a true sense of how comparable these numbers are. Nevertheless, the figures do provide some indication that there is widespread variation in workforce patterns across countries. Even countries with similar demographic, geographic and health system characteristics have widely varying numbers of specialists. For example, Norway has more than twice the number of cardiologists as Finland.

The specialist workforce increased substantially in OECD countries. For those countries that provided time series data, the total number of cardiologists and neurologists increased by 4.6% and 3.9% per year, respectively. Growth in the number of cardiologists was particularly high in Ireland (21% pa), the Czech Republic (9.1% pa) and Poland (8.8% pa). In Denmark and Iceland, though, the number of cardiologists remained virtually unchanged between 2005 and 2011. The number of neurologists increased substantially in Germany (8.5% pa), Korea (6.6% pa) and Norway (5.8% pa).

The increasing number of specialist staff in many countries indicates that, while the age-standardised incidence rates of some CVD may be falling, the absolute numbers will continue to grow. This is likely to place additional pressure on staff and other resources in years to come. In a number of other countries, the rise can also be explained by the perceived shortage of skills. In Ireland, for example, the national CVD policy plan explicitly links CVD workforce policy with the recommendations that are made for future service delivery models (DHC, 2010). While the data shown above relate to some aspects of the specialised CVD workforce, it is important to consider other clinical staff, including nurses, not just in terms of numbers, but also in terms of their functions in treating CVD.

Figure 4.4. **Specialist medical workforce, 2011 (or latest year)**

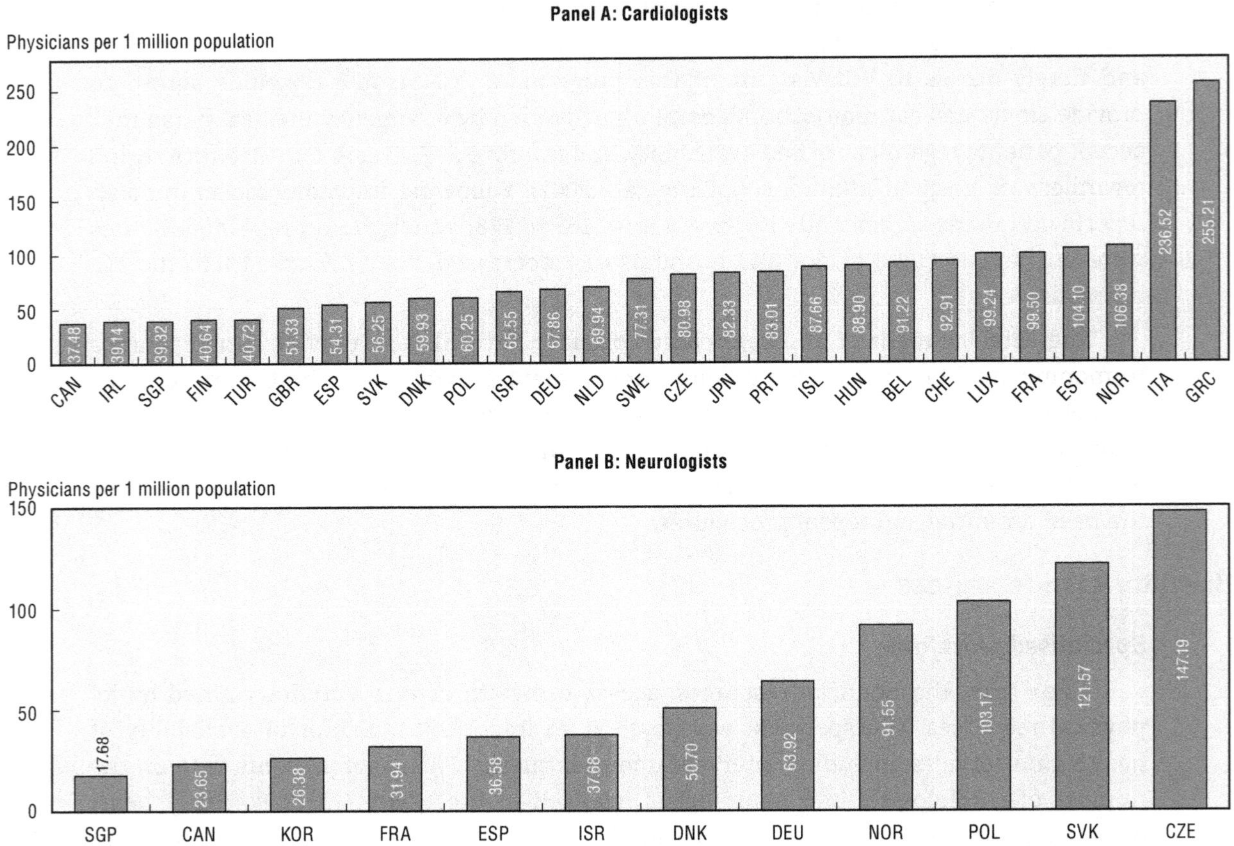

Source: Cardiologists: EUROSTAT, 2014 except Canada, Czech Republic, Denmark, France, Germany, Israel, Japan, Norway, Poland, Singapore, the Slovak Republic and Spain, OECD Cardiovascular Disease and Diabetes Health System Characteristics Survey, unpublished, 2014; Neurologists: OECD Cardiovascular Disease and Diabetes Health System Characteristics Survey, unpublished, 2014.

Expenditure

Figure 4.5 shows hospital expenditure on cardiovascular diseases across eight OECD countries. These estimates are part of the work on estimating expenditure by disease, age and gender under the System of Health Accounts (SHA) framework. The expenditure has been converted using the OECD's GDP PPP conversion and are reported in constant 2005 US dollars. Variation in hospital expenditure is extensive across countries, ranging from only USD PPP 30 in Israel to USD PPP 202 in Japan. For three countries, it is possible to examine expenditure by type of cardiovascular disease. In Sweden, heart failure accounts for the biggest proportion of hospital expenditure on cardiovascular disease whereas it accounts for a relatively small proportion in Canada and Korea. In Korea, cerebrovascular diseases (primarily stroke) accounts for the biggest proportion of in-hospital cardiovascular disease expenditure. The "others" category includes hypertensive disease, pulmonary heart disease and atheroscherosis.

Figure 4.6 presents information on per capita hospital expenditure relating to endocrine, nutritional and metabolic disease, which includes diabetes. For those where it is possible to isolate diabetes expenditure, the figure reveals that diabetes account for around 60% of endocrine, nutritional and metabolic disease expenditure, although this percentage is considerably lower in Sweden (35%). The pattern of expenditures across countries shows considerably similarity between cardiovascular disease and diabetes, reflecting not only that diabetes is a major risk factor for cardiovascular disease, but may also reflects the role and functions of hospitals in managing disease. Although expenditure has been converted using purchasing power parities, these conversion rates are based on the respective price levels of the entire economy (GDP) rather conversion rates than take specific health or hospital price levels into account. Hence, part of the cross-country variation observed in Figures 4.5 and 4.6 may also be reflect different in the prices paid for hospital care.

Figure 4.5. **Per capita hospital expenditure on cardiovascular diseases (USD PPP, 2005)**

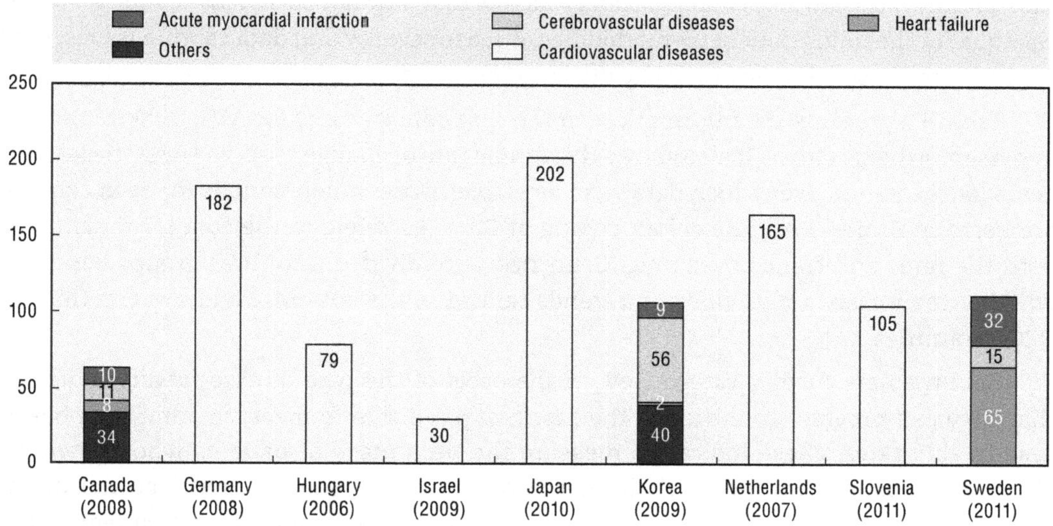

Note: Japan: OECD calculations using published data.

Source: *OECD Health Statistics 2013, http://dx.doi.org/10.1787/health-data-en.*

Figure 4.6. **Per capita hospital expenditure on endocrine, nutritional and metabolic disease (USD PPP, 2005)**

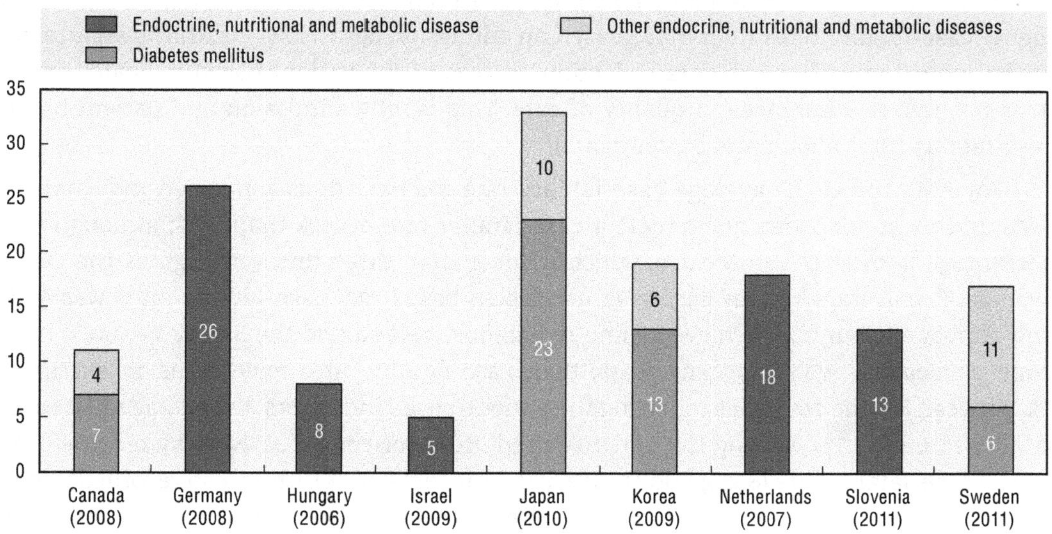

Note: Japan: OECD calculations using published data.

Source: *OECD Health Statistics 2013, http://dx.doi.org/10.1787/health-data-en.*

Better access and quality of care have improved survival after a heart attack and stroke

Results from the OECD's Health Care Quality Indicators (HCQI) project reveal that the acute care sector has performed well over the last ten years. Thirty day case-fatality rates for both AMI and stroke have fallen across the OECD as a whole, as well as in almost every single OECD country. Case-fatality rates reflect the percentage of patients who die within the 30 days following an admission to hospital for AMI, ischemic stroke and haemorrhagic stroke. These indicators reflect the processes of care, including timely transportation of patients and the use of medical interventions that are within the realm of health system control. While case-fatality rates can also be influenced by factors that may not be directly related to health care quality, including patient co-morbidities, disease severity and data capture issues, they are commonly used in many OECD health systems as a measure of acute care quality.

Table 4.2 presents the information on the case-fatality rates for AMI, ischemic stroke and haemorrhagic stroke. It also shows the annual rate of change observed over the last ten years (or the period over which data were available). Observation periods for each country are listed in Annex 4.A1. The colour coding of Table 4.2 refers to the country ranking for both the rates and trends over time. Countries were divided into three groups based on whether their case-fatality rates and trends ranked in the bottom, middle or top third of OECD countries.

Countries are further categorised on the basis of the type of case-fatality indicator that they can provide. Countries in the first group are able to measure admission-based case-fatality rates. These indicators measure the percentage of patients who die within 30 days of hospital admission if the death occurs in the same hospital as the initial admission. Countries in the second group provide the more comprehensive patient-based indicator; their case-fatality rates refer to the percentage of patients who die within 30 days of hospital admission, but the data capture a patient's death even if it occurs in another hospital or outside of hospital. The latter indicator is a preferred measure of acute care quality but requires more sophisticated data infrastructure to be able to track patients, which is a capacity not shared by all countries. Patient-based indicators typically return higher case-fatality rates than those based on admission data. However, this is an artefact of the more comprehensive data collection process of the patient-based indicator and it does not reflect differences in quality of care. This is why admission and patient-based case-fatality rates should not be compared.

For AMI, the OECD average case-fatality rate for the admission-based indicators is 8.8% and most countries now report a case-fatality rate of less than 10%; although this percentage is over 27% in Mexico, which is more than three times as high as the OECD average. The average rate of decline in admission-based AMI case-fatality rates was 4.9% and almost all countries achieved some reductions. Ireland and the Slovak Republic have done particularly well in recent years; their case-fatality rates have fallen in excess of 7% per year. For the countries reporting the patient-based indicators, the average AMI case-fatality rate is 11.1%. Among the patient-based indicator countries, Norway recorded the lowest case-fatality rate (8.2%) and Hungary the highest (18.8%). Chile also recorded a high case-fatality rate (13.8%) but the rate of decline between 2007 and 2010 in this country was an impressive 9.6%. The average rate of decline in patient-based countries was -4.2%.

For ischemic stroke, the average case-fatality rate is 8.7% for admission-based countries, which is very similar to the AMI average of 8.8%. Countries in the top third reported rates in excess of 9.8% and those in the bottom third had rates that were less than or equal to

6.8%. Almost all countries exhibited a negative trend, indicating that case-fatality rates are falling. The two exceptions were Iceland and Mexico, where the case-fatality rates for ischemic stroke have been increasing over recent years. For the countries reporting the patient-based indicators, the average ischemic stroke case-fatality rate was 11.9%, ranging from 5.4% in Korea to 22.4% in Latvia. The average annual rate of decline was 3.8% and all countries with patient-based indicators reported some falls in their case-fatality rates. The United Kingdom and Slovenia have been able to reduce their case-fatality rates by more than 8% in recent years.

For haemorrhagic stroke, case-fatality rates are much higher than for either AMI or ischemic stroke. Among the admission-based countries, rates averaged 22%, but these showed considerable variation. Countries such as Austria and Japan recorded rates lower than 15% and Belgium and Turkey reported case-fatality rates in excess of 30%. While most countries reported a decline in case-fatality rates, the falls were not as high as those reported for AMI or ischemic stroke. That said, there are some positive signs that the fall in case-fatality rates has accelerated since 2005 in a large number of countries. In Japan, case-fatality rates are relatively low (11.8%), but it reported a rise in case-fatality rates between 2008 and 2011. For countries with patient-based indicators, the average haemorrhagic stroke case-fatality rate was 30.1%, and ranged from 18.5% in Korea to 45.9% in Hungary. Case-fatality rates in Latvia were also very high (36.3%), but between 2008 and 2009 rates fell by 8.3%. The average rate of decline across countries was 2.4% (virtually identical to the average rate of decline for admission-based countries).

There are encouraging signs across most countries that case-fatality rates are falling, and that these are reflecting better access to high-quality acute care for patients. Nevertheless, the figures also provide some warning signs for countries with very high case-fatality rates or where the fall in rates over time is not as great as for their country peers, or, worse, where trends are showing a rise in case-fatality rates.

From onset to discharge: Full pathway monitoring and governance

This chapter has examined the individual aspects of what is needed to deliver highly effective acute care services: public awareness and first response capabilities, high functioning emergency response teams, adequate resources and access to specialised care and treatments. What is evident is that each of these aspects forms a chain that need to come together in order to optimise health care outcomes.

In Korea, the Health Insurance Review and Assessment Service's Value Incentive Program (VIP) provides a good example of a systematic programme to improve acute care quality. As part of its focus on AMI, the VIP benchmarks the relative improvements in performance of each of Korea's tertiary hospitals through collecting indicators such as timely reperfusion, adherence to medication recommendations (including medication upon discharge) and 30-day case-fatality. A composite indicator score is calculated from these measures, which is reported publicly. The programme carries a small financial incentive for high performing hospitals or improving hospitals as well as potential penalty for scoring less than a predetermined benchmark score. In 2009, a total of around KRW 250 million (around USD 250 000) was awarded to 26 hospital for the AMI incentive, but no penalties were applied (Kim et al., 2012). Although the VIP has only been evaluated on a before and after basis, the programme's implementation has coincided with an increase in the composite quality score achieved by hospitals. The more remarkable result, however, has been the decrease in variation in scores across hospitals. Scores among the poorly performing

Table 4.2. **Case-fatality rates and trends for AMI, ischemic and haemorrhagic stroke, 2011 (or nearest year)**

	AMI		Ischemic stroke		Haemorrhagic stroke	
	Case-fatality rate %	Annual % change	Case-fatality rate %	Annual % change	Case-fatality rate %	Annual % change
			Admission-based			
Australia	4.8	-6.9	10	-1.6	22.2	-1.5
Austria	7.7	-6.7	6	-3.6	14.4	-2.9
Belgium	7.6	-6.5	9.2	-1.4	30.5	-0.6
Canada	5.7	-5.3	9.7	-3.1	22.2	-3.1
France	6.2	-4.7	8.5	-4.3	24	-1.2
Germany	8.9	-3.6	6.7	-4.4	17.5	-3.7
Iceland	5.7	-4.3	7.4	6.7	16.7	-10.4
Ireland	6.8	-7.4	9.9	-3.4	26.2	-1.2
Italy	5.8	-4.4	6.5	-2.4	19.9	-0.5
Japan	12.2	-1.8	3	-1.1	11.8	0.9
Mexico	27.2	1.5	19.6	1.3	29.7	-1.6
Portugal	8.4	-5.5	10.5	-2.5	23.8	-0.6
Singapore	12.5	-1.5	7.6	-0.4	22	-1.5
Slovak Republic	7.6	-10.4	11	-4.8	28	-4.5
Switzerland	5.9	-6.3	7	-3.2	16.5	-3.8
Turkey	10.7		11.8		32	
United States	5.5	-4.4	4.3	-2.1	22.3	-2.2
			Patient-based			
Chile	13.8	-9.6	13.9	-2.9	29.9	-1.4
Czech Republic	11	-4.7	12.4	-3.9	32.5	-2.4
Denmark	9.6	-5.0	10.9	-1.5	33.2	-0.8
Finland	12.6	-3.4	10.3	-1.5	24.5	0.5
Hungary	18.8	-2.7	13.7	-2.1	45.9	-0.3
Israel	10.3	-3.3	8.9	-2.9	28.3	-1.8
Korea	11.2	-4.6	5.4	-4.9	18.5	-2.4
Latvia	17	-2.9	22.4	-3.0	36.3	-8.3
Luxembourg	11.9	-4.1	12.6	-0.7	23.3	-7.1
Netherlands	9.8	-5.0	10.3	-5.1	31.7	-2.3
New Zealand	8.4	-4.0	13.1	-1.3	34.7	-0.2
Norway	8.2	2.5	8.8	0.0	24.3	-1.2
Poland	8.9	-7.4				
Slovenia	10.5	-3.2	14.8	-8.6	34.4	-5.2
Spain	9	-4.4	10.4	-2.0	26.8	-1.1
Sweden	8.5	-4.5	9.8	-1.7	24	-1.3
United Kingdom	10	-5.9	12.4	-10.0	33.7	-1.4

Best third | Middle third | Worst third

Note: Trends reflect average annual growth rates over the observation period for which country data was available. Observation periods are shown in Annex 4.A1.

Source: OECD Health Statistics 2013, http://dx.doi.org/10.1787/health-data-en.

hospitals witnessed the biggest overall improvement, with almost all hospitals attaining a score higher than the benchmark that was set to indicate poor performance (Kim et al., 2012). Plans are afoot to expand the programme to a broader range of health sectors (including primary care) and diseases such a stroke. The VIP provides a good example of the potential for good measurement alongside strong governance to deliver better quality.

While acute care is an important focus of the quality improvement initiatives in Korea, the Korean Ministry of Health and Welfare also implemented a Comprehensive Plan for CVD that encompassed prevention and primary care as well as acute CVD care. One key policy initiative was the creation of regional cardio and cerebrovascular centres throughout the country not only to fund the upgrade of facilities and enhance specialised services but also to establish prevention and management centres to provide community education for early CVD signs/symptoms and form links with prevention and management programmes in local government (OECD, 2012).

Such moves are part of a wider movement to create stronger ties and governance over the full pathway of patient care, including a greater emphasis on indicators. Monitoring of hospital performance for stroke in France, for example, includes the date and time of onset of symptoms to the initial management of stroke, first-line imaging, medications and assessment by a professional rehabilitation during the initial management of stroke. These indicators incorporate aspects that are part of the pre- and post-hospital phases of an acute CVD event. Furthermore, there is a strong emphasis on process-related indicators (e.g. door-to-balloon times or use of medications) that are within the realm the of health care sector control.

The diagram below summarises some of the many initiatives that countries have used to deliver better CVD acute care for their patients. These initiatives provide an example of a full pathway starting at the onset of a patient's CVD event and incorporating first responders, emergency care, diagnosis, acute care treatment and rehabilitative services, and the return back home. Such a wider perspective of optimum care among policy makers and clinical managers could help identify potential weak links in the acute care chain as well as develop more comprehensive plans to improve health outcomes.

Figure 4.7. **Governance and performance measurement of the full pathway of CVD acute care**

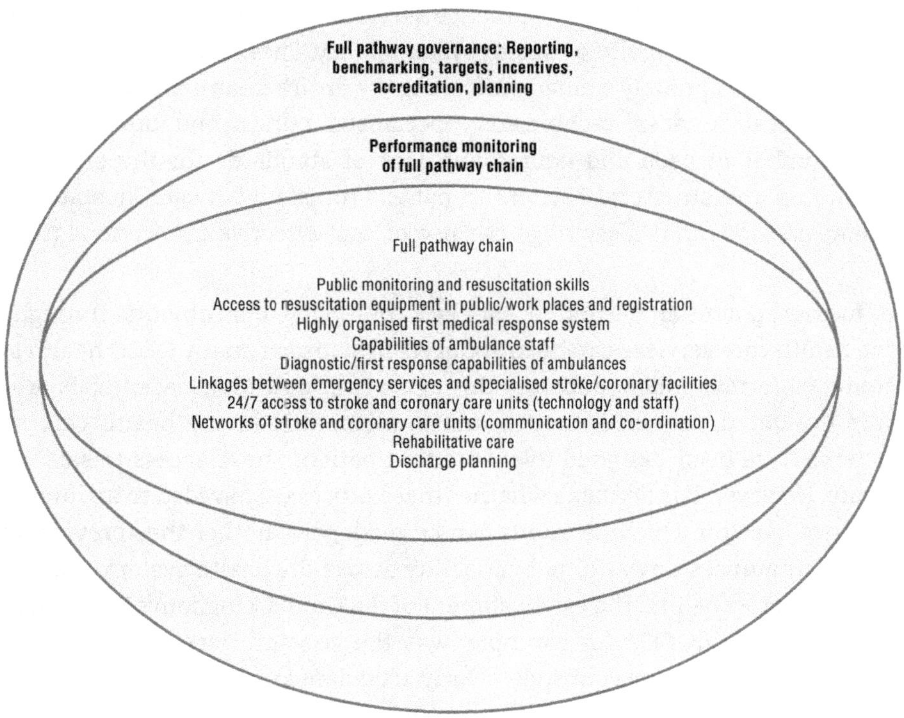

Summary

Despite the many advances in CVD prevention as described in Chapters 2 and 3, patients will continue to rely on their acute care facilities to deliver life-saving care. The pressure on hospitals to deliver high-quality care is unlikely to diminish in the near future. While incidence rates have been fairly stable, the rise in some risk factors including obesity, diabetes and ageing are likely to lead to rising numbers of acute care cases. Furthermore, the complexity of cases may also rise, with more patients suffering multiple morbidities that can have important bearings on the type and method of treatments.

The recommended care guidelines that have been published in recent years have challenged many acute care systems. Guidelines have set strict protocols around the timeliness of care, the type of care and the facilities in which care is provided. While many of these guidelines relate to the delivery of technological innovations, there are important health care service implications as well.

There is little doubt that many OECD countries have had difficulty in consistently implementing recommended care. The available data reveal substantial variations in the process of care, such as the timeliness of treatment, as well as access to specialised facilities like stroke units. In the field of CVD, there is a wealth of evidence that sub-optimal care processes have a real and long-lasting effect on patient outcomes.

Perhaps the most alarming aspect of these statistics is that the evidence on what constitutes good quality care has been in the public domain for well over 30 years. Health systems have now had more than three decades to implement the various changes needed to deliver high-quality care that is in line with the best available evidence. Despite substantial efforts, it is clear that some countries have been more successful than others in implementing much needed change in CVD acute care.

The delays in implementing best-practice services may be explained by a number of factors that are within the realm of health system policy. These factors include: shortages in the number of appropriately trained staff along the entire treatment pathway, including emergency medical services, technicians, specialised nurses and other related staff; insufficient number of beds and equipment; lack of standards for the organisation of systems; funding and structural barriers to patient transfers between hospitals/regions; and payment methods that discourage the use of cost-effective innovations (Laut et al., 2011).

One further potential barrier is the lack of policy instruments through which innovative health care services can be introduced. By contrast, many OECD health systems have introduced formal policy processes through which new pharmaceuticals or medical devices are evaluated, assessed, funded and implemented in the health care systems. These systems have been designed to ensure that patients have access to safe and cost-effective care. However, it is arguable whether these processes have led to an improvement in the evidence base on which decisions can be made, or whether they provide a unified structure that minimises unwarranted variability across the health system. Indeed, one of the motivating factors behind the establishment of the United Kingdom's National Institute of Clinical Excellence (NICE),[6] for example, was the concern over postcode prescribing (Cookson et al., 2001). In many countries, clearly articulated policy instruments are lacking when it comes to the introduction of new and innovative health care services, including acute care services.

Improvements in CVD acute care services have often been instigated at the regional level, frequently relying on local clinical leaders with the support of professional and patient groups. This reliance on local-level factors has resulted in many success stories, but may also help explain why there is such heterogeneity between and within countries in the diffusion of evidence-based acute health care services. This could potentially call for a stronger role for national governments in supporting the diffusion of best practices in acute CVD care. This could include the development of better indicators and information systems to capture performance along the full pathway of acute care performance, including pre-hospital, hospital and post-hospital care, which can be used to strengthen wider governance structures and create a culture of continuous quality of improvement from the patient's home to the hospital door, and back again.

Notes

1. Administration of a controlled electric shock to the heart to allow restoration of the normal rhythm.
2. Data from British Columbia.
3. HIQR: Hospital Inpatient Quality Reporting; ACTION-GWTG: Acute Coronary Treatment and Intervention Outcomes Registry–Get With The Guidelines.
4. Of the 19 OECD CVD/Diabetes Survey responses received, 12 responded that either door-to-balloon or door-to-needle times were part of their suite of hospital performance indicators.
5. See: *www.stentforlife.org for more details.*
6. Now called the National Institute for Health and Care Excellence.

References

Atwood, C. et al. (2005), "Incidence of EMS-treated Out-of-hospital Cardiac Arrest in Europe", *Resuscitation*, Vol. 67, No. 1, pp. 75-80.

Bagai, A. et al. (2013), "Emergency Department Bypass for ST-segment-elevation Myocardial Infarction Patients Identified with a Prehospital Electrocardiogram: A Report from the American Heart Association Mission: Lifeline Program", *Circulation*, Vol. 128, No. 4, pp. 352-359.

Bassand, J.P. et al. (2005), "Implementation of Reperfusion Therapy in Acute Myocardial Infarction. A Policy Statement from the European Society of Cardiology", *European Heart Journal*, Vol. 26, No. 24, pp. 2733-2741.

Berdowski, J. et al. (2010), "Global Incidences of Out-of-hospital Cardiac Arrest and Survival Rates: Systematic Review of 67 Prospective Studies", *Resuscitation*, Vol. 81, No. 11, pp. 1479-1487.

Bradley, E.H. et al. (2009), "National Efforts to Improve Door-to-Balloon Time Results from the Door-to-Balloon Alliance", *Journal of the American College of Cardiology*, Vol. 54, No. 25, pp. 2423-2429.

Concannon, T.W. et al. (2012), "A Percutaneous Coronary Intervention Lab in Every Hospital?", *Cardiovascular Quality and Outcomes*, Vol. 5, pp. 14-20.

Cookson, R., D. McDaid, D. and A. Maynard (2001), "Wrong SIGN, NICE Mess: Is National Guidance Distorting Allocation of Resources?", *British Medical Journal*, Vol. 323, No. 7315, p. 743.

Deb, S. et al. (2013), "Coronary Artery Bypass Graft Surgery vs Percutaneous Interventions in Coronary Revascularization: A Systematic Review", *Journal of the American Medical Association*, Vol. 310, No. 19, pp. 2086-2095.

DHC – Department of Health and Children (2010), *Changing Cardiovascular Health National Cardiovascular Health Policy 2010-2019*, Department of Health and Children, Dublin, *http://health.gov.ie/blog/publications/changing-cardiovascular-health-national-cardiovascular-health-policy-2010-2019/*.

EMS – Emergency Medical Services Division, (2013), *Annual Report to the King County Council*, Public Health, Seattle and King County, *www.kingcounty.gov/healthservices/health/ems.aspx*.

Epstein, A.J. et al. (2011), "Coronary Revascularization Trends in the United States, 2001-2008", *Journal of the American Medical Association*, Vol. 305, No. 17, pp. 1769-1776.

ESO – European Stroke Organisation (2008), "Guidelines for Management of Ischaemic Stroke and Transient Ischaemic Attack 2008", *Cerebrovascular Disease*, Vol. 25, pp. 457-507.

Fonarow, G.C. et al. (2011a), "Timeliness of Tissue-type Plasminogen Activator Therapy in Acute Ischemic Stroke: Patient Characteristics, Hospital Factors, and Outcomes Associated with Door-to-needle Times within 60 Minutes", *Circulation*, Vol. 123, pp. 750-758.

Fonarow, G.C. et al. (2011b), "Improving Door-to-needle Times in Acute Ischemic Stroke: The Design and Rationale for the American Heart Association/American Stroke Association's Target: Stroke Initiative", *Stroke*, Vol. 42, No. 10, pp. 2983-2989.

Fothergill, R.T. et al. (2013), "Increases in Survival from Out-of-hospital Cardiac Arrest: A Five Year Study", *Resuscitation*, Vol. 84, No. 8, pp. 1089-1092.

Gilligan, A.K. et al. (2005), "Stroke Units, Tissue Plasminogen Activator, Aspirin and Neuroprotection: Which Stroke Intervention Could Provide the Greatest Community Benefit?", *Cerebrovascular Disease*, Vol. 20, pp. 239-244.

Go, A.S. et al. (2013), "Heart Disease and Stroke Statistics 2013 Update: A Report from the American Heart Association", *Circulation*, Vol. 127, No. 1, p. e6.

Hacke, W. et al. (1998), "Thrombolysis in Acute Ischemic Stroke: Controlled Trials and Clinical Experience", *Neurology*, Vol. 53, No. 7, Suppl. 4, pp. S3-14.

Hasin, Y. et al. (2005), "Recommendations for the Structure, Organization, and Operation of Intensive Cardiac Care Units", *European Heart Journal*, Vol. 26, No. 16, pp. 1676-1682.

Henry, T. et al. (2007), "A Regional System to Provide Timely Access to Percutaneous Coronary Intervention for ST-elevation Myocardial Infarction", *Circulation*, Vol. 116, No. 7, pp. 721-728.

Hollenberg, J. et al. (2005), "Difference in Survival After Out-of-hospital Cardiac Arrest between the Two Largest Cities in Sweden: A Matter of Time?", *Journal of Internal Medicine*, Vol. 257, pp. 247-254.

Hölscher, T. et al. (2013), "Prehospital Stroke Diagnosis and Treatment in Ambulances and Helicopters – A Concept Paper", *American Journal of Emergency Medicine*, Vol. 31, No. 4, pp. 743-747.

Jauch, E.C. et al. (2013), "Guidelines for the Early Management of Patients with Acute Ischemic Stroke: A Guideline for Healthcare Professionals From the American Heart Association/American Stroke Association", *Stroke*, Vol. 44, No. 3, pp. 870-947.

Jaworski, R. et al. (2012), "Costs of Management of Patients with Coronary Artery Disease in Poland: The Multicenter RECENT Study", *Polish Archives of Internal Medicine*, Vol. 122, No. 12, pp. 599-607.

Jollis, J.G. et al. (2007), "Implementation of a Statewide System for Coronary Reperfusion for ST-segment Elevation Myocardial Infarction", *Journal of the American Medical Association*, Vol. 298, No. 20, pp. 2371-2380.

Karla, L. et al. (2005), *A Randomised Controlled Comparison of Alternative Strategies in Stroke Care*, York Publishing.

Kim, S.M. et al. (2012), "Korean National Health Insurance Value Incentive Program: Achievements and Future Directions", *Journal of Preventive Medicine and Public Health*, Vol. 45, No. 3, pp. 148-155.

Kjellström T. et al. (2007), "Declaration 2006 on European stroke strategies", *Cerebrovascular Disease*, Vol. 23, pp. 231–241.

Kramer, A.H. (2013), "Treatment of Haemorrhagic Stroke", *Stroke*, pp.78-102.

Kristensen, S.D. et al. (2014), "Reperfusion Therapy for ST Elevation Acute Myocardial Infarction 2010/2011: Current Status in 37 ESC Countries", *European Heart Journal*, eht529.

Krumholz, H.M. et al. (2008), "A Campaign to Improve the Timeliness of Primary Percutaneous Coronary Intervention Door-to-Balloon: An Alliance for Quality", *Journal of the American College of Cardiology: Cardiovascular Interventions*, Vol. 1, No. 1, pp. 97-104.

Langhorne, P. et al. (1993), "Do Stroke Units Save Lives?", *The Lancet*, Vol. 342, No. 8868, pp. 395-398.

Launois, R. et al. (2004), "Estimating the Cost-effectiveness of Stroke Units in France Compared with Conventional Care", *Stroke*, Vol. 35, No. 3, pp.770-775.

Laut, K.G. et al. (2013), "Determinants and Patterns of Utilization of Primary Percutaneous Coronary Intervention Across 12 European Countries: 2003-2008", *International Journal of Cardiology*, Vol. 168, No. 3, pp. 2745-2753.

Lees, K.R. et al.; ECASS, ATLANTIS, NINDS and EPITHET rt-PA Study Group (2010), "Time to Treatment with Intravenous Alteplase and Outcome in Stroke: An Updated Pooled Aanalysis of ECASS, ATLANTIS, NINDS, and EPITHET Trials", *The Lancet*, Vol. 375, pp. 1695-1703.

Leys, D. et al. (2007), "Facilities Available in European Hospitals Treating Stroke Patients", *Stroke*, Vol. 38, No. 11, pp. 2985-2991.

Lloyd-Jones, D. et al. (2010), "Heart Disease and Stroke Statistics – 2010 update. A Report from the American Heart Association", *Circulation*, Vol. 121, No. 7, pp. e46-e215.

Luepker, R.V. et al. (2000), "Effect of a Community Intervention on Patient Delay and Emergency Medical Service Use in Acute Coronary Heart Disease: The Rapid Early Action for Coronary Treatment (REACT) Trial", *Journal of the American Medical Association*, Vol. 284, pp. 60–67.

Malhotra, A. and R. Rakhit (2013), "Improving the UK's Performance on Survival After Cardiac Arrest", *British Medical Journal*, Vol. 347.

Marler, J.R. et al. (2000), "Early Stroke Treatment Associated with Better Outcome: The NINDS rt-PA Stroke Study", *Neurology*, Vol. 55, pp. 1649-1655.

Meretoja, A. et al. (2014), "Stroke Thrombolysis Save a Minute, Save a Day", *Stroke*, Vol. 45, No. 4, pp. 1053-1058.

Meretoja, A. et al. (2010), "Effectiveness of Primary and Comprehensive Stroke Centers: PERFECT Stroke: A Nationwide Observational Study from Finland", *Stroke*, Vol. 41, pp. 1102-1107.

Moodie, M. et al. (2006), "Economic Evaluation of Australian Stroke Services A Prospective, Multicenter Study Comparing Dedicated Stroke Units with Other Care Modalities", *Stroke*, Vol. 37, No. 11, pp. 2790-2795.

Neumar, R.W. et al. (2011), "Implementation Strategies for Improving Survival After Out-of-Hospital Cardiac Arrest in the United States Consensus Recommendations From the 2009 American Heart Association Cardiac Arrest Survival Summit", *Circulation*, Vol. 123, No. 24, pp. 2898-2910.

NINDS rt-PA Stroke Study Group. (1995), "Tissue Plasminogen Activator for Acute Ischemic Stroke", *New England Journal of Medicine*, Vol. 333, pp. 1581-1587.

OECD (2012), *OECD Reviews of Health Care Quality: Korea 2012: Raising Standards*, OECD Publishing, Paris, *http://dx.doi.org/10.1787/9789264173446-en*.

OECD (2005), *Health Technologies and Decision Making*, OECD Publishing, Paris, *http://dx.doi.org/10.1787/9789264016224-en*.

Perkins, G.D. and M.W. Cooke (2012), "Variability in Cardiac Arrest Survival: The NHS Ambulance Service Quality Indicators", *Emergency Medicine Journal*, Vol. 29, No. 1, pp. 3-5.

Rea, T.D. et al. (2010), "Resuscitation Outcomes Consortium Investigators. Predicting Survival After Out-of-hospital Cardiac Arrest: Role of the Utstein Data Elements", *Annals of Emergency Medicine*, Vol. 55, pp. 249-257.

Ringelstein, E.B. et al. (2013), "European Stroke Organisation Recommendations to Establish a Stroke Unit and Stroke Center", *Stroke*, Vol. 44, No. 3, pp. 828-840.

Saka, Ö. et al. (2009), "Cost-effectiveness of Stroke Unit Care Followed by Early Supported Discharge", *Stroke*, Vol. 40, No. 1, pp. 24-29.

Sasson, C. et al. (2010), "Predictors of Survival from Out-of-hospital Cardiac Arrest", *Circulation: Cardiovascular Quality and Outcomes*, Vol. 3, pp. 63-81.

Schwamm, L.H. et al. (2005), "Recommendations for the Establishment of Stroke Systems of Care Recommendations from the American Stroke Association's Task Force on the Development of Stroke Systems", *Circulation*, Vol. 111, No. 8, pp. 1078-1091.

Seenan, P., M. Long, M. and P. Langhorne (2007), "Stroke Units in their Natural Habitat Systematic Review of Observational Studies", *Stroke*, Vol. 38, No. 6, pp. 1886-1892.

Smith, E.E. et al.; Registry of the Canadian Stroke Network (RCSN); Stroke Outcome Research Canada (SORCan) Working Group (2010), "Do All Ischemic Stroke Subtypes Benefit from Organized Inpatient Stroke Care?", *Neurology*, Vol. 75, pp. 456-462.

Steg, P.G. et al. (2012), "ESC Guidelines for the Management of Acute Myocardial Infarction in Patients Presenting with ST-segment Elevation. The Task Force on the Management of ST-segment Elevation Acute Myocardial Infarction of the European Society of Cardiology (ESC)", *European Heart Journal*, Vol. 33, No. 20, pp. 2569-2619.

Tamis-Holland, J.E. and P. O'Gara (2014), "Highlights from the 2013 ACCF/AHA Guidelines for the Management of ST-elevation Myocardial Infarction and Beyond", *Clinical Cardiology*, Vol. 37, No. 4, pp. 252-259.

Wardlaw, J.M. et al. (2003), "Thrombolysis for Acute Ischaemic Stroke", *Cochrane Database Systematic Review*.

Weisfeldt, M.L. and S.J. Zieman (2007), "Advances in the Prevention and Treatment of Ccardiovascular Disease", *Health Affairs*, Vol. 26, No. 1, pp. 25-37.

Widimsky, P. and S.D. Kristensen (2012), "Stent for Life Initiative: Where Are We Standing and Where Are We Going?", *European Heart Journal: Acute Cardiovascular Care*, Vol. 1, No. 1, pp. 48-49.

Widimsky, P. et al. (2010), "Reperfusion Therapy for ST-elevation Acute Myocardial Infarction in Europe: Description of the Current Situation in 30 Countries", *European Heart Journal*, Vol. 31, No. 8, pp. 943-957.

Zhu, H.F. et al. (2009), "Impact of a Stroke Unit on Length of Hospital Stay and In-hospital Case Fatality", *Stroke*, Vol. 40, No. 1, pp. 18-23.

ANNEX 4.A1

Data coverage for case-fatality indicators

Table 4.A1.1. **Observation periods for AMI, ischemic and haemorrhagic stroke case-fatality data**

	AMI		Ischemic stroke		Haemorrhagic stroke	
	Rank (2011)	Trend	Rank (2011)	Trend	Rank (2011)	Trend
			Admission-based			
Australia	2011	2000-2011	2011	2000-2011	2011	2000-2011
Austria	2011	2001-2009	2011	2001-2011	2011	2001-2011
Belgium	2009	2000-2009	2009	2000-2009	2009	2000-2009
Canada	2011	2002-2011	2011	2002-2011	2011	2002-2011
France	2010	2005-2010	2010	2005-2010	2011	2005-2010
Germany	2011	2005-2011	2011	2005-2011	2011	2005-2011
Iceland	2011	2003-2011	2011	2003-2011	2011	2003-2011
Ireland	2011	2000-2011	2011	2000-2011	2011	2000-2011
Italy	2011	2001-2011	2011	2001-2011	2011	2001-2011
Japan	2011	2008-2011	2011	2008-2011	2011	2008-2011
Mexico	2011	2009-2011	2011	2009-2011	2013	2009-2011
Portugal	2011	2000-2011	2011	2000-2011	2011	2000-2011
Singapore	2011	2001-2011	2011	2001-2011	2011	2001-2011
Slovak Republic	2011	2007-2011	2011	2007-2011	2012	2007-2011
Switzerland	2010	2004-2010	2010	2004-2010	2012	2005-2010
Turkey	2012		2012		2012	
United States	2010	2000-2010	2010	2000-2010	2011	2000-2010
			Patient-based			
Chile	2010	2007-2010	2010	2007-2010	2011	2007-2010
Czech Republic	2011	2000-2011	2011	2000-2011	2011	2000-2011
Denmark	2011	2000-2011	2011	2000-2011	2011	2000-2011
Finland	2011	2005-2011	2011	2005-2011	2009	2005-2011
Hungary	2009	2004-2009	2009	2004-2009	2010	2004-2009
Israel	2010	2000-2010	2010	2000-2010	2011	2000-2010
Korea	2011	2004-2011	2011	2004-2011	2009	2004-2011
Latvia	2009	2008-2009	2009	2008-2009	2011	2008-2009
Luxembourg	2011	2002-2011	2011	2002-2011	2009	2002-2011
Netherlands	2010	2000-2010	2010	2000-2010	2011	2000-2010
New Zealand	2011	2000-2011	2011	2000-2011	2011	2000-2011
Norway	2011	2010-2011	2011	2010-2011	2009	2010-2011
Poland	2011	2004-2011				
Slovenia	2011	2009-2011	2011	2009-2011	2011	2009-2011
Spain	2011	2000-2011	2011	2000-2011	2009	2000-2011
Sweden	2011	2000-2011	2011	2000-2011	2009	2000-2011
United Kingdom	2011	2008-2011	2011	2008-2011	2011	2008-2011

Best third | Middle third | Worst third

Source: *OECD Health Statistics 2013, http://dx.doi.org/10.1787/health-data-en.*

Cardiovascular Disease and Diabetes
Policies for Better Health and Quality of Care

Chapter 5

Acute care cardiovascular disease: Examining hospital performance

This report has primarily focused on a descriptive analysis of how countries compare with respect to CVD outcomes and health care access, resources and quality. Chapter 5 seeks to develop a better understanding of how health system characteristics and policies can influence the relationship between the health system's inputs and outcomes. It presents the analytical results on how countries have performed in improving the quality of acute care by focusing on 30-day case-fatality rates for both heart attack and stroke. It examines the relationship between the deployment of health care resources such as financial resources and medical equipment and improvements in the quality of acute care. This analysis examines whether this relationship varies across countries. Importantly, it also looks at the role of specific health system characteristics and policies to determine their importance in explaining cross-country variation in the quality of CVD acute care.

The statistical data for Israel are supplied by and under the responsibility of the relevant Israeli authorities. The use of such data by the OECD is without prejudice to the status of the Golan Heights, East Jerusalem and Israeli settlements in the West Bank under the terms of international law.

Examining the links between hospital expenditure and quality

Thus far, this report has primarily focused on a descriptive analysis of how countries compare with respect to CVD outcomes and health care access, resources and quality. The key messages from this analysis are that: 1) countries have been able to reduce the mortality burden of cardiovascular disease (CVD); 2) there remains considerable variation between countries in terms of the overall burden of CVD, as well as the rate of decline that countries have been able to achieve; and 3) while the health care system's capacity to prevent, treat and manage CVD has improved, not all countries have been able to take full advantage of this enhanced capacity.

This chapter takes the next analytical step by investigating the relationship between the health care system and CVD outcomes. It seeks to develop a better understanding of how health system characteristics and policies can influence the relationship between the health system's inputs and outcomes. Its focus is on the performance of acute care in relation to heart attacks and stroke (Chapter 6 will focus on heart failure). In particular, the analysis will examine the contribution that acute care resources have made in improving the quality of CVD care. The analysis has three objectives:

- Explore the relationship between acute care inputs (hospital expenditure) and acute care quality, measured through 30-day case-fatality rates.
- Examine whether the relationship between inputs and quality differs across countries.
- Determine the role that health system characteristics play in explaining the relationship between acute care inputs and quality of care.

The working hypothesis in this chapter is that more inputs lead to better quality of care. With the focus on case-fatality rates, this would imply that greater hospital expenditure is associated with a fall in the percentage of patients who die within 30 days of an acute myocardial infarction (AMI) or stroke admission. A second hypothesis is that the relationship between inputs and quality is not the same across countries. The analysis will test whether some countries have been able to obtain greater quality improvements from additional hospital expenditure than others. This part of the analysis focuses on the within-country relationships between expenditure and quality by looking at country trends over time. Third, this chapter seeks to explain potential cross-country differences by exploring the role of health system characteristics. It will examine the extent to which the relationship between expenditure and quality across countries is influenced by: 1) access to health care; 2) the use of technologies; 3) payment mechanisms; and 4) quality measurement.

New opportunities to measure hospital performance

While there is an extensive body of work on hospital performance, this work is fairly narrow in its focus. The main analytical tools used in this literature have been Data Envelope Analysis (DEA) and Stochastic Frontier Analysis (SFA). Most of these studies examine the relationship between hospital inputs and outputs, but many do not incorporate issues of quality and health outcomes into their analysis (Hollingsworth, 2008). More recently, however, a small number of studies have started to look at performance more broadly by taking the quality of hospital care into account, using indicators such as post-treatment survival and re-admission rates (Street et al., 2010; Hvenegaard et al., 2011; Gutacker et al., 2011; Schreyögg et al., 2011). Projects such as EUROHOPE and the European Collaboration in Healthcare Optimisation (ECHO) Project, for example, have developed methods to measure hospital activity and quality at the institutional level across a number of countries (Häkkinen et al., 2013; see ECHO for more details). The inclusion of quality indicators is an important development in the evolution of hospital performance analysis; it allows policy makers to make a more holistic assessment of the impact of hospital-based reforms.

Despite the large volume of studies in this field, only a handful of papers have undertaken hospital performance analysis at the international level. Typically these studies look at hospital performance in only two or three countries at a time.[1] This is an important gap in knowledge, especially considering that international comparative analysis can provide a better understanding of the role of national health system characteristics in hospital performance.

To date, the major barrier to international analysis of hospital performance has been the lack of comparable data, particularly in relation to quality of care. However, since 2007, the OECD's Health Care Quality Indicators (HCQI) project has undertaken important work with respect to developing and standardising indicators to compare health care quality, including acute care. Of particular relevance to this analysis are the indicators relating to 30-day case-fatality rates.

The OECD HCQI project collects data on case-fatality rates that are directly relevant to the acute care of CVD. These indicators reflect the percentage of patients who die within the 30 days following an admission to hospital for AMI, ischemic stroke and haemorrhagic stroke. These indicators reflect the processes of care, including the timely transportation of patients and the use of medical interventions that are within the realm of health system control. That said, the indicator can also be influenced by factors that are not directly related to health care quality, including patient co-morbidities, disease severity, and data capture issues. Nevertheless, case-fatality rates are commonly used in many OECD health systems as an indicator of acute care quality, and have become a standard feature of international comparative analysis (e.g. OECD, 2013). All 34 OECD member countries contribute to the HCQI data collection and almost all have been able to supply information on the CVD case-fatality indicators, dating back as far as 2000.

In addition, the OECD's Health System Characteristics (HSC) and CVD and Diabetes Surveys provide information on some of the main institutional features of OECD health systems. The surveys include information on the type of payment mechanisms and performance management systems which are in place across countries. Alongside this data sits the existing OECD Health Statistics, which offers longitudinal data on health system resources, health care use and outcomes, updated every year.

Measuring hospital performance

The analysis in this chapter is based on multi-level modelling econometric techniques. Such models are commonly used in quantitative analysis, particularly when the data involve units at different "levels" of observation. For example, it is frequently used in education analysis and health services research. At a micro-level, its strength lies in its ability to simultaneously examine the role of, for example, patient-level factors (e.g. socio-economic status of the patient) and hospital-level factors (e.g. number of nurses) on hospital performance. Multi-level modelling can also be used at a more aggregated level when there are repeated observations over time for multiple countries. Analysis of this type of data can help disentangle "within effects" (variations over time) and "between effects" (variation between countries). This is the nature of the data used in the current analysis.

The analysis looks at the relationship between health care inputs (hospital expenditure) and the quality of acute care, measured in terms of 30-day case-fatality rates. The empirical framework is based on the approach used by Or et al. (2005), who used the repeated observations over time for each country to estimate multi-level models. Or et al. (2005) examined the relationship between doctor numbers and a range of health-related outcomes consisting of life expectancy, infant mortality and potential years of life lost. Their analysis was based on data observed between 1970 and 1998. For a more detailed discussion of the empirical framework, please refer to Annex 5.A1 of this chapter.

Alternative econometric approaches are feasible, but there are some salient features of the multi-level approach that make it an appealing option for this analysis. The first of these features is that it provides an efficient way to determine whether the relationship between health care inputs and quality varies across countries. The model not only estimates the average relationship across countries but also the extent to which the relationship deviates from the average for individual countries. These estimates can then be used to determine whether such country-specific deviations are statistically important. The second important feature of multi-level models is that they allow further exploration of the country-level characteristics that may help explain why the relationship between inputs and quality deviates for some countries. The characteristics that will be used to help explain cross-country variation relate aspects of the health system to each other, such as access to technology, funding arrangements, equity, payment systems and quality measurement.

Dependent variables

To assess the relationship between health care inputs and hospital quality, three different dependent variables will be used in the analysis: 30-day case-fatality rates for 1) AMI; 2) ischemic stroke; and 3) haemorrhagic stroke. Separate models will be estimated for males and females. All case-fatality rates have been age standardised to reflect the 2010 OECD population aged 45 and older who have been admitted to hospital for AMI or stroke, depending on the indicator.

The analysis will use admission-based case-fatality rates. These data refer to the percentage of patients who die of any cause within 30 days of being admitted to hospital for one of the conditions of interest (AMI, ischemic or haemorrhagic stroke). The indicator only captures deaths that occur within the same hospital in which the initial admission took place.[2] Data for these indicators are widely available, with 34 and 33 countries reporting the AMI and stroke case-fatality rates, respectively. The first available year these indicators were collected as part of the OECD HCQI project was 2000 and some countries now report a maximum of 13 observations. On average, countries report just over eight observations. The observation period for this analysis is between 2000 and 2012, although most countries have thus far reported data up to 2011. While 30-day case-fatality rates reflect the quality of care including timely transport of patients and effective medical interventions, the indicator is also influenced by non-quality factors such as hospital transfers, coding practices and disease severity. However, these limitations are negated to a considerable extend in this empirical approach if the non-quality influences are reasonably stable within a country over the observation period.

Explanatory variables: Health care input

The analysis will explore the relationship between case-fatality rates and two types of health care inputs measured in terms of hospital expenditure. Financial resources are a key input into the production of *health care* which, in turn, is a factor in the production of *health*. These data are derived from OECD Health Statistics under the Systems of Health Accounts (SHA). Hospital-level expenditures are reported by 32 countries and collected on an annual basis. The data used in the analysis are based on per capita expenditure and have been converted using 2005 purchasing power parities (PPP) rates with US dollars as the reference currency.[3]

However, it should be noted that expenditure data are a broad measure of hospital resources and do not reflect the amount of hospital resources directed towards CVD care. Hence, these explanatory variables should be interpreted as indicators of hospital resources rather than CVD resources.

Explanatory variables: Control (time-varying)

A number of variables will be used in the analysis to control for factors that are outside the realm of hospital control but may impact on hospital quality. Given the strong relationship between socio-economic status and health, per capita GDP is used to account for the income effect that may influence quality of care. Lifestyle factors may also be a determinant of hospital quality. For example, patients in some countries may, on average, have worse lifestyles that diminish their chances of survival. However, such factors are outside of the control of the acute hospital sector and therefore their influence on case-fatality rates would not reflect the quality of care provided to inpatients. To help account for this, the percentage of adults who smoke daily and the percentage of the adult population who are obese are included in the model.

OECD Health Statistics reports two types of obesity indicators. The first indicator is the percentage of people who are measured as obese (e.g. by asking respondents to weigh themselves in the presence of the survey administrator). The second obesity indicator is based on the self-reported weight and height of the respondent. The analysis uses measured obesity data when available. For countries that do not provide measured data, self-reported data is used. Typically, self-reported data shows considerably lower levels of obesity than measured data. To account for systematic differences between the two measures, a variable is used to indicate which obesity indicator is added to the models.

The average length of hospital stay is also added to the model because it is an important statistical determinant of case-fatality rates. In effect, in countries where patients tend to spend more days in hospital, the chances of a death being recorded in hospital are higher than in countries with shorter lengths of stay. However, this may just be an artefact of how the data are collected because deaths that occur outside of hospital are not captured in this indicator.[4] It is also unclear whether longer lengths of stay reflect sicker patients or whether they reflect institutional characteristics such as financial (dis)incentives to discharge patients later. The length of stay is therefore an important control variable, but its direct relevance to assessing hospital performance is limited.

Health system characteristics (non-time varying)

The analysis will use a number of health system characteristics to help explain the relationship between hospital expenditure and hospital quality. A number of variables have been selected to proxy the characteristics, such as health care access, technology use, payment systems and quality performance policy. More specifically, the percentage of health care funded by public sources is used as a proxy for access. The use of diagnostic machines such as computed tomography (CT) and magnetic resonance imaging (MRI) scanners is included to indicate access to sophisticated technology. Although both technologies have wider applications, they are used in the diagnosis of CVD. Hospital payment mechanism will be proxied by whether or not a country uses global budgets to pay for hospital care. Quality performance is indicated by whether hospital performance is measured in a country.

One restriction of the multi-level approach is that the selected health system characteristic variables cannot vary over time. That is, each health system characteristic must remain consistent over the entire observation period for each country. This restriction has some important implications. First, variables such as the use of technology do clearly vary over time, but only the average use within a country over the observation period was incorporated into the model. Second, the restriction does not allow for important policy changes that may have occurred during the observation period. In other words, the model assumes that variables such as hospital payment systems and measurement of hospital performance were consistent throughout the observation period.

All variables, except the dummy variables, were transformed into their log values. The key independent variable of interest (hospital expenditure) and continuous health system characteristic variables were centred on the overall OECD mean. The Stata 13 software package was used for all analysis and models were estimated using a maximum likelihood approach.

Performance is linked to resources but some countries derive more quality for money

Descriptive results

Table 5.1 presents the descriptive statistics for all dependent and independent variables used in the models for selected years, along with a brief description of each variable and its data source. The statistics shown are the mean and standard error of the mean across countries, as well as the number of countries reporting the data. While the majority of variables are sourced from OECD Health Statistics, this dataset has been supplemented with important economic data from the OECD Social Protection and Wellbeing and National Accounts databases. In addition, the OECD's Health System Characteristics and CVD/Diabetes surveys have been used to derive information on hospital payment systems and the measurement of hospital performance.

An important observation is that the number of countries reporting data is limited in any given year. For example, while most OECD countries have reported case-fatality rates at some point in time, some substantial gaps in the data remain because not all countries have reported these data for all years. This was particularly true for the earlier years of the observation period. The implication is that, in the regression analysis, the number of observations will fluctuate depending on the availability of each variable. The low number of observations restricts the analytical possibilities. In particular, it will not be possible to examine the role of multiple health system characteristics within the same model. Instead, the analysis will examine the role of such characteristics one at a time.

Table 5.1. **Variable definitions, descriptive statistics (selected years) and data sources**

	Definition	2001			2006			2011			Source
		Mean	Std.dev	Observ.	Mean	Std.dev	Observ.	Mean	Std.dev	Observ.	
AMI_fem	30-day AMI case-fatality females (age std)	11.96	2.88	16	8.90	2.51	24	8.42	5.87	24	1
Isc_stroke_fem	30-day ischemic stroke case-fatality females (age std)	10.16	3.08	16	8.96	2.55	23	8.85	3.59	23	1
Hem_stroke_fem	30-day haemorrhagic stroke case-fatality females (age std)	25.94	6.08	16	25.09	6.35	23	21.87	6.35	23	1
AMI_male	30-day AMI case-fatality males (age std)	10.81	2.29	16	8.93	2.83	24	7.61	4.16	24	1
Isc_stroke_male	30-day ischemic stroke case-fatality males (age std)	9.46	3.04	16	8.23	2.60	23	8.03	3.91	23	1
Hem_stroke_male	30-day haemorrhagic stroke case-fatality males (age std)	24.62	5.35	16	22.95	7.08	23	19.95	5.45	23	1
GDP	GDP per capita (US PPP)	24158	9579	34	31190	12770	34	35508	14365	34	2
Smok15_fem	% females age 15 and over smoke daily	19.52	6.33	32	17.85	5.81	34	14.01	3.91	15	1
Smok15_male	% males age 15 and over smoke daily	32.34	8.82	32	29.05	8.40	34	23.98	8.83	15	1
Obese_fem	% females obese	14.05	7.09	29	16.16	7.84	34	18.43	10.03	14	1
Obese_male	% males obese	13.28	5.81	29	15.46	6.67	34	18.23	8.80	14	1
ALOS_circ	Average length of hospital stay (circulatory disease - days)	8.94	2.74	29	8.63	2.77	31	10.40	5.32	20	1
He_hosp	Hospital expenditure per capita (US PPP)	804	422	23	934	449	29	1020	470	25	1
CT_scan	CT exams per 1000 population	100	55	3	112	50	11	143	78	17	1
MRI_scan	MRI exams per 1000 population	32.87	29.86	3	37.52	24.11	11	54.72	27.24	17	1
HE_public	% of health expenditure publicly funded	0.72	0.11	30	0.71	0.12	33	0.73	0.10	28	1
Gini	Gini coefficient[1]	0.32	0.07	29	0.32	0.06	34				3
Hosp_GB	Countries that pay hospitals with global budgets (yes = 1)	0.41	0.50	34	0.41	0.50	34	0.41	0.50	34	4
Hosp_perf	Countries that measure hospital performance (yes =1)	0.72	0.46	32	0.72	0.46	32	0.72	0.46	32	4

Note: The Gini coefficient is measure of inequality of income or wealth. A Gini coefficient of zero expresses perfect equality, where all individuals (households) have equal income. A Gini coefficient of one expresses maximal inequality where only one person (household) has all the income within a country. The Gini coefficient used in this analysis is for the population measured after the transfer of taxes and government benefits.

Source: 1) OECD Health Statistics 2013, *http://dx.doi.org/10.1787/health-data-en.*; 2) OECD Social Protection and Well-Being Statistics, 2013; 3) OECD National Account Statistics, 2013; 4) OECD Health Systems Characteristics Survey 2012 and CVD/Diabetes Surveys 2014.

Analytical results part 1: Higher spending is related to better quality

Table 5.2 presents the results on the average relationship between health care inputs and the three case-fatality indicators described above. Separate models are estimated for males and females. In most models hospital care expenditure is negatively related to 30-day case-fatality rates. This indicates that, on average, greater health care inputs are associated with improved quality of care. For both genders, the relationship becomes statistically significant for AMI and ischemic stroke case-fatality rates. For haemorrhagic stroke, however, the relationship between expenditure and case fatality is not significantly different from zero for either females or males.

Table 5.2. **Regression results: Case-fatality rates by gender**

VARIABLES (log)	Females AMI	Females Isch_stroke	Females Hem_stroke	Males AMI	Males Isch_stroke	Males Hem_stroke
HE_hosp	-0.37***	-0.61***	0.01	-0.52***	-0.69***	-0.05
	(0.14)	(0.16)	(0.09)	(0.17)	(0.17)	(0.10)
GDP	-0.72***	-0.09	-0.42***	-0.78***	-0.60***	-0.19*
	(0.12)	(0.12)	(0.09)	(0.13)	(0.14)	(0.10)
Smok15_fem/male	0.28***	0.34***	0.26***	0.08	-0.13	0.76***
	(0.11)	(0.11)	(0.08)	(0.14)	(0.15)	(0.13)
Obese_fem/male	-0.17	0.19*	-0.00	-0.06	0.29**	0.16*
	(0.11)	(0.10)	(0.08)	(0.13)	(0.13)	(0.09)
Obese_selfreport	-0.09	0.02	-0.11	-0.07	0.10	-0.07
	(0.08)	(0.08)	(0.07)	(0.08)	(0.08)	(0.07)
ALOS_circ	0.34***	-0.14	-0.22***	0.35***	-0.03	-0.32***
	(0.11)	(0.11)	(0.08)	(0.12)	(0.11)	(0.08)
Constant	8.63***	1.98	7.40***	9.39***	8.02***	2.96**
	(1.40)	(1.41)	(1.14)	(1.63)	(1.71)	(1.35)
Observations	177	171	170	177	171	170
Number of groups	26	25	25	26	25	25

Note: Standard errors in parentheses; *** $p < 0.01$, ** $p < 0.05$, * $p < 0.10$; random slope and intercept models.

All models are expressed in log-log form, which means that coefficients are expressed in percentage terms. For example, a 1% *increase* in health expenditure is associated with an approximate 0.37% and 0.52% *decrease* in the female and male AMI 30-day case fatality, respectively. The decrease is because of the negative sign in front of the coefficient. Health expenditure is even more strongly related to ischemic stroke, with a 1% increase in expenditure associated with a 0.61% drop for female case fatalities and a 0.69% drop for males.

Higher income countries generally had lower case-fatality rates, although this relationship was only weakly significant in one model (haemorrhagic stroke males) and not at all significant for the female ischemic stroke model. Obesity was associated with greater case-fatality rates in most models, although this indicator was not statistically significant in the case of AMI or ischemic stroke in females or males. Smoking was associated with higher case-fatality rates in the models where it was statistically significant. In the other models, smoking was not significantly different from zero (no relationship). A longer average length of stay was significant in a number of models and justifies the inclusion of this variable in the analysis. However, as previously mentioned, the resultant coefficient has limited interpretability.

Analytical results part 2: The relationship between spending and quality differs by country

Having established that hospital expenditure plays a significant role in inpatient AMI and ischemic stroke care, the next step is to test whether this relationship varies across countries. To do this, two models were estimated and tested: one model with only random country intercepts, and the other with random country intercepts and random country slopes. This concept is shown diagrammatically in Figure 5.1.

Panel A of Figure 5.1 shows a model with a country-specific intercept, estimated on the basis of each country's residuals after estimating the model. Line A`A represents the overall OECD relationship between hospital expenditure and case-fatality rates. As revealed in the first result section of this chapter, this relationship is found to be negative, indicating that, on average, when hospital expenditure rises, case fatality falls. The random intercept model, shown in Panel A, estimates a country-specific error term U_0 for each country, j in the sample. Hence, each country has its own estimated intercept indicated by line B`B and C`C. The size and sign of U_0 indicates how far the country-specific intercept deviates from the overall intercept, which is given by the model's estimated constant. As the hospital expenditure variable has been centred, the constant represents the case-fatality rate (in log form) when hospital expenditure is at the cross-country average. Note that the slope of country "B" and "C" are the same as the OECD slope, "A". This indicates that the relationship between expenditure case-fatality rates is assumed to be fixed across countries.

Panel B illustrates a model where the assumption of a fixed relationship between expenditure and case fatality across countries is relaxed. In addition to random intercepts (as per Panel A), the model now also estimates a random slope component, U_1, for each country, j. This random component indicates the extent to which the relationship between expenditure and quality for country, j, deviates from the OECD average. In the diagram shown, the U_1 estimated for country B would be negative, which indicates that the relationship between expenditure and case fatality has a steeper slope than the overall OECD average slope (A`A). The interpretation is that country B has been able to extract greater benefits, in terms of its case-fatality rates, from each additional amount of hospital expenditure, compared to the OECD average. The U_1 for country C, however, would be positive, indicating that its slope is not as steep as the OECD average. For country C, the result would indicate that, compared to the OECD average, it has extracted fewer greater benefits, in terms of its case-fatality rates, from each additional amount of hospital expenditure.

Figure 5.1. **Cross-country variation in the relationship between expenditure and quality: A hypothetical example**

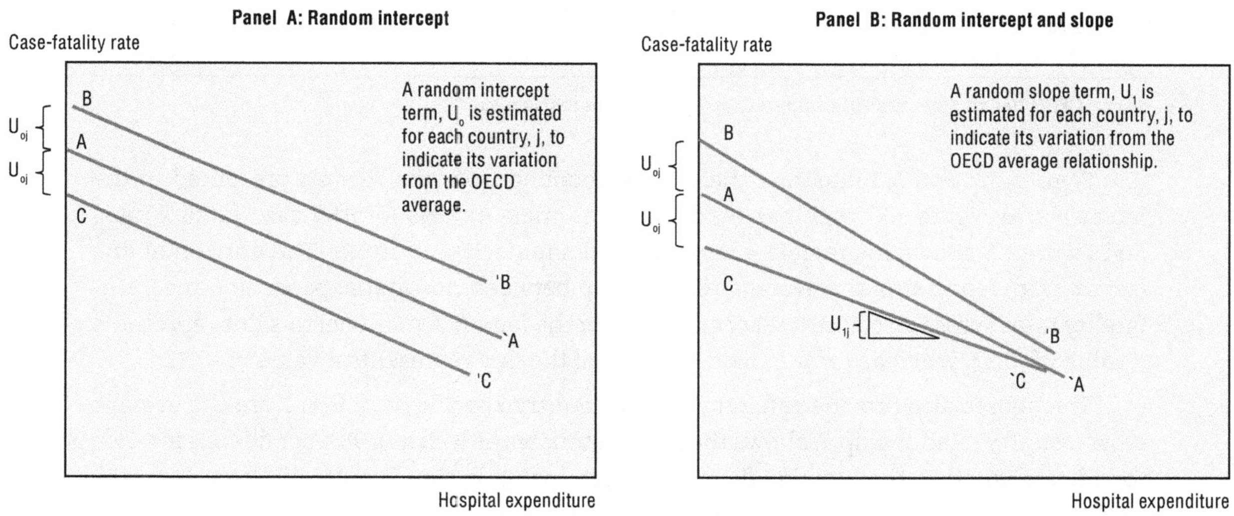

This part of the analysis tests whether allowing country slopes to vary in the models (Panel B) improves the fit of the model when compared to just random intercepts (Panel A). This is done formally on the basis of a likelihood ratio test. Table 5.3 reports the results of this test, along with the 95% confidence interval for the hospital expenditure coefficient and the covariance between the random country intercepts and random country slopes. Results are only shown for the AMI and ischemic stroke models, as the hospital expenditure coefficient for the haemorrhagic stroke models failed to reach conventional levels of statistical significance.

The p-values for the likelihood ratio test are presented in the first row. The values indicate that the relationship between hospital expenditure and acute care CVD quality differs between countries. This evidence is strong with respect to the ischemic stroke models as well as the AMI model for males. Evidence on country differences for female AMI case-fatality rates is weaker. Table 5.3 also presents the 95% confidence interval for hospital expenditure coefficient. For the female AMI model, the interval suggests that for 95% of countries the relationship between hospital expenditure and case fatality is between -1.013 and 0.273. This implies that, for countries on the lower bound, every 1% increase in hospital expenditure is associated with a 1.013% fall in the female AMI case-fatality rate. Importantly, the upper bounds for all models exhibit positive values, indicating that for a small number of countries additional hospital expenditure is not associated with improved quality. The last row in Table 5.3 shows the degree of covariance between the two random components of the model: country intercepts and hospital expenditure. Across all models, the covariance between the random terms takes on a negative value which suggests that differences between countries in case-fatality rates diminish as hospital expenditure rises (as is drawn in Figure 5.1, Panel B).

Table 5.3. **Testing for country differences in the relationship between hospital expenditure and CVD quality**

	Females		Males	
	AMI	Isch_ stroke	AMI	Isch_ stroke
Likelihood ratio test (p-value)	0.060	0.009	0.005	0.001
HE_hosp coefficient (from Table 5.2)	-0.37	-0.61	-0.52	-0.69
95% confidence interval of HE_hosp coefficient:				
lower bound	-1.013	-1.528	-1.604	-1.745
upper bound	0.273	0.308	0.564	0.365
Covariance (HE_hosp; country intercept)	-0.044	-0.055	-0.132	-0.161

Source: OECD Health Statistics 2013, *http://dx.doi.org/10.1787/health-data-en*.

Figures 5.2 and 5.3 illustrate the results obtained from the models presented in the tables above. Figure 5.2 combines the female and male models for AMI case-fatality rates and Figure 5.3 shows the female and male results for ischemic stroke. The horizontal line (set at zero) represents the average relationship between hospital expenditure and case-fatality rates across all countries. For example, for the female AMI model this line represents a value of -0.37, whereas for the male AMI model the line represents a value of -0.52.

The figures also provide estimates of the country-specific deviation from the average cross-country relationship. It shows the point estimates as well as a 95% confidence interval to indicate whether the individual country relationship is significantly different from the OECD average relationship. The interpretation of this is quite specific. For countries that are above the central OECD line, any additional hospital expenditure has had a relatively lower impact on quality than the OECD average. It implies a lower performance than the OECD average. Importantly, being above the line does not automatically imply that higher expenditures are associated with worse quality. It only implies that, for these countries, higher expenditure has not led to the same degree of quality improvement compared to the OECD average. For countries below the OECD line, additional health expenditures have resulted in better than average improvements in the quality of CVD acute care. These countries have witnessed a better than average improvement in case-fatality rates for every unit of additional expenditure put into the hospital system.

Figure 5.2 shows, that for the majority of countries, the relationship between expenditure and case fatality is not statistically different from the OECD average. In terms of female AMI case-fatality rates and hospital expenditure, performance in Finland and Poland is lower than the OECD average, whereas Denmark has a significantly better than average performance. For males, Finland and Poland are joined by Spain and Chile in the lower than average performance, whereas Luxembourg joins Denmark in the better than average performance ledger.

Figure 5.2. **Country-specific relationships between health expenditure and AMI case fatality**

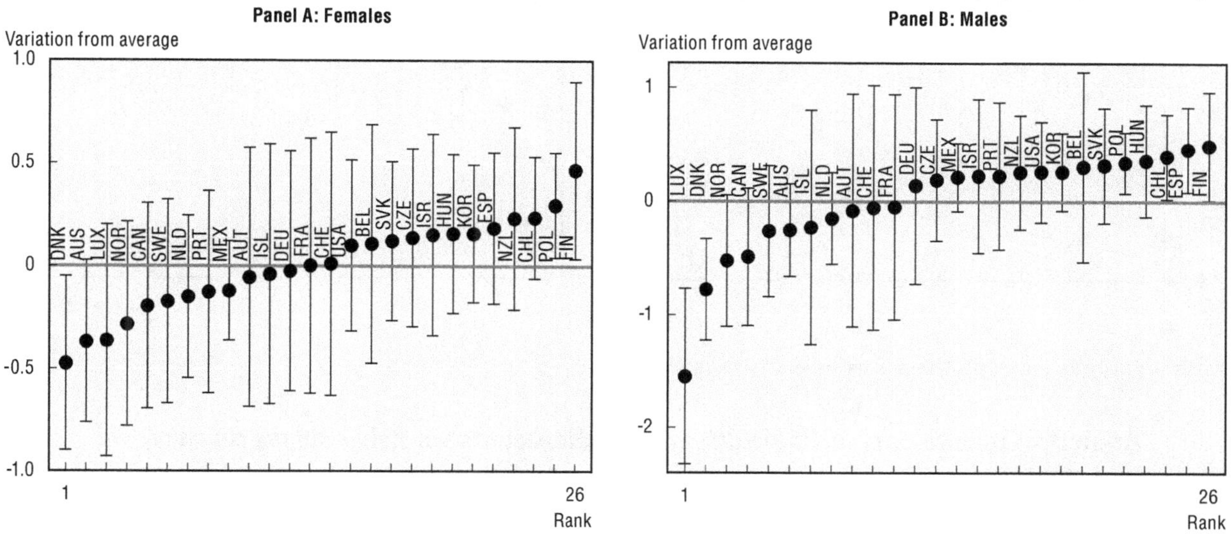

Source: OECD Health Statistics 2013, *http://dx.doi.org/10.1787/health-data-en.*

Figure 5.3 presents the country-specific estimates on the relationship between hospital expenditure and the 30-day case-fatality rates for ischemic stroke. The strongest estimated performances were found in the Netherlands for both males and females. For male case-fatality rates, performance was also significantly better than average for Luxembourg and Norway. Less than average performances were estimated for Chile, Hungary, Mexico and Israel. The figure also shows that there is slightly more variation across countries for males than females. The 95% confidence interval encompassed the OECD average for 20 out of 25 countries in the case of female ischemic case fatalities, whereas, for males, country performance was not significantly different to the OECD average for 16 countries. A similar pattern can be observed for AMI case-fatality rates.

The results from Figures 5.2 and 5.3 are summarised in Table 5.4. The table indicates that there is a substantial degree of consistency in country rankings across all models. The numbers in the boxes refer to the country ranking, with lower numbers representing better performing countries. The shading of the cells indicates the statistical significance of the results. Countries such as Denmark, Luxembourg and Norway consistently rank in the top five of high performing countries. For a few countries, there is considerable variation in performance depending on which indicators are used. For example, Australia's performance ranks highly in terms of AMI case fatality but is low for ischemic stroke. For New Zealand, the opposite result is shown with a relatively good performance in stroke quality but a lower ranking recorded for AMI. It should be noted, however, that the estimated relationships between expenditure and quality are not significantly different from the OECD average for either Australia or New Zealand.[5]

Figure 5.3. **Country-specific relationships between health expenditure and ischemic stroke case fatality**

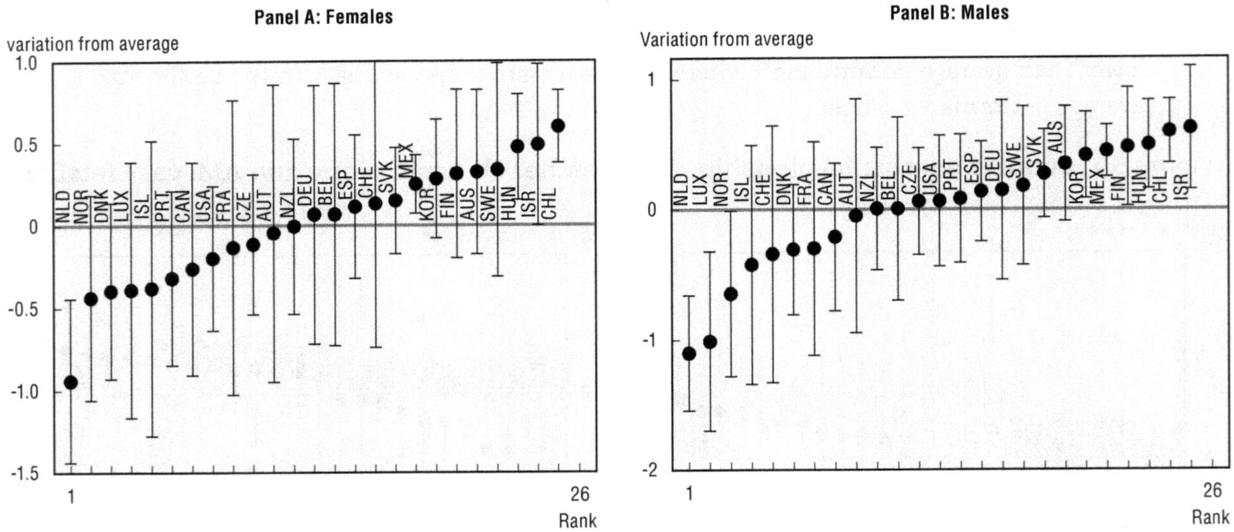

Source: *OECD Health Statistics 2013, http://dx.doi.org/10.1787/health-data-en.*

Analytical results part 3: Do health system characteristics help explain country performance?

In this final stage of the analysis, attention turns to exploring whether health system characteristics can help explain the relationship between hospital expenditure and acute care quality for CVD. In essence, this part of the analysis explores whether certain health system characteristics are associated with better or worse performance when it comes to the relationship between expenditure and quality. The analysis is necessarily exploratory and its results should be regarded as an initial investigation into potential drivers of performance.

The analysis builds on the previously reported results and introduces a set of health system characteristic variables into the model. These variables are brought into interaction with hospital expenditure. Figure 5.4 illustrates the concept of using interaction terms. Panel A shows the models that have been estimated thus far. It illustrates the relationship between hospital expenditure (horizontal axis) with the case-fatality rates (vertical axis). The slope of line A`A is negative, consistent with the results shown in Table 5.3 where, on average, an increase in hospital expenditure is associated with a fall in the case-fatality rate.

Panel B illustrates the next step in the analysis, whereby the model includes a health system characteristic variable that is brought into interaction with the health expenditure variable. In the first instance, consider a dichotomous health system characteristic variable. For example, the variable could indicate whether or not a country pays hospitals on a diagnosis-related group (DRG) basis. The variable would take on the value of one for countries that use DRGs, and zero otherwise. The line B`B now represents the average relationship between health expenditure and case-fatality rates for countries that do not pay hospitals through DRG mechanisms. The line C`C represents the relationship between expenditure and case-fatality rates in countries that do use DRG payments systems.

Table 5.4. **Country rankings for case-fatality performance**

	AMI		Ischemic stroke	
	Female	Male	Female	Male
Australia	2	6	21	19
Austria	10	9	11	9
Belgium	16	20	14	11
Canada	5	4	7	8
Chile	24	23	25	25
Czech Republic	18	13	10	12
Denmark	1	2	3	6
Estonia				
Finland	26	26	20	22
France	13	11	9	7
Germany	12	12	13	16
Greece				
Hungary	20	24	23	23
Iceland	11	7	5	4
Ireland				
Israel	19	15	24	24
Italy				
Japan				
Korea	21	19	19	20
Luxembourg	3	1	4	2
Mexico	9	14	18	21
Netherlands	7	8	1	1
New Zealand	23	17	12	10
Norway	4	3	2	3
Poland	25	22		
Portugal	8	16	6	14
Slovak Republic	17	21	17	18
Slovenia				
Spain	22	5	15	15
Sweden	6	5	22	5
Switzerland	14	10	16	17
Turkey				
United Kingdom				
United States	15	18	8	13

Better than average		Average performance		Worse than average	

Source: OECD Health Statistics 2013, *http://dx.doi.org/10.1787/health-data-en.*

The estimated slope for line C`C is derived by adding the hospital expenditure coefficient to the estimated coefficient of the interaction term. The line C`C is drawn on the basis that the interaction coefficient has a positive value. In this hypothetical case, this implies that, in countries with DRG payments, additional hospital expenditure produces less quality than countries without DRG payments. Of course, the value of the interaction coefficient could also have a negative value, in which case the line C`C would be underneath the B`B line.[6] Importantly, the interaction coefficient should not be interpreted as having a direct effect on case-fatality rates, but rather as having an indirect effect through hospital expenditure.

The health system characteristic variables are listed in Table 5.5. These variables are measured at a national level and can only be considered as a very broad representation of a national health system. At this level of measurement, the within-country variation that is very likely to exist is not captured. The HSC variables have been selected as proxies of health technology access (MRI and CT exams), equitable access to care (proportion of hospital spending that is publicly funded), payment systems (dichotomous variable indicating whether a country funds hospitals on the basis of a global budget, or not) and quality initiatives (dichotomous variable indicating whether a country actively measures the quality of hospital performance).

Figure 5.4. **The role of health system characteristics in explaining performance: A hypothetical example**

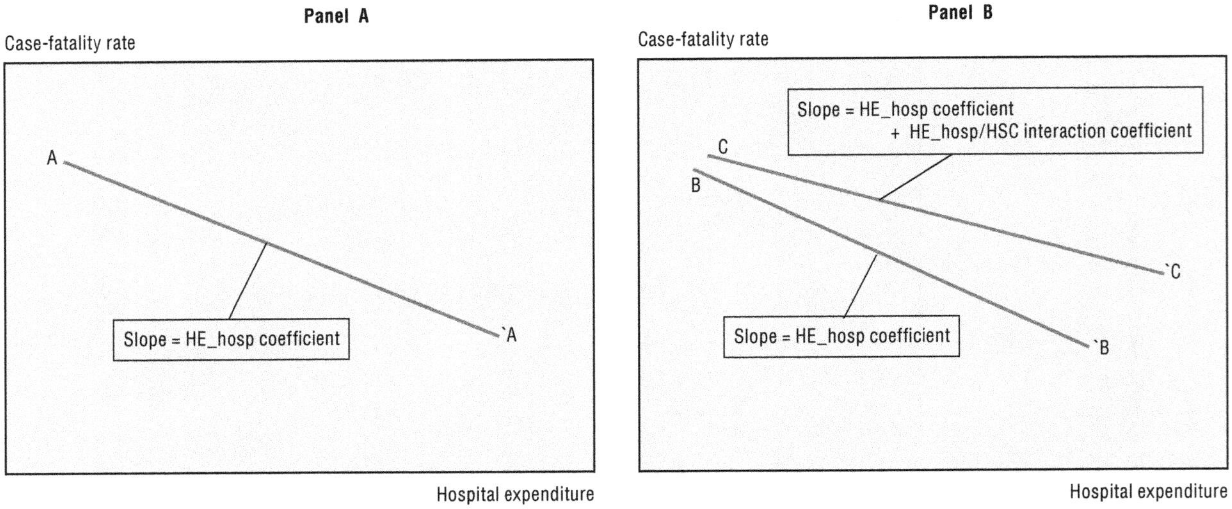

As noted previously, due to the restrictions of the modelling technique, the selected health system characteristic variables cannot vary over time. Each health system characteristic remains constant for each country over the observation period. A further restriction is the available sample size. This limits our capacity to introduce multiple health system characteristics within the one model. This is why only one health system characteristic is modelled at a time. Separate models are estimated for each health system characteristic. This implies a total of 24 models, with gender specific models for six health system characteristic variables and two CVD case-fatality outcomes (AMI and ischemic stroke) ($2 \times 6 \times 2 = 24$).

Table 5.5 summarises the results of the models showing only the coefficients of the interaction terms. The full model results are presented in Annex 5.A2. The value of this coefficient reflects the difference between the hospital expenditure slope (line B`B in Figure 5.4) and the health expenditure line that is brought into interaction with the health system characteristic variable (line C`C). A negative coefficient suggests that the interacted term improves performance with respect to the relationship between health expenditure and case-fatality rates. A positive value would indicate a reduction in performance. The conventional p-values to indicate whether the interaction term is significant are marked by the asterisks (*).

The results shown in Table 5.5 and Annex 5.A2 were estimated using random intercepts models. Please note that for some models the sample size is reduced to only 68 observations obtained from 16 countries. This particularly affects the models that examine the role of technology-related HSC variables such as CT scans and MRI scans.

Most interaction terms were not statistically significant. Out of the 24 models with interaction terms, 14 were not statistically significant at conventional levels. None of the models that included the gini coefficient turned out to be statistically significant. The technology variables also produced non-significant results with the exception of the male case-fatality rate for ischemic stroke. Here, greater access to high CT and MRI scanners improves quality performance. There is more consistent evidence that the percentage of publicly funded hospital expenditure is associated with improved quality performance, although this evidence was not significant for female AMI case-fatality rates. There is also some evidence that countries that pay hospitals on the basis of global budgets have been able to extract greater quality improvements from additional expenditure. However, this health system characteristic appears to be significant only for AMI case-fatality rates, and less so for ischemic stroke. Countries that systematically measure hospital performance also extract greater value from hospital expenditure.

Table 5.5. **Summary of health system characteristic results**

Interacted terms with HE_hosp	Females		Males	
	AMI	Isch. stroke	AMI	Isch. stroke
MRI scans	-0.09	-0.13	-0.10	-0.26***
	(0.10)	(0.08)	(0.09)	(0.10)
CT scans	-0.13	-0.08	-0.14	-0.30**
	(0.14)	(0.11)	(0.13)	(0.13)
HE_public	-0.48	-1.03***	-0.85**	-1.43***
	(0.35)	(0.33)	(0.35)	(0.36)
Gini	-0.10	0.20	0.34	0.45
	(0.34)	(0.30)	(0.33)	(0.33)
Hosp_GB	-0.51***	-0.25*	-0.50***	-0.19
	(0.14)	(0.14)	(0.14)	(0.16)
Hosp_perf	-0.37**	-0.26	-0.26*	-0.08
	(0.15)	(0.22)	(0.16)	(0.23)

Note: Standard errors in parentheses; *** p < 0.01, ** p < 0.05, * p < 0.10; based on random intercept models; controls for GDP, smoking rates, obesity and length of stay. Full results reported in Annex 5.A2.

Source: OECD Health Statistics 2013 and OECD HSC Survey 2012.

Payment systems, technology, quality measurement are linked to better hospital performance

This chapter has shown that there is a strong relationship between hospital expenditure and the quality of acute CVD care. Greater hospital expenditure is associated with lower case-fatality rates for AMI and ischemic stroke. This relationship persists after controlling for a number of factors that may affect case-fatality rates but that are not associated with hospital performance. The relationship is not statistically significant for haemorrhagic stroke. This may reflect less within country variation in case fatality rates particularly during the first half of observation period.

The results also show that there is evidence that the relationship between hospital expenditure and acute care CVD quality varies across countries; although, it should be acknowledged that performance in most countries does not significantly deviate from the overall OECD average. Nevertheless, some countries do perform better than others. The estimated results for countries such as Denmark, Luxembourg, Netherlands and Norway show that additional expenditure has been associated with greater than average improvement in CVD acute care quality. In countries such as Chile, Finland, Hungary, Israel, Korea, Mexico, Poland and Spain, some models indicate that additional hospital expenditures have had less impact on CVD quality compared to the OECD average. It should be noted that these results may not reflect the quality of the care provided in hospitals. For example, the Finnish result is likely to reflect the large increases in health care expenditures over the observation period, but only average quality improvements for some case-fatality rates.

Despite the lack of statistical significance in the relationship between hospital expenditure and quality for most countries, the results show considerable consistency across different case-fatality measures and genders. For all four models considered in this analysis, countries that perform well in one area tend to perform well in another, and vice versa. The consistency for most country rankings provides somewhat greater confidence in the performance estimates.

The results also indicate that certain health system characteristics may have a bearing on the performance of the acute care system. The results of this exploratory analysis show that global payment systems and greater health care access are associated with better performance. In addition, a quality of care initiative such as hospital performance measurement also appears to have a beneficial relationship with hospital performance. These findings should be interpreted with care. The results were not consistent across all models and in some cases the association was only weakly significant. Furthermore, the health system variables can only be considered as proxies for certain characteristics. It is possible that these proxy variables confound other unobserved characteristics.

There are several other limitations in this analysis that should be taken into account when interpreting the findings. First and foremost is the small sample size. Although the vast majority of OECD countries have reported some case-fatality rates since 2000, there is a substantial amount of missing data in any given year. The same is true for other variables in OECD Health Statistics, which restricts the ability to infer strong results from longitudinal analysis. For most models in this analysis there were around 170 observations available from 25 to 26 countries, but for some of the models that explored the effect of health system characteristics, this number dropped to less than 70 observations. The small sample size restricts the analysis in several ways. In particular, it limits the number of explanatory variables that can be used in the analysis and may also underestimate some of the relationships.

Another limitation is that the analysis has focused on only one objective of the health care system. While the relationship between hospital expenditure and CVD quality is important, countries also invest in hospital care to provide greater access to care and reduce morbidity. These aspects have not been examined here and therefore the analysis can only shed light on one, albeit important, part of hospital performance.

The key explanatory variable in this analysis has been hospital expenditure, obtained under the Systems of Health Accounts. This variable serves as a proxy for the hospital resources devoted to CVD care. Obviously, the key underlying assumption is that the proportion of hospital expenditure devoted to CVD does not vary within countries over time. Unfortunately, it is not possible to test the validity of this assumption, although work is currently being undertaken to develop disease-specific expenditures using the Systems of Health Accounts methodology. This work may in future years provide more detailed data that can be used to examine the relationship between disease-specific resources and outcomes. Similarly, work is also being undertaken to develop health-specific purchasing power parity (PPP) estimates that will permit a more appropriate method of converting expenditure data into common resource units.

Summary

Notwithstanding the limitations outlined above, this analysis has developed a better understanding of the relationship between acute care quality and hospital resources in the field of CVD care. It has looked at some of the potential factors that may account for the differences in acute care quality that are routinely used in international comparisons. This chapter has shown that improvements in the quality of CVD acute care are associated with higher hospital care expenditure. This is particularly true for AMI and ischemic stroke care. The results are consistent with the notion that acute care resources remain an important determinant of health care quality. These results are not predictive of future success because the relationship between resources and quality may change over time. This is particular true, for example, when increasing amounts of resources are required to make smaller gains in quality. Nevertheless, there are indications that some health-system characteristics can help explain why the relationship between expenditure and quality differs between countries. The results show that greater access to acute care (as proxied by the percentage of hospital expenditure that is public funded) is associated with improved hospital performance. There is also some evidence that countries that pay hospitals on the basis of global budgets and those that systematically measure hospital performance have been able to extract greater quality improvements from additional expenditure. Given the short time span of the data on which this study is based, it may be of value to repeat this type of analysis in future years, as the OECD Health Statistics develops into a stronger longitudinal dataset.

Notes

1. See, for example, Mobley and Magnussen (1998), Steinmann et al. (2004), Dervaux (2004) and Linna et al. (2006).
2. A better measure of hospital quality is an indicator that captures mortality more broadly than just those that occur in the same hospital as the initial admission. While the OECD does collect such broader indicators, only a limited (albeit growing) number of countries have the infrastructure to collect these data. The number of countries able to report this information is too small for the purposes of this analysis.
3. Economy-wide GDP PPPs were used for this analysis. In future years, it will become possible to convert expenditure data using health-specific PPPs that will more accurately reflect cross-country hospital price variations.
4. A better indicator of case fatality would be to collect mortality data regardless of whether the death occurred in or outside of hospital. See note 2.
5. One potential reason for the differences between countries observed in Figures 5.2 and 5.3 is that it may take increasing resources to continually improve quality of care. If this type of relationship were true, it would imply that countries at high level of quality would need to invest greater resources to achieve the same amount of improvement compared to countries who have lower quality levels. This suggests a non-linear relationship between expenditure and quality. To test for this, a quadratic health expenditure term was added to the model. The results showed that the quadratic relationship was not statistically significant at conventional levels. However, this results may be related to the short time-frame over which the analysis is conducted and the small number of observations per country. It would be important to test for non-linear relationships if longer time-periods are evaluated.
6. The interpretation of the interaction term is slightly more complicated when the health system characteristic variable is continuous (e.g. average number of CT exams in a country) compared to a dichotomous variable, although the same principle shown in Figure 5.4 applies. In the case of a continuous health system characteristic interaction term, instead of having just one potential alternative line (as in C`C) there are many alternative lines, depending on the multiple potential values that the health system characteristic variable can take.

References

Dervaux, B. (2004), "Comparing French and US Hospital Technologies: A Directional Input Distance Function Approach", *Applied Economics*, Vol. 36, pp. 1065-1081.

ECHO – European Collaboration for Healthcare Optimisation, *www.echo-health.eu* for more details.

Gutacker, N. et al. (2011), "Truly Inefficient or Providing Better Quality of Care? Analysing the Relationship Between Risk-adjusted Hospital Costs and Patients' Health Outcomes", Centre for Health Economics, University of York.

Häkkinen, U. et al. (2013), "Health Care Performance Comparison Using a Disease-based Approach: The EuroHOPE Project", *Health Policy*, Vol. 112, No. 1, pp. 100-109.

Hollingsworth, B. (2008), "The Measurement of Efficiency and Productivity of Health Care Delivery", *Health Economics*, Vol. 17, pp. 1107-1128.

Hvenegaard, A. et al. (2011), "Does the Joint Evaluation of Costs and Quality Alter the Ranking of Danish Hospital Departments", *European Journal of Health Economics*, Vol. 12, pp. 541-551.

Linna, M., U. Hakkinen and J. Magnussen (2006), "Comparing Hospital Cost Efficiency Between Norway and Finland", *Health Policy*, Vol. 77, No. 3, pp. 268-278.

Mobley, L. and J. Magnussen (1998), "An International Comparison of Hospital Efficiency: Does Institutional Environment Matter?", *Applied Economics*, Vol. 30, No. 8, pp. 1089-1100.

OECD (2013), *Health at a Glance 2013: OECD Indicators*, OECD Publishing, Paris, *http://dx.doi.org/10.1787/health_glance-2013-en*.

Or, Z., J. Wang and D. Jamison (2005), "International Differences in the Impact of Doctors on Health: A Multilevel Analysis of OECD Countries", *Journal of Health Economics*, Vol. 24, pp. 531-560.

Schreyögg, J., T. Stargardt and O. Tiemann (2011), "Costs and Quality of Hospitals in Different Health Care Systems: A Multi-level Approach with Propensity Score Matching", *Health Economics*, Vol. 20, pp. 85-100.

Steinmann, L. et al. (2004), "Measuring and Comparing the (In)efficiency of German and Swiss Hospitals", *European Journal of Health Economics*, Vol. 3, pp. 216-226.

Street, A. et al.. (2010), "Determinants of Hospital Costs and Performance Variation: Methods, Models and Variables for the EuroDRG Project", *Working Papers in Health Policy and Management*, University of Berlin.

ANNEX 5.A1

Empirical framework for analysing acute care CVD performance

Econometric techniques are employed to assess health system performance in CVD outcomes. The empirical strategy is based on the Or et al. (2005) study using a multilevel model approach to estimate the relationship between health care resources and CVD outcomes across countries and over time. Or et al. (2005) exploited the longitudinal nature of OECD Health Data. The model will use the repeated observations over time (level 1) nested at a higher country level (level 2). In the first instance, the analysis will examine the relationship between health care inputs and outcomes, after controlling for a range of health and non-health factors: At this most basic level, the model will look like this:

$$\mathbf{y}_{it} = \beta_{oi} + \beta_{1i} I_{it} + \alpha_p \mathbf{x}_{pit} + e_{it} \qquad \text{(equation 1)}$$

where $\mathbf{y}_{it}$ represents an indicator of health outcome, y, for country *i* at time period *t*. The set of variables *I* represent a health care input that varies by country and over time. The vector **x** is a set of *p* control variables that can vary over time. The coefficient β_{0i} varies by country while *e* is the residual error term for the *i*th country in year *t* and is assumed to be normally distributed with a mean of zero.

The first model assumes that the relationship between the input and outcome is the same across countries; however, the use of multi-level models provides greater flexibility to estimate country-specific slopes. Equation 2 estimates performance on the basis of the country's own performance in converting inputs to outputs, compared to the average OECD level:

$$\mathbf{y}_{it} = \beta_{oi} + \beta_{1i} I_{it} + \alpha_p \mathbf{x}_{pit} + e_{it} \qquad \text{(equation 2)}$$

Equation 2 is an extension of equation 1 where both coefficients β_{0i} and β_{1i} vary by country. Under this model, each country is characterised by a different intercept, $\beta_{0i,}$ as well as a different slope coefficient, β_{1i} for health care inputs. Across all countries, these coefficients have a distribution with a given mean and variance. Each country's β coefficient comprises an average effect across countries as well as a country-specific deviation from that average. Exploring the variability around β_{1i} will be of particular interest in assessing each country's capacity to convert health care inputs into health care outputs.

ANNEX 5.A2

Full CVD acute care performance analysis results

Table 5.A2.1. **CVD acute care performance analysis results**

VARIABLES	Females											
	AMI case-fatality							Ischemic stroke case-fatality				
HE_hosp	-0.28*	-0.25	-0.41***	-0.22*	-0.13	-0.03	-0.47***	-0.40***	-0.66***	-0.32***	-0.24**	-0.12
	(0.17)	(0.16)	(0.13)	(0.13)	(0.11)	(0.15)	(0.15)	(0.14)	(0.15)	(0.11)	(0.12)	(0.22)
MRI scans * HE_hosp	-0.09						-0.13					
	(0.10)						(0.08)					
CT scans * HE_hosp		-0.13						-0.08				
		(0.14)						(0.11)				
He_pbl * HE_hosp			-0.48						-1.03***			
			(0.35)						(0.33)			
Gini coefficient * HE_hosp				-0.10						0.20		
				(0.34)						(0.30)		
Global budget payment * HE_hosp					-0.51***						-0.25*	
					(0.14)						(0.14)	
Hosp. perf. * HE_hosp						-0.37**						-0.26
						(0.15)						(0.22)
GDP	-0.47**	-0.46**	-0.70***	-0.81***	-0.69***	-0.74***	-0.10	-0.13	-0.09	-0.30***	-0.17	-0.20
	(0.19)	(0.19)	(0.12)	(0.12)	(0.12)	(0.12)	(0.16)	(0.16)	(0.13)	(0.10)	(0.13)	(0.13)
Smok15	0.32**	0.32**	0.28***	0.30***	0.33***	0.28***	0.27**	0.29**	0.29***	0.24***	0.35***	0.33***
	(0.15)	(0.15)	(0.10)	(0.10)	(0.10)	(0.10)	(0.13)	(0.13)	(0.10)	(0.09)	(0.10)	(0.10)
Obese	-0.13	-0.11	-0.12	-0.15	-0.21**	-0.10	0.08	0.11	0.21**	0.08	0.15	0.21**
	(0.15)	(0.15)	(0.11)	(0.11)	(0.10)	(0.11)	(0.15)	(0.15)	(0.10)	(0.10)	(0.10)	(0.10)
Obese_ selfreport	-0.12	-0.11	-0.06	-0.08	-0.10	-0.04	0.01	0.03	0.07	0.01	0.05	0.08
	(0.11)	(0.11)	(0.08)	(0.08)	(0.08)	(0.08)	(0.09)	(0.09)	(0.08)	(0.07)	(0.08)	(0.08)
ALOS_circ	0.17	0.20	0.41***	0.49***	0.40***	0.48***	-0.12	-0.01	-0.01	0.19*	0.10	0.14
	(0.19)	(0.18)	(0.12)	(0.12)	(0.10)	(0.11)	(0.17)	(0.16)	(0.12)	(0.10)	(0.11)	(0.11)
Constant	6.19***	6.01***	8.12***	9.10***	8.15***	8.26***	2.48	2.39	1.72	3.92***	2.22	2.40
	(2.10)	(2.08)	(1.39)	(1.42)	(1.34)	(1.37)	(1.79)	(1.79)	(1.48)	(1.22)	(1.47)	(1.49)
Observations	68	68	177	170	177	177	68	68	171	164	171	171
Number of groups	16	16	26	26	26	26	16	16	25	25	25	25

Table 5.A2.1. **CVD acute care performance analysis results** *(cont.)*

VARIABLES	Males											
	AMI case-fatality							Ischemic stroke case-fatality				
HE_hosp	-0.25	-0.22	-0.50***	-0.30**	-0.19*	-0.13	-0.58***	-0.47***	-0.75***	-0.27**	-0.33**	-0.34
	(0.17)	(0.16)	(0.13)	(0.12)	(0.11)	(0.15)	(0.18)	(0.17)	(0.15)	(0.13)	(0.13)	(0.23)
MRI scans * HE_hosp	-0.10						-0.26***					
	(0.09)						(0.10)					
CT scans * HE_hosp		-0.14						-0.30**				
		(0.13)						(0.13)				
He_pbl * HE_hosp			-0.85**						-1.43***			
			(0.35)						(0.36)			
Gini coefficient * HE_hosp				0.34						0.45		
				(0.33)						(0.33)		
Global budget payment * HE_hosp					-0.50***						-0.19	
					(0.14)						(0.16)	
Hosp. perf. * HE_hosp						-0.26*						-0.08
						(0.16)						(0.23)
GDP	-0.35	-0.33	-0.67***	-0.71***	-0.72***	-0.73***	-0.40*	-0.42*	-0.44***	-0.57***	-0.57***	-0.58***
	(0.21)	(0.21)	(0.14)	(0.14)	(0.13)	(0.14)	(0.24)	(0.24)	(0.15)	(0.14)	(0.15)	(0.15)
Smok15	0.46*	0.50*	0.25*	0.37**	0.20	0.20	0.02	0.06	-0.03	0.29*	-0.04	-0.04
	(0.26)	(0.25)	(0.14)	(0.14)	(0.13)	(0.14)	(0.26)	(0.26)	(0.15)	(0.15)	(0.16)	(0.16)
Obese	0.08	0.12	-0.00	-0.07	-0.06	-0.05	0.45**	0.52**	0.28**	0.28**	0.25*	0.26*
	(0.18)	(0.18)	(0.13)	(0.13)	(0.13)	(0.13)	(0.20)	(0.21)	(0.14)	(0.13)	(0.14)	(0.14)
Obese_selfreport	-0.05	-0.03	-0.01	-0.03	-0.04	-0.01	0.15	0.19	0.13	0.11	0.12	0.13
	(0.11)	(0.11)	(0.08)	(0.08)	(0.08)	(0.08)	(0.12)	(0.12)	(0.08)	(0.08)	(0.09)	(0.09)
ALOS_circ	0.04	0.09	0.42***	0.44***	0.51***	0.54***	-0.08	0.04	0.11	0.22**	0.32***	0.33***
	(0.19)	(0.17)	(0.12)	(0.11)	(0.10)	(0.10)	(0.20)	(0.19)	(0.12)	(0.11)	(0.12)	(0.12)
Constant	3.95	3.39	7.35***	7.49***	7.96***	7.96***	5.12*	4.72	5.69***	5.78***	6.65***	6.65***
	(2.85)	(2.79)	(1.63)	(1.63)	(1.59)	(1.64)	(3.10)	(3.16)	(1.79)	(1.65)	(1.84)	(1.85)
Observations	68	68	177	170	177	177	68	68	171	164	171	171
Number of groups	16	16	26	26	26	26	16	16	25	25	25	25

Note: Standard errors in parentheses; *** p<0.01, ** p<0.05, * p<0.10; based on random intercept models.

Source: OECD Health Statistics 2013 and *OECD Health Systems Characteristics Survey 2012*.

Cardiovascular Disease and Diabetes
Policies for Better Health and Quality of Care

Chapter 6

Adherence to recommended cardiovascular care in OECD health systems

Despite the potential for practice guidelines to improve health care outcomes, there is evidence that they are adopted too slowly or are applied inconsistently within and across countries. The lack of adherence to recommended clinical practice can have adverse effects on patient outcomes as well as higher health care costs. Chapter 6 reports on the analysis of the European Society of Cardiology's long-term registry of heart failure. It examines cross-country and within-country variations in recommended heart failure practice and analyses whether the degree of adherence can be explained by health system characteristics and policies across countries.

The statistical data for Israel are supplied by and under the responsibility of the relevant Israeli authorities. The use of such data by the OECD is without prejudice to the status of the Golan Heights, East Jerusalem and Israeli settlements in the West Bank under the terms of international law.

Improving adherence to chronic heart failure treatment is an important health care issue

Heart failure[1] is a common and serious condition in industrialised countries, affecting approximately 2% to 3% of the population; rising to around 10% among those aged 70 years and older. Patients suffer poor quality of life with constant fatigue and fluid accumulation and congestion in the lungs as well as a high risk of mortality (Dickstein, 2008; McMurray, 2012). In Sweden, for example, the three year mortality rate after first diagnosis was between 17% and 19% and for those aged 65 and older it was between 36% and 41% (Shafazand et al., 2009). Heart failure is a common reason for admissions and accounts for around 14% of all CVD-related hospital admissions in OECD countries (OECD, 2013).

Survival of patients with chronic heart failure (CHF) has improved over the last two decades. Several trials have concluded that outpatient medical treatment with blockers of the renin-angiotensin-aldosterone system (ACE inhibitors, angiotensin receptor blockers and mineralo-corticoid antagonists) and beta-adrenergic, combined with fluid management and controlled exercise can improve survival rates of heart failure (CONCENSUS, 1987; SOLVD Investigators, 1991; SOLVD Investigators, 1992; CIBIS-II, 1999; MERIT-HF, 1999; Packer et al., 2002; Pitt et al., 1999). This evidence has now been widely incorporated in clinical practice guidelines that provide practitioners and patients with recommendations on optimum care. Patients receiving recommended care have been shown to improve survival and quality of life (Dickstein et al., 2008; Bonnow et al., 2011; Jessup et al., 2009; McMurray et al., 2012).

However, despite the potential for practice guidelines to improve health care outcomes, there is evidence that they are adopted too slowly or are applied inconsistently (Fonarow et al., 2005; Stafford et al., 2003; Maggioni et al., 2013a; Maggioni et al., 2013b). This often leads to suboptimal care and fails to deliver further improvements in the quality of patient care and health outcomes.

Previous research has indicated that some aspects of the structure and organisation of the health system play an important role in explaining patient adherence to guideline recommendations. Among Medicare beneficiaries with chronic heart failure, for example, a USD 10 increase in out-of-pocket costs for pharmaceuticals was associated with a decrease with patients filling prescriptions and, in turn, a 6% to 9% increase in the risk of hospitalisation for CHF (Cole et al., 2006). Enrolment in a disease management programme has also shown to improve survival amongst CHF patients (Galbreath et al., 2004). The studies provide some indication that health systems that can provide patients with greater access to high quality care can improve outcomes.

This evidence suggests that there is considerable room for improvement in the management of chronic heart failure patients. However, one of the limitations of many adherence studies is that they often define the use of guideline-recommended "optimal therapy", usually as the proportion of patients who received these treatments, without due regard to the potential clinical reasons why a patient may not be adherent to a particular recommendation.

A more recent study using ESC's Heart Failure Long-Term Registry data from 21 European and Mediterranean countries, found considerable evidence of non-adherence to current guidelines (Maggioni et al., 2013b). While only around 5% of CHF patients were considered undertreated with respect to any specific type of medication they were using, between 70% and 82% of CHF patients had failed to reach their recommended target dosage. For around 1/3 of those patients there was no reason why the recommended dosage had not been adhered to.

One of the conclusions of this paper was that the lack of adherence could be due to 1) the preferences of physicians in not prescribing all recommended treatments because they consider that there is sufficient evidence underpinning the guidelines or 2) to their lack of knowledge of current standards, or 3) due to external constraints imposed by the health care system, funding and infrastructure. Another potential reason for non-adherence is related to patient characteristics. These may relate to clinical reasons such as contraindications or comorbidities, but may also relate to socio-economic variables including costs and access to care as well as the patient's perceived benefits of care.

When taking these factors into consideration, there is an important need to develop a better understanding of the role of health system structures and organisation to help explain adherence to recommended treatments. Such an exploration can produce important information for both clinicians and policy makers to better understand the sources of cross-country and within country variation in guideline adherence. Ultimately, this understanding can help improve the design of health systems policies for the benefit of patients.

The purpose of this study was to investigate whether a patient's country of residence is an independent determinant of non-adherence to clinical practice guidelines. It also examines the extent to which patient adherence varies within countries. Finally, the analysis seeks to develop a better understanding of the role of patients' clinical characteristics and health system characteristics can have on non-adherence to recommended care.

Combining individual patient and national health system data to study the problem of adherence

Data and variable selection

To undertake the analysis, three different sources of data were combined: the ESC's Heart Failure Long-Term Registry, the OECD's Health System Characteristics Survey and the *OECD Health Statistics 2013 Database*.

Patient level data: The ESC's Long-Term Heart failure Registry

The ESC's Heart Failure Long-Term Registry is a prospective observational study, conducted in 211 Cardiology Centres across 21 European and Mediterranean countries. Centres were selected by the national cardiology societies of each country in a way that it involved a broad spectrum of cardiology and/or HF units following outpatients with HF and admitting patients with acute, pre-existing or new-onset of HF. The number of participating centres for each country was decided according to the number of inhabitants in each country. From May 2011 to December 2013, a total of 17 901 patients aged over 18 years old were enrolled on a "one day per week" basis for 12 consecutive months. Patients were recruited via their presentation at one of the participating Cardiology Centres and classified on the basis of their presentation at an outpatient (chronic HF patients) or inpatient setting (acute HF patients). The registry collects information on the clinical epidemiology as well as the diagnostic and therapeutic processes applied for these patients in each country.

The ESC Long-Term Registry aimed to reflect "real-world" management from a variety of hospitals, representing all levels of complexity, and from all regions of Europe and Mediterranean countries. In the ESC Long-Term Registry detailed information has been obtained not only on patient characteristics and the use of procedures and treatments, but also on the reasons why recommended pharmacological or non-pharmacological treatments are not appropriately utilised in patients with HF. This information has generally not been available from previous administrative datasets, trials, or registries.

To maximise representativeness of participating centers, the number of centres for each country was decided according to the number of inhabitants in that country. As far as possible, the centres were selected to represent a balanced proportion across a different range of facilities for cardiology.

For the purpose of this analysis, only patients living in OECD countries were considered. Acute HF patients were excluded as well as chronic HF patients for whom the ejection fraction was not available or preserved (i.e. higher than 45%). This is because the clinical practice guidelines recognise that for these patients there is considerable heterogeneity in trial evidence about the effect of different treatments on patient outcomes. In the absence of evidence-based recommendations, adherence is harder to define for acute HF patients and for those with chronic HF and preserved ejection fraction. Figure 6.1 provides patient disposition information for this analysis.

Figure 6.1. **ESC-HFA Heart Failure Long-Term Registry: Patient disposition**

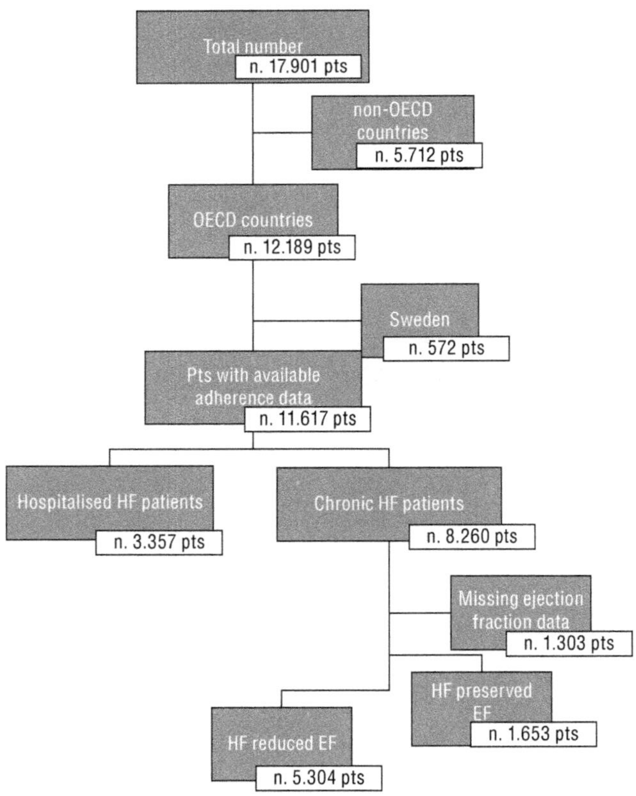

Source: ESC Long-Term Heart Failure Registry, 2013.

For drug treatment of patients with chronic heart failure and reduced ejection fraction, non-adherence to ESC guidelines was defined as all patients:

- not treated with at least one of the two recommended treatments (ACE inhibitors/ARBs and beta-blockers); or
- treated with both ACE inhibitors/ARBs and beta-blockers, but with a dosage of at least one of the two drugs with less than 100% of the recommended dosage; and
- absence of a documented contraindication or intolerance (reported as unknown and other in non-adherent).

All patients for whom information on non-adherence to drug treatment was unknown were excluded.

Selected variables for patient-level characteristics

Twenty-one variables were selected as the most suitable patient-level candidates to be examined for their association with non-adherence to ESC guidelines on drug treatment. These variables include demographic characteristics (age and gender), presenting vital signs and symptoms (systolic blood pressure – SBP), heart rate, NYHA class, etiology of heart failure, laboratory test results [left bundle branch block at ECG, ejection fraction (EF), sodium, creatinine], classical cardiac risk factors [body mass index (BMI), diabetes mellitus, hypertension], comorbid condition and vascular history [history of stroke, atrial fibrillation, mitral regurgitation, depression, chronic obstructive pulmonary disease (COPD), chronic kidney dysfunction (CKD), peripheral arterial diseases (PAD)], indication for a device [implantable cardioverter defibrillator (ICD) or cardiac resynchronisation therapy (CRT)].

National level data: OECD Health System Characteristics survey and OECD Health Statistics 2013 Database

The OECD Health System Characteristics survey collects information on a wide range of health system characteristics including coverage of health services and products, provider payment systems, health care financing arrangements, provision of health care and governance structures (Paris et al., 2010). One questionnaire is completed per country and responses are generally co-ordinated by national bodies such as the Ministry of Health. In all 33 out of 34 member countries responded to the survey, although not all countries completed all questions. This analysis used responses from the 2012 survey wave.

Some quantitative national level variables were drawn from OECD Health Statistics 2013. This dataset offers the most comprehensive source of comparable statistics on health and health systems across OECD countries. It includes numerous data on a wide range of topics including health resources and activities as well as health expenditures. In addition, the 2011 wave of Eurostat's Statistics on Income and Living Conditions (EU-SILC) was used to obtain data on the percentage of people who reported that they did not visit their doctor in the previous 12 months when they felt they needed health care.

Selected variables for country-level characteristics

Fifteen variables related to access, resources and quality were selected for the analysis and used as "group-level" variables. These variables are described in Table 6.1 along with their country-level values. For the access to care variables, the proportion of the population reporting that they had skipped a doctor consultation, the out-of-pocket expenditures for medical goods and outpatient care, the patient payment mode for health care services (free at the point of care, co-payments or full payment but reimbursed afterwards) as well as the annual number of doctor consultations per capita per year were examined in this analysis. With regards to resources, the share of ambulatory care on total health expenditure, the number of generalists per 1 000 population and variables related to how the primary care system is organised (main employment status for generalists, payment status, incentives or obligation to register with a general practitioner) were included. The variables related to quality describe the way medical education is managed, whether patient information are stored and exchanged across providers and if incentives or obligation to comply with drug treatment guidelines exist.

Table 6.1. **Descriptive national health system characteristics data by country**

Variable description	Country level values														
	AUT	CZE	DNK	EST	FRA	GRC	HUN	ISR	ITA	POL	PRT	SVK	SVN	ESP	TUR
Percentage share of ambulatory care expenditure of total health expenditure	19	20.3	22.5	15.8	23.6	17.6	19.4	47.2		24.3	33.1	22.7	20	21.1	14.8
Number of GPs (per 1 000 population)	1.58	0.7	0.73	0.82	1.59	0.3	0.34	0.69	0.96	0.45	2	0.41	0.51	0.75	0.56
Average out of pocket costs on outpatient care (per capita USD PPP)	274	80	196	67	92	366	156	280		86	136	116	266	320	
Average out of pocket costs on medical goods (per capita USD PPP)	255	174	218	137	150	191	222	169		205	254	299	148	227	
Average annual doctor consultations (per capita)	6.9	11	4.6	6	6.7	4	11.6	6.2		6.6	4.1	11.6	6.4	7.4	7.3
Percentage of population skipping a doctor consultation	2.4	3.5	3.8	5.9	4.7	7.7	7.8		7.2	14.3	2.6	5.3	0.3	6.8	18.3
Health services free at the point of care (1 = co-pay; 0 = free)	0	1	0	1	1	1	0	0	1	0	1		1	0	1
GPs employment status (1 = mostly publicly employed; 0 = mostly self-employed)	0		0	0		0	0	0	1	1	0	1		1	1
GP payment system (1= others; 0 = fee for service)	0		1	1		1	0	1	1	1		1		1	1
Obligation or incentives to register with a GP (1 = no; 0 = yes)	1	0	0		0	1	0	1	0	0	0		0	0	
Formal requirements for accreditation needed for primary care practices (1 = no; 0 = yes)	1	0	1		0	0	0	1	1	0	0		0	0	
Formal system of continuous medical education (1 = no; 0 = yes)	0	0	1		0	1	0	0	0	0	1		0	0	
Use of a patient registration system (1 = no; 0 = yes)	0	0	0		0	0	0	0	0	1	0		0	0	
Electronic exchange of information between providers (1 = no; 0 = yes)	0	0	0		0	0	1	0	1	1	0		1	0	
Incentives to comply with treatment guidelines (1 = no incentives; 0 = yes)		1	1		0	1	0	0	0	0	0		0	0	

Source: *OECD Health Statistics 2013*; OECE Health Systems Characteristics Survey 2012 and OECD HCQI Questionnaire on Health Information Infrastructure 2012.

Statistical analysis

The first step aimed to identify those patient-level and country-level variables that could significantly predict adherence to guideline drug treatment. In selecting these, each variable was examined for their univariate association with non-adherence using simple logistic regression. In the second step, given the hierarchical nature of the data (patients nested within countries), the suitability for a hierarchical model was tested in an empty model with the country identifier as random intercept. All patient-level variables were then included in the model. Next, group-level covariates were added and examined one at a time. The association between non-adherence and each covariate was calculated using odds ratios (OR) with 95% confidence intervals (CI).

Results show substantial cross and within country variation found in adherence

Descriptive statistics

Out of the initial 17 901 patients who were included in the ESC's Heart Failure Long-Term Registry, 5 304 were retained for the analysis of non-adherence to drug treatment. Table 6.2 lists the number of patients enrolled, the number of centres and the non-adherence to guidelines for drug treatment (expressed in percentage) within each country. A total of 1 290 (24.3%) patients were respectively non-adherent to ESC guidelines on drug treatment (Table 6.2). Estonia and Greece had the highest percentage of patients being non-adherent to drug treatment (respectively 73.3% and 72.9%) while Portugal and the Slovak Republic had the lowest percentage (10.5% and 16.5%).

Table 6.2. **Number of patients enrolled, number of centres and non-adherence to drug treatment**

	Number of centres		Number of patients	Non-adherence to drug treatment (%)
	All in sample	With ≥ 10 patients		
Austria	4	4	135	17.0
Czech Republic	7	7	379	21.1
Denmark	23	3	185	38.4
Estonia	2	1	30	73.3
France	12	10	370	17.8
Greece	4	1	59	72.9
Hungary	5	4	271	15.9
Israel	2	2	309	17.8
Italy	17	15	896	30.6
Poland	17	5	269	30.9
Portugal	10	9	428	10.5
Slovak Republic	4	2	121	16.5
Slovenia	8	5	92	18.5
Spain	20	17	1655	25.6
Turkey	5	3	105	23.8
Total	140	52	5304	24.3

Source: ESC Long-Term Heart Failure Registry 2013.

Non-adherence to medication guidelines: Across and within country variation

To examine within and across country variation, patients were grouped on the basis of their treating centre. For each of the 140 centres, the level of non-adherence was calculated. Figure 6.2 shows the median level of non-adherence within each country as well as the range of non-adherence results, using treating centres as the unit of analysis. The line inside the box shows the median level of non-adherence within a country. This is the level where 50% of centres have a better level of non-adherence and 50% record worse levels. The box indicates the interquartile range of non-adherence within each country. Twenty-five percent of centres within a country perform better that the top line of the box and 25% perform worse than the bottom line of the box. Hence, the size of the box is one measure of the extent of variation within a country. When the box is relatively narrow, the difference in non-adherence across centres is small. The "whiskers" extending beyond the box, represent the distance between the 25th percentile and the 10th percentile centre. Thus each "whisker" captures a further 15% of centres. The absence of a box or whisper indicates that there are too few centres within a country to calculate these ranges.

The variability of non-adherence across all centres was relatively high, particularly in countries such as Denmark, Poland and the Slovak Republic where non-adherence ranged from 0% to 100% within these countries (Figure 6.2, Panel A). However, these extreme values were mostly reported by centres with very small patient samples. Panel B shows the within country variability when very small centres returning fewer than ten patients to the sample are excluded from the sample.[2] This further restriction has a marked effect on within-country variation in countries such as Denmark and Poland, but has reduced the number of centres in the sample to just one in Estonia and Greece.

Figure 6.2. **Non-adherence in participating centres, within and across country variation**

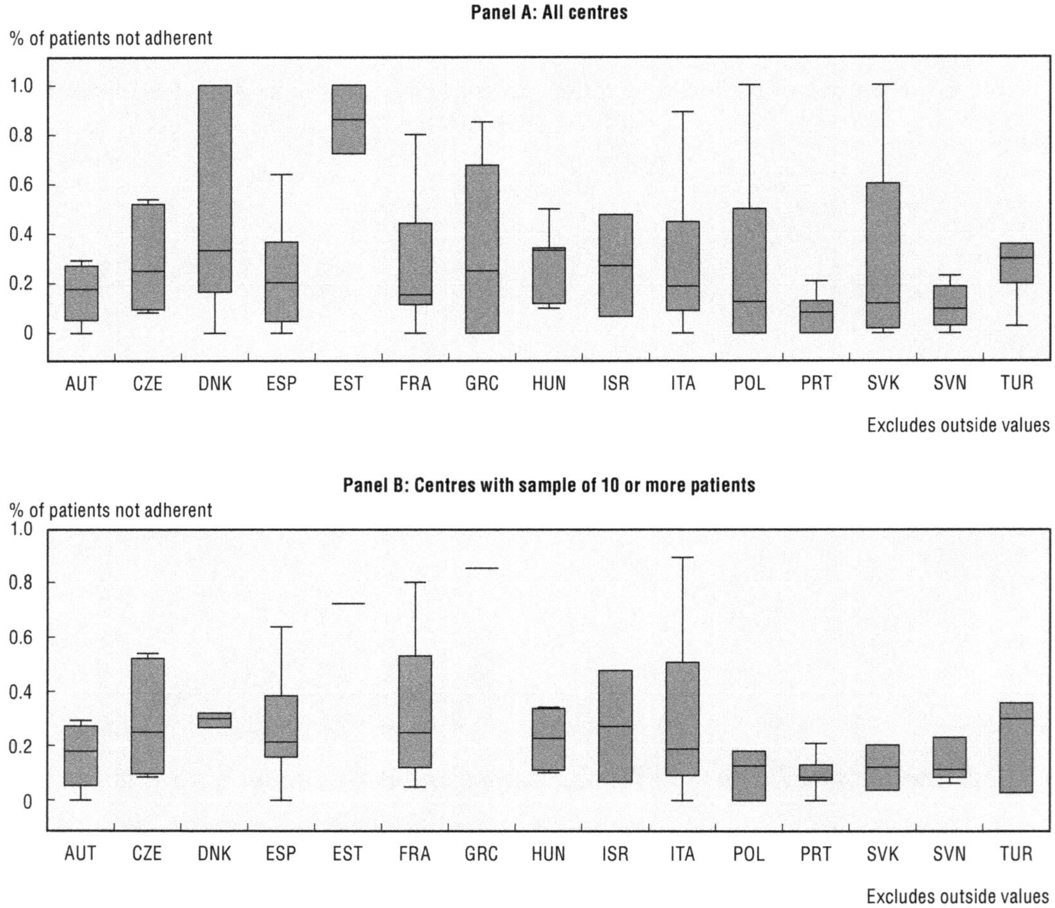

Source: ESC Long-Term Heart Failure Registry, 2013.

As shown in Panel B of Figure 6.2, participating centres in Portugal and Slovenia report the lowest levels of non-adherence with median levels of 8% and 10%, respectively. Along with Denmark, the within-country variation is also very low in Portugal, with interquartile ranges of less than six percentage points reported among participating centres with at least ten patients. Variability was relatively high, with interquartile ranges of more than 40% in the Czech Republic, France, Israel and Italy.

To some extent the variability within a country may be driven by the fact that there are more participating centres in some countries than others, depending on the number of inhabitants in each country. Variability may rise with more centres. Some care therefore needs to be taken when comparing the degree of within country across countries. However, even when comparing countries with large sample sizes, considerable differences remain. For example, while Italy has better overall adherence, the degree of variation is considerable lower in Spain. This suggest that while Italian patients are more likely to be adherent to treatment guidelines, the choice (or location) of treating centre has less of a bearing on adherence in Spain.

Patient and country baseline characteristics associated with non-adherence

Table 6.3 shows the characteristics of the study population as well as odds ratios for non-adherence estimated by univariate models. Non-adherent patients for drug treatment were more likely to be older, have an EF between 30% and 45%, be classified in NYHA I or II and have mitral regurgitation but were less likely to have COPD and be indicated for an ICD than adherent patients.

A number of country's characteristics were significant predictors of non-adherence in the univariate analysis. Some country-level variables such as the average out-of-pocket costs and share of health expenditure on ambulatory care were statistically significant but returned odds ratios very close to one. This indicates very low predictive power for these variables.

A number of the resource, payment and quality variables had strong associations with non-adherence. More GPs per 1 000 population was linked to lower levels of non-adherence. Countries where GPs were mostly privately employed or were paid on a fee-for-service basis also had lower levels of non-adherence.

Higher levels of non-adherence were observed in countries with no formal requirements for primary care practices to be accredited, where there was no patient registration system, electronic exchange of information between providers were not in use and where there were no incentives to comply with treatment guidelines or practice protocols.

Explaining non-adherence with patient and country-level information: Results from multivariate analysis

Having examined the univariate relationships between non-adherence, patient and country level characteristics, the analysis will now examine whether country of residence is significant driver of adherence to treatment guidelines. This part of the analysis utilises the hierarchical nature of the data where both patient-level and country-level characteristics can be examined simultaneously.

The multi-level multiple logistic regression results are summarised in Table 6.4. To test the suitability of a multilevel model, the intraclass correlation[3] was examined in the empty multilevel model, which only included the identifiers for patients and countries without any predictor variable. It shows that 17.5% of the total variability is explained by differences between countries.

Having established the significance of country of residence, patient-level characteristics were added to the analysis (Model 1). This slightly reduced the ICC by 0.3%. The results suggest that having mitral regurgitation (OR = 1.3, CI = 1.1-1.6) significantly increases the probability of being non-adherent while having an ejection fraction below 30% (OR = 0.8, CI = 0.7-1.0), having a COPD (OR = 0.6, CI = 0.5-0.8), being classified in NYHA III or IV (OR = 0.8, CI = 0.6-1.0) significantly decrease the probability of being non-adherent.

Table 6.3. **Characteristics of the study population and odds ratio for non-adherence estimated by univariate models**

PATIENT-LEVEL variables	Adherent (n = 4014)		Non-adherent (n = 1290)		OR	95% CI	P-value
	N	%	N	%			
Age							0.00
Below 65 years old	2 083	51.9	609	47.2	Ref		
65-75 years old	1 155	28.8	368	28.5	1.1	0.9-1.3	0.30
Above 75 years old	776	19.3	313	24.3	1.4	1.2-1.6	0.00
Men	3 118	77.7	978	75.8	0.8	0.8-1.0	0.17
Body mass index					1.0		0.94
Below 22 kg/m²	361	9.0	114	8.9	1	0.8-1.2	0.86
22-25 kg/m²	792	19.8	259	20.3	Ref		
Above 25 kg/m²	2 846	71.2	905	70.8	1.0	0.8-1.1	0.89
Ejection fraction below 30%	2 001	49.9	570	44.2	0.8	0.7-0.9	0.00
NYHA III or IV	1 048	26.1	289	22.4	0.8	0.7-1.0	0.01
Heart rate above 70 bpm	1 755	43.7	563	43.6	1.0	0.9-1.1	0.96
SBP (%)							0.32
Below 110 mm Hg	1 348	33.6	411	31.9	1.0	0.8-1.1	0.21
110-130 mm Hg	1 614	40.2	516	40.0	Ref		
Above 130 mm Hg	1 051	26.2	363	28.1	1.1	0.9-1.3	0.16
Creatinine above 1.5 mg/dL	728	19.4	247	20.6	1.1	0.9-1.3	0.37
Sodium below 136 mEq/L	392	10.9	139	12.2	1.1	0.9-1.4	0.21
Ischemic aetiology	1 883	46.9	635	49.2	1.1	1.0-1.2	0.15
Atrial fibrillation	1 363	34.0	444	34.4	1.0	0.9-1.2	0.76
Left bundle branch block	807	22.1	263	23.9	1.1	0.9-1.3	0.23
Mitral regurgitation	1 128	28.5	405	32.6	1.2	1.1-1.4	0.01
COPD	634	15.8	156	12.1	0.7	0.6-0.9	0.00
PAD	478	11.9	170	13.2	1.1	0.9-1.4	0.23
CKD	793	19.8	242	18.8	0.9	0.8-1.1	0.43
Diabetes mellitus	1 344	33.5	432	33.5	1.0	0.9-1.1	1.00
Prior stroke	365	9.1	122	9.5	1.1	0.8-1.3	0.69
Depression	305	7.6	80	6.2	0.8	0.6-1.0	0.09
COUNTRY-LEVEL variables							
ACCESS							
Population skipping a doctor consultation	6.3 + 3.2		6.8 + 3.1		1.1	1.0-1.1	< .0001
Health services free at the point of care	2 126	54.3	698.00	55.0	1.0	0.9-1.2	0.70
Out of pocket expenditures on medical goods (per capita USD ppp)	213 + 36		210 + 31		1.0	1.0-1.0	0.03
Out of pocket expenditures on outpatient care (per capita USD ppp)	215 + 100		229 + 104		1.0	1.0-1.0	< .0001
Annual doctor consultations (per capita)	7.4 + 2.2		7.2 + 2.0		1.0	0.9-1.0	0.02
RESSOURCES							
Share of ambulatory care on total expenditure	24.5 + 7.7		23.0 + 6.6		1.0	1.0-1.0	< .0001
Number of GPs (per 1 000 population)	0.9 + 0.5		0.8 + 0.4		0.6	0.5-0.7	< .0001
GPs mostly self-employed or privately employed	1 115	33.4	302	26.8	0.7	0.6-0.9	< .0001
GP's payment using fee-for-services	340	11.5	66.00	6.1	0.5	0.4-0.7	< .0001
Obligation or incentives for registration with a GP	3 443	90.0	1 102	90.1	1.0	0.8-1.3	0.92
QUALITY							
Formal requirements needed for primary care practices	2 723	71.2	800	65.4	0.8	0.7-0.9	0.00
Formal system of continuous medical education	3 312	86.6	1 064	87.0	1.0	0.9-1.3	0.71
Use of a patient registration system	3 639	95.1	1 140	93.2	0.7	0.5-0.9	0.01
Electronic exchange of information between providers	2 714	71.0	806	65.9	0.8	0.7-0.9	0.00
Incentives to comply with treatment guidelines	3 284	88.5	1 006	83.8	0.7	0.6-0.8	< .0001

Source: ESC Long-Term Heart Failure Registry, 2013; OECD Health Statistics 2013, *http://dx.doi.org/10.1787/health-data-en; OECD Health* Systems Characteristics Survey 2012 and OECD HCQI Questionnaire on Health Information Infrastructure 2012.

Table 6.4. **Odds ratios by the multi-level logistic model**

	OR	95% CI	P-value
Model 0. Empty model			
Model 1. Controlled for patient-level characteristics			
Age			
Below 65 years old	Ref		
65-75 years old	1.0	0.9-1.3	0.77
Above 75 years old	1.1	0.9-1.4	0.23
Men	0.9	0.7-1.1	0.21
Body mass index			
Below 22 kg/m²	0.9	0.7-1.3	0.61
22-25 kg/m²	Ref		
Above 25 kg/m²	1.0	0.8-1.2	0.56
Ejection fraction below 30%	0.8	0.7-1.0	0.05
NYHA III or IV	0.8	0.6-1.0	0.03
Heart rate above 70 bpm	1.1	1.0-1.3	0.15
SBP			
Below 110 mm Hg	1.0	0.8-1.2	0.87
110-130 mm Hg	Ref		
Above 130 mm Hg	0.9	0.7-1.1	0.26
Creatinine above 1.5 mg/dL	1.1	0.9-1.5	0.37
Sodium below 136 mEq/L	1.3	1.0-1.7	0.05
Ischemic aetiology	1.1	0.9-1.3	0.17
Atrial fibrillation	1.1	0.9-1.3	0.33
Left bundle branch block	1.2	1.0-1.4	0.13
Mitral regurgitation	1.3	1.1-1.6	0.01
COPD	0.6	0.5-0.8	0.00
PAD	1.1	0.9-1.5	0.35
CKD	0.9	0.7-1.2	0.38
Diabetes mellitus	1.0	0.9-1.2	0.68
Prior stroke	1.3	0.9-1.6	0.14
Depression	0.8	0.6-1.1	0.13
Model 2. Controlled for patient-level characteristics and country-level characteristics			
Age			
Below 65 years old	Ref		
65-75 years old	1.0	0.8-1.2	1.00
Above 75 years old	1.1	0.9-1.4	0.27
Men	0.9	0.7-1.1	0.31
Body mass index			
Below 22 kg/m²	0.9	0.7-1.1	0.57
22-25 kg/m²	Ref		
Above 25 kg/m²	0.9	0.7-1.3	0.38
Ejection fraction below 30%	0.8	0.7-1.0	0.06
NYHA III or IV	0.8	0.7-1.0	0.09
Heart rate above 70 bpm	1.1	0.9-1.3	0.22
SBP			
Below 110 mm Hg	1.0	0.8-1.3	0.80
110-130 mm Hg	Ref		
Above 130 mm Hg	0.9	0.7-1.1	0.18
Creatinine above 1.5 mg/dL	1.1	0.8-1.4	0.53
Sodium below 136 mEq/L	1.2	0.9-1.6	0.12
Ischemic aetiology	1.1	0.9-1.4	0.18
Atrial Fibrillation	1.1	0.9-1.4	0.20
Left bundle branch block	1.2	1.0-1.5	0.08
Mitral regurgitation	1.3	1.1-1.6	0.01

Table 6.4. **Odds ratios by the multi-level logistic model** *(cont.)*

	OR	95% CI	P-value
COPD	0.6	0.5-0.8	0.00
PAD	1.1	0.8-1.5	0.43
CKD	0.9	0.7-1.2	0.57
Diabetes mellitus	1.0	0.9-1.3	0.75
Prior stroke	1.3	0.9-1.7	0.11
Depression	0.8	0.6-1.1	0.17
Incentives to comply with treatment guidelines	0.4	0.2-1.1	0.08

Source: ESC Long-Term Heart Failure Registry 2013; OECD Health Systems Characteristics Survey 2012.

Country-level variables were tested one at a time, but no significant contribution was found, except for the variable related to incentives to implement drug treatment guidelines (Model 2), although this was only weakly significant. The OR of 0.4 (CI = 0.2-1.1) suggests that incentives or obligation to comply with treatment guidelines decreases the probability of being non-adherent. Adding this variable, the ICC decreased from 17.2% to 10.6%.

Four countries were excluded from Model 2 as information was missing for incentives or obligation to comply with guidelines: Austria, Turkey, Estonia and Slovak Republic. Re-running the analysis for model 1 with these countries excluded did not qualitatively change the results.

Better adherence is linked to some national health system characteristics but within-country variation needs to be better understood

This paper has found that there is significant country variation in adherence to guideline recommendations for chronic heart failure patients. Across countries 24.3% of patients were not being treated in line with pharmacological recommendations, but this percentage ranged from more than 70% in Greece and Estonia to around 10% in Portugal. That said, it should be noted that the sample sizes for both Estonia and Greece were relatively small.

The study showed that a large number of clinical patient characteristics were influential in predicting non-adherence. While statistically important, these patient-level characteristics only explained a further 0.3% of the adherence variation across the sample population. This may be because the study defined patients as non-adherent if no contraindication was recorded. This would have meant that many of the clinical reasons for being non-adherent had already been accounted for in study. This may also help explain why adherence was relatively high in this study population. Nevertheless, the results reported here are in line with a previous European study which showed that non-adherence to evidence-based treatment for chronic heart failure ranged between 12% and 64% depending on pharmacological intervention (Komajda, 2005).

The analysis also found that within-country variation was even more extensive than cross-country variations. While participating centres in Portugal displayed a relatively small degree of variation, the level of non-adherence between centres in a number of other countries ranged from the extreme values of 0% to 100%. To some extent this result was driven by the very small centres in some countries. Once these were removed, the within country variation diminished for countries including Denmark, Poland and the Slovak Republic but remained extensive in most other countries in the sample.

Both within and across country variation has important implications for patients. Portuguese patients were not only more likely to be adherent to guidelines, their choice of centre was also less important in the likelihood of being adherent compared to any other country. Among participating Hungarian centres, overall adherence is also high but there the patient's likelihood of being treated according to the guideline recommendations is, to a greater extent, dependent on the choice of treating centre. These results also have important implications for policy makers. Good overall adherence but with extensive within-country variation suggests that a more targeted approach to improve access and quality of care in certain areas may be more beneficial. Poor overall adherence on the other hand may warrant more comprehensive measures.

The within-country variations found in this study also points to the potential role for further research to better understand this phenomenon. Further work could examine data on treatment centre characteristics as well as local geographic information to explore whether these variables can help explain within-country variation of guidelines adherence. It would be important to see whether these characteristics can explain within-country variation not just in one country but across several countries.

This study explored a number of national health system characteristics to help explain the cross-country variation in adherence. A number of these were found to be significant in the univariate analysis. While these results are only simple associations, there is a fairly consistent pattern which indicates that countries with greater access, resourcing and quality programmes have better levels of adherence than in countries without these characteristics. However, it should be noted that the study found only weak evidence for one health system characteristic in the full multivariate model, suggesting that provider incentives to comply with guidelines does improve adherence. Care should be taken in interpreting this finding, as information on the use of guideline incentives was unavailable for four countries in the sample.

Aside from the small sample for some country-level data, some further limitations are worth noting. The health system characteristics survey represents a very high level overview of a health system's institutional features and may obscure many internal differences within a health system. Furthermore, the health system characteristics selected for this analysis, while relevant, may not directly reflect the unique features of heart failure care. They should therefore only be regarded as proxies for health system access, resources and quality.

Despite its strengths, the registry data also has some important limitations. First, heart failure patients were diagnosed on the basis of the investigators' clinical judgement but were not validated centrally. Secondly, despite the methodological desirability of consecutive enrolment this cannot be fully proven in the sample of ambulatory patients with chronic HF. That said, administrative records for the acute heart failure patient population showed a satisfactory degree of consecutive enrolment. Thirdly, while representativeness is a frequent limitation of observational studies, the centres in the registry sample were selected in proportion to the size of the population of the participating countries as well as taking into account the different technological levels of the cardiology centres. Fourthly, the patients were enrolled through cardiology clinics and therefore the study population may not be representative the entire CHF population (Maggioni et al., 2013a).

Notwithstanding these limitations, this analysis has shown the value of combining individual level registry data together with national health system data to undertake cross-country analysis. This analysis reveals that national borders can help explain some of the variation in the treatment patterns, it also points to the importance of within country variation.

Greater adherence to recommended guidelines can play a vital role in reducing health care use and costs. In the United Kingdom, heart failure accounted for 1.9% of total NHS expenditure, with hospitalisation accounting for nearly 70% of these costs (Stewart et al., 2002). Given the poor prognosis for many patients and the high health care costs associated with hospital readmissions, even small improvements in heart failure care can have a substantial impact on patient quality of life and health care cost and (Lee et al., 2004).

Summary

The lack of adherence to recommended clinical practice can have adverse effects on patient outcomes as well as higher health care costs. More efforts should be made towards understanding the role of health system characteristics in explaining adherence to guidelines both within and across countries. Such an understanding can aid decision makers design more effective policies which will ultimately help providers in their quest to improve adherence and health care outcomes as well as potentially reduce costs.

Notes

1. This chapter is co-authored by Professors Aldo Maggioni (EURObservational Research Programme Department, European Society of Cardiology) and Renato Urso (Pharmacology Unit "Giorgio Segre", University of Siena, Siena, Italy) and members of the Secretariat.
2. This reduced the number of centres from 140 to 52 but only reduced the patient sample by 220.
3. The intraclass correlation coefficient (ICC) estimates the variability in non-adherence between countries.

References

Bonow, R.O. et al. (2012), "ACCF/AHA/AMA-PCPI 2011 Performance Measures for Adults with Heart Failure: A Report of the American College of Cardiology Foundation/American Heart Association Task Force on Performance Measures and the American Medical Association–Physician Consortium for Performance Improvement", *Circulation*, Vol. 125, pp. 2382-2401.

CIBIS-11 (1999), "The Cardiac Insufficiency Bisoprolol Study II (CIBIS-II): A Randomised Trial", *The Lancet*, Vol. 353, pp. 9-13.

Cole, J.A. et al. (2006), "Drug Copayment and Adherence in Chronic Heart Failure: Effect on Cost and Outcomes", *Pharmacotherapy: The Journal of Human Pharmacology and Drug Therapy*, Vol. 26, No. 8, pp. 1157-1164.

CONSENSUS (1987), "Effects of Enalapril on Mortality in Severe Congestive Heart Failure. Results of the Cooperative North Scandinavian Enalapril Survival Study (CONSENSUS). The CONSENSUS Trial Study Group", *New England Journal of Medicine*, Vol. 316, pp. 1429-1435.

Dickstein, K. et al. (2008), "ESC Guidelines for the Diagnosis and Treatment of Acute and Chronic Heart Failure 2008", *European Journal of Heart Failure*, Vol. 10, No. 10, pp. 933-989.

Fonarow, G.C., C.W. Yancy and J.T. Heywood (2005), "Adherence to Heart Failure Quality-of-care Indicators in US Hospitals: Analysis of the ADHERE Registry", *Archives of Internal Medicine*, Vol. 165, No. 13, pp. 1469-1477.

Galbreath, A.D. et al. (2004), "Long-term Healthcare and Cost Outcomes of Disease Management in a Large, Randomized, Community-based Population with Heart Failure", *Circulation*, Vol. 110, No. 23, pp. 3518-3526.

Jessup, M. et al., writing on behalf of the 2005 Guideline Update for the Diagnosis and Management of Chronic Heart Failure in the Adult Writing Committee (2009), "Focused Update: ACCF/AHA Guidelines for the Diagnosis and Management of Heart Failure in Adults: A Report of the American College of Cardiology Foundation/American Heart Association Task Force on Practice Guidelines", *Circulation*, Vol. 119, pp. 1977-2016

Komajda, M. et al. (2005), "Adherence to Guidelines is a Predictor of Outcome in Chronic Heart Failure: The MAHLER Survey", *European Heart Journal*, Vol. 26, No. 16, pp. 1653-1659.

Lee, W.C. et al. (2004), "Economic Burden of Heart Failure: A Summary of Recent Literature", *Heart and Lung*, Vol. 33, No. 6, pp. 362-371.

McMurray, J.J. et al. (2012), "ESC Guidelines for the Diagnosis and Treatment of Acute and Chronic Heart Failure 2012. The Task Force for the Diagnosis and Treatment of Acute and Chronic Heart Failure 2012 of the European Society of Cardiology. Developed in collaboration with the Heart Failure Association (HFA) of the ESC", *European Heart Journal*, Vol. 33, No. 14, pp. 1787-1847.

Maggioni, A.P. et al. on behalf of the Heart Failure Association of the European Society of Cardiology (HFA) (2013a), "EURObservational Research Programme: Regional Differences and 1-year Follow-up Results of the Heart Failure Pilot Survey (ESC-HF Pilot)", *European Journal of Heart Failure*, Vol. 15, pp. 808-817.

Maggioni, A.P. et al. (2013b), "Are Hospitalized or Ambulatory Patients with Heart Failure Treated in Accordance with European Society of Cardiology guidelines? Evidence from 12 440 Patients of the ESC Heart Failure Long-Term Registry", *European Journal of Heart Failure*, Vol. 15, pp. 1173-1184.

MERIT-HF (1999), "Effect of Metoprolol CR/XL in Chronic Heart Failure: Metoprolol CR/XL Randomised Intervention Trial in Congestive Heart Failure (MERIT-HF)", *The Lancet*, Vol. 353, pp. 2001–2007.

OECD (2013), *OECD Health Statistics*, OECD Publishing, Paris, *http://dx.doi.org/10.1787/health-data-en*.

Packer, M. et al. (2002), "Effect of Carvedilol on the Morbidity of Patients with Severe Chronic Heart Failure: Results of the Carvedilol Prospective Randomized Cumulative Survival (COPERNICUS) Study", *Circulation*, Vol. 106, pp. 2194-2199.

Paris, V., M. Devaux and L. Wei (2010), "Health Systems Institutional Characteristics: A Survey of 29 OECD Countries", *OECD Health Working Papers*, No. 50, OECD Publishing, Paris, *http://dx.doi.org/10.1787/5kmfxfq9qbnr-en*.

Pitt, B. et al. (1999), "The Effect of Spironolactone on Morbidity and Mortality in Patients with Severe Heart Failure. Randomized Aldactone Evaluation Study Investigators", *New England Journal of Medicine*, Vol. 341, pp. 709-717.

Shafazand, M. et al. (2009), "Survival Trends in Men and Women with Heart Failure of Ischaemic and Non-ischaemic Origin: Data for the Period 1987-2003 from the Swedish Hospital Discharge Registry", *European Heart Journal*, Vol. 30, No. 6, pp. 671-678.

SOLVD Investigators (1991), "Effect of Enalapril on Survival in Patients with Reduced Left Ventricular Ejection Fractions and Congestive Heart Failure. The SOLVD Investigators", *New England Journal of Medicine*, Vol. 325, pp. 293-302.

SOLVD Investigators (1992), "Effect of Enalapril on Mortality and the Development of Heart Failure in Asymptomatic Patients with Reduced Left Ventricular Ejection Fractions", *New England Journal of Medicine*, Vol. 327, pp. 685-691.

Stafford, R.S. et al. (2003), "Chronic Disease Medication Use in Managed Care and Indemnity Insurance Plans", *Health Services Research*, Vol. 38, No. 2, pp. 595-612.

Stewart, S. et al.(2002), "The Current Cost of Heart Failure to the National Health Service in the UK", *European Journal of Heart Failure*, Vol. 4, No. 3, pp. 361-371.

Zannad, F. et al. (2011), "Eplerenone in Patients with Systolic Heart Failure and Mild Symptoms", *New England Journal of Medicine*, Vol. 364, pp. 11-21.

ORGANISATION FOR ECONOMIC CO-OPERATION AND DEVELOPMENT

The OECD is a unique forum where governments work together to address the economic, social and environmental challenges of globalisation. The OECD is also at the forefront of efforts to understand and to help governments respond to new developments and concerns, such as corporate governance, the information economy and the challenges of an ageing population. The Organisation provides a setting where governments can compare policy experiences, seek answers to common problems, identify good practice and work to co-ordinate domestic and international policies.

The OECD member countries are: Australia, Austria, Belgium, Canada, Chile, the Czech Republic, Denmark, Estonia, Finland, France, Germany, Greece, Hungary, Iceland, Ireland, Israel, Italy, Japan, Korea, Luxembourg, Mexico, the Netherlands, New Zealand, Norway, Poland, Portugal, the Slovak Republic, Slovenia, Spain, Sweden, Switzerland, Turkey, the United Kingdom and the United States. The European Union takes part in the work of the OECD.

OECD Publishing disseminates widely the results of the Organisation's statistics gathering and research on economic, social and environmental issues, as well as the conventions, guidelines and standards agreed by its members.

OECD PUBLISHING, 2, rue André-Pascal, 75775 PARIS CEDEX 16
(81 2015 10 1 P 1) ISBN 978-92-64-23300-3 – 2015